MEXICAN AMERICAN BASEBALL IN THE SAN GABRIEL VALLEY

OLD SAN GABRIEL

Our little city of San Gabriel lies
By the foothills and the mountains' crest
In the rich San Gabriel Valley,
Great, historic center of the West.
Since the days of Father Serra
And all the brave men that came
To discover, trade and to settle,
They gave our fair city its name.

You were quite an important "pueblo"
For many miles around,
As people came from near and far
To worship on your sacred ground.
The ruins that now silently stand
Of old adobe homes that used to be,
Are rich with tales of the Dons,
So fascinating for you and me.

You have grown to serve your people,
Yes, you are a city with a "Mission."
Oh! How we love you Old San Gabriel,
We enjoy your heritage and rich tradition.

—Steve "Rico" Salazar (1921–2011), 1964

FRONT COVER: Hank John Aguirre, nicknamed "the Tall Mexican," was a major-league pitcher for four different teams from 1955 to 1970, including the Los Angeles Dodgers in 1968. He was born and raised in the San Gabriel Valley and worked for his father's San Gabriel business, the Aguirre Market. He went on to become a successful businessman and humanitarian in Detroit. He is buried at the San Gabriel Mission Cemetery. (Courtesy of Pamela Aguirre.)

COVER BACKGROUND: The 1958 Montebello Braves were boys from Montebello, San Gabriel, Whittier, Pico Rivera, Monterey Park, and East Los Angeles. Players included Chris Jaramillo Jr., Mike Sepulveda, Ralph Arzate, Eddie Garza, and Jim Kreutzer. The team was sponsored by Local 11 of the International Brotherhood of Electrical Workers. (Courtesy of Jim Kreutzer.)

BACK COVER: The 1952 little league Pirates played in Pico Rivera, California. The team included childhood friends Julian Barry Aguirre and Bob and Art Lagunas. All three were born and raised in the city of Pico Rivera in the San Gabriel Valley. They remained friends for 60 years until the passing of Julian. (Courtesy of James Henninger Aguirre.)

MEXICAN AMERICAN BASEBALL IN THE SAN GABRIEL VALLEY

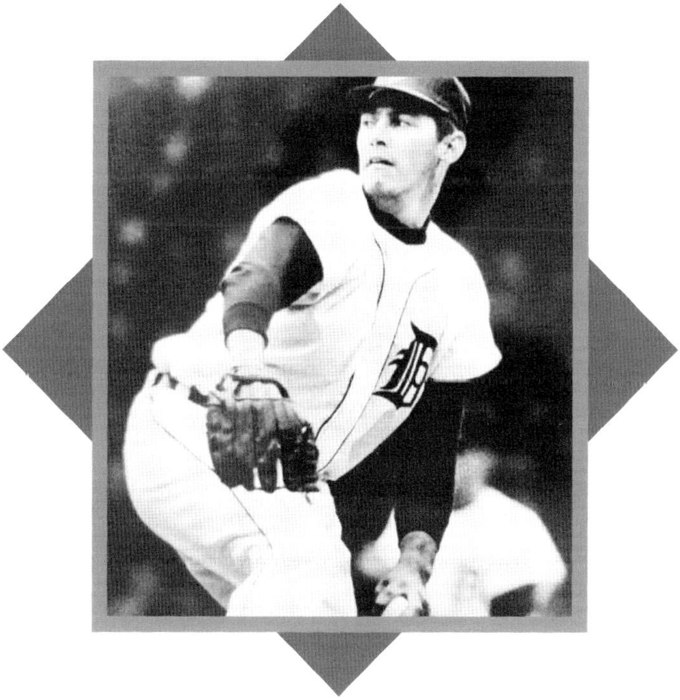

Richard A. Santillán, Camila Alva López, James H. Aguirre, Donna Galván, and Mark R. García
Foreword by the Hank Aguirre family

ARCADIA PUBLISHING

ISBN 978-1-4671-2970-1

Published by Arcadia Publishing
Charleston, South Carolina

Printed in the United States of America

Library of Congress Control Number: 2018951443

For all general information, please contact Arcadia Publishing:
Telephone 843-853-2070
Fax 843-853-0044
E-mail sales@arcadiapublishing.com
For customer service and orders:
Toll-Free 1-888-313-2665

Visit us on the Internet at www.arcadiapublishing.com

I dedicate this book to my family members who played ball in Alhambra, son John Talamantes, grandchildren Román and Rhiannon Mejía, and team moms: daughter Dianne Sánchez and wife Teresa M. Santillán. To all my Norwalk memories, and finally to my extraordinary wife, Teresa.

—*Richard*

To the Gabrieleño-Tongva who lived in the San Gabriel Valley, of whom I am a descendant, and to my rich Mexican heritage and a new generation of Native and Mexican Americans who play baseball. To my parents, Henry and Beatrice Salazar Alva, to my grandparents, and to my husband, Sal, and our daughters, Alicia and Lucinda, for their love, encouragement, and support. To God be the Glory.

—*Camila*

To my parents, Julian Barry Aguirre and Lucille Henninger Aguirre, who were born in the San Gabriel Valley and were a combination of Gabrieleño/Diegueño, Spanish, Mexican, German, and Irish. To my girlfriend, Donna Galván, for believing in me, and to my baseball coaches, including Orlando González, Carl Tilander, Willie Rubalcava, Nicholas Jannis, and Jerry Schlegelmilch.

—*James*

To my parents, Ray and Gloria Galván; my siblings, Lorraine, Ray, Manuel, and Denise; my soulmate, James, and my friends, who are my family: R.C., Mama K., and Mama L. I love you more than mere words can say.

—*Donna*

I dedicate this book to my great parents, Adolph and Carmen García, who raised three remarkable young Latino sons. My heartfelt appreciation to Dr. Richard A. Santillán (Latino Baseball History Project), David Brown (Pasadena Red Birds), William Rogers, and manager Joe Amaya (East Los Angeles Monarchs) for their advice and encouragement.

—*Mark*

CONTENTS

ACKNOWLEDGMENTS

This project to record the rich history of Mexican American baseball and softball in the San Gabriel Valley is part of the remarkable work of the Latino Baseball History Project at California State University at San Bernardino (CSUSB). Supporters of the project at the John M. Pfau Library are César and Sue Caballero, Jill Vassilakos-Long, Manny Verón, Mark Ocegueda, Tomás Benítez, Cherstin Lyon, Ericka Saucedo, Catrina Mancha, and Stephen Picanco.

The authors are indebted to the players, their families, and other community members for sharing their wonderful stories and remarkable photographs, including Beatrice Alva, Frank Andrade, Rick J. Arnold, Virginia Flores, Linda Hollyfield, Irene Aguirre Juárez, Steve Juárez, Richard and Dolly Salazar, Paula Taizon, the San Gabriel Historical Association Archives, Richard Aguirre, Joe Aguirre, the Orozco family, Paul Cole Padilla, Carlos Salazar, Hank and Lucy Vera Pedregón, Jack Arenas, Eris Pérez, George and Maria Van Dyke, Anthony González and the Route 66 Inland Empire California Association, Bob and Diane Morales, Alfredo and Linda Hernández, Stella Domínguez, Teresa M. Santillán, Dianne Sánchez, Mel Sánchez Sr., Fred Padilla, Lauro Montes, Helen Fuentes Gonzáles, Gene Aguilera, Victor Pimentel, Fidel Elizarrez, Jim Kreutzer, Tony Pérez, the Nieto family, Maynard and Pauli Horst, Ralph Martínez, the Pérez family, Christina González Magoni, Tony Ortega, the Santillán family, the Toney family, Mike Álvarez, John Echeveste, John Lemos, Ramiro Gallegos Jr., David Gallegos, Tomás Espinoza, Rod Martínez, Jerry Rocha, Richard Villaseñor, Bob Lagunas, Phil Torres, Joe Laski, Jim Irwin, Dick Guzmán, Julian Barry Aguirre, Lucille Henninger Aguirre, Billie Henninger Jeffredo, and Davey Escobedo.

The coauthors especially acknowledge and pay special tribute to Steve Gewecke, the current head baseball coach at Alhambra High School, for his time, his relentless get-up-and-go attitude, his invaluable community resources, and his wonderful networks in the world of high school baseball in the San Gabriel Valley. The coauthors also thank the Steve "Rico" Salazar family for sharing his poem on page 2. Steve was a World War II US Marine, school counselor, writer, and poet. We enthusiastically thank once again our priceless in-house editor, Elisa Grajeda-Urmston, for her great enthusiasm, tireless energy, and professional expertise, and we bestow our immeasurable endorsement to our technical consultant Monse Segura. Both Elisa and Monse have now collaborated on 11 books since 2013. We are perpetually indebted to their extraordinary work. Finally, the Latino Baseball History Project Planning Committee, director César Caballero, and lead author Richard A. Santillán extend their utmost respect and endless gratitude to Arcadia Publishing's Jim Kempert and to our longtime editor, friend, champion, and mentor Jeff Ruetsche for his exceptional relationship with the Mexican American baseball and softball communities. Your endorsement of our book series will live forever in the hearts of Mexican Americans.

FOREWORD

This foreword is a collection of memories by members of the Hank Aguirre family.

My brother Henry (Hank) was the comic of the family. He had a great sense of humor, and was friendly, easy-going, gentle, compassionate, and very generous. He had faith in God and Our Lady of Guadalupe. He left home to follow his dream and married his beautiful first wife, Barbara, who became my closest friend. After my husband, David, lost his eyesight due to diabetes, Hank immediately arranged for us to move to Arizona and work at his Mexican Industries factory. He never forgot his family roots. My brother Hank will forever live in my heart.

—sister Irene Aguirre Juárez

When I was at San Gabriel Mission Grammar School, the Detroit Tigers were in town playing against the Angels, which meant that Uncle Hank would visit Grandma and Grandpa's house behind the store. They were in Grandma's kitchen laughing, eating, and talking to neighbors. It was so surreal. Bill Freehan, Al Kaline, Gates Brown, Mickey Stanley, Norm Cash, Mickey Lolich, Eddie Matthews, Larry Sherry, Willie Horton, Johnny Podres, Dick McAuliffe, just to name a few—it was unbelievable!

—nephew Steve Juárez

My fondest memories of Hank are when he would come home to San Gabriel and take us to eat at local restaurants like Panchito's, or just an old-fashioned dinner with the family at home. Our mom, Jenny, was an excellent cook. Family always came first for my brother Hank, and I enjoyed his visits home very much. He was kind, loving, and generous, and I love him to this day.

—sister Linda Aguirre Hollyfield

Hank had a second funeral at the San Gabriel Mission. Terry Barton, one of Hank's early baseball coaches, was quite elderly and ran his car into the hearse carrying Hank's remains. Even though we were all grieving, we had a moment of laughter saying that it was Terry's way of saying farewell to Hank, and Hank would have laughed the hardest.

—brother Joe Aguirre

Hank would take me to Tiger Stadium and we would pick up Al Kaline—who happened to be my baseball idol! Hank lost his life to prostate cancer, and Detroit lowered all the flags in his honor. The police department escorted the funeral procession, and the fire trucks flashed their lights and the firefighters saluted. It was quite a tribute to a special man and city hero.

—brother Richard Aguirre

INTRODUCTION

In many areas with Mexican American neighborhoods, there is often disagreement as to the precise borders. Some attempt, for example, to define specific perimeters along natural features like rivers, mountains, hills, and valleys. The previous titles in our Mexican American Baseball history series, however, have by and large incorporated different criteria to define demarcation lines based on several factors, including ethnicity, family networks, places of labor, military service, cultural interactions, school enrollment, language, immigration patterns, prejudice and discrimination, sports rivalries, and the incalculable spirit of a proud people with a common past and common destiny. Therefore, this San Gabriel Valley book generally examines Mexican American baseball and softball in the area encircled by the 710 freeway to the west, the 210 freeway to the north, the 57 freeway to the east, and the 91 freeway to the south.

The San Gabriel Valley derives its name from the San Gabriel River, which flows through the center of the valley. The river itself was named for the Spanish Mission San Gabriel Arcángel, built in Whittier Narrows in 1771. The mission served as the starting point for the original Spanish settlers (*Los Pobladores*) in the founding of Los Angeles in 1781. The nine-mile trek is still reenacted each year to celebrate the beginning of Los Angeles. Initially, the San Gabriel Valley's economy relied largely on agriculture and ranching. Besides cattle and crops, the region produced a variety of wines. After the Civil War, the economy expanded into manufacturing, packinghouses, railroads, foundries, oilfields, canneries, the leisure industry, domestic labor, small businesses, auto and tire plants, and construction. Mexican American workers have been a significant financial force that has helped generate prosperity in the valley, mostly by their backbreaking labor.

There are at least 31 cities and five unincorporated neighborhoods in the San Gabriel Valley, with more than two million residents, 20 percent of the population of Los Angeles County. Most of the cities have significant Mexican American populations. Baseball and softball took root in these neighborhoods. Mexican American baseball can be traced to at least the early 1900s. As elsewhere, baseball and later softball played important social and cultural roles in the development of these ethnic enclaves. Baseball and softball allowed these otherwise isolated neighborhoods to come together via games and tournaments. Many Mexican American leaders received their first political lessons on the diamond. Moreover, baseball and softball networks eventually promoted organizational and community networks, civil rights, and the ongoing constitutional struggle for social, educational, and cultural equality. Baseball and softball were and continue to be safe havens where Mexican heritage and language are respected and encouraged.

1

San Gabriel

Long before the Spanish, Mexicans, and Europeans discovered the vast San Gabriel Valley, stretching from the deserts to the mountains to the Pacific Ocean, it was inhabited by a proud indigenous people known as the Tongva ("People from the Earth"), a branch of the Shosonean-speaking people (Uto-Aztecan language group) that had migrated out of the Great Basin. These powerful indigenous people roamed free throughout this lush valley, living off the land and sea. Their village *rancheria*, then named Sibangna, was on what became San Gabriel Mission land. The priests named the Tongva people living on the mission land the Gabrieleño (Gabrielino)-Tongva Band of Mission Indians. Today, their living descendants are still known as the Gabrieleño-Tongva Band of Mission Indians. Some families are also known as the Gabrieleño Band of Mission Indians–Kizh Nation. The San Gabriel Mission was the fourth built and was known as the "Queen of the Missions." The city of San Gabriel was one of the first townships in Los Angeles County and celebrated its centennial in 2013.

The city of San Gabriel has always been multiethnic, starting with the Tongva people, Spaniards, Mexicans, Europeans, Japanese, and Chinese. A community was formed south of the Southern Pacific Railroad tracks known as El Barrio. A few Native American, Mexican American, Japanese American, and Anglo American families owned property, built homes, and started businesses. Their children attended the neighborhood Lincoln Elementary School. During World War II, many young men from the neighborhood volunteered or were drafted to defend their country. The residents were shaken and appalled when their Japanese American neighbors were hauled off to internment camps after the government classified them as "enemy aliens." These uprooted US citizens lost properties, businesses, constitutional rights, and even their identities as Americans. The entire community of El Barrio did everything to resist this clear racial discrimination by hiding their Japanese American neighbors' private belongings and cash and taking care of their properties and businesses before they were ultimately confiscated by the US government.

From the 1940s through the 1960s, there was a significant population of Anglo Americans along with a large Italian community and small pockets of Mexican Americans and Japanese Americans. Today, the San Gabriel Valley hears English, Spanish, Chinese, Vietnamese, and Polish daily, including on the baseball and softball diamonds. San Gabriel has produced outstanding teams, players, and coaches. This is part of their remarkable story.

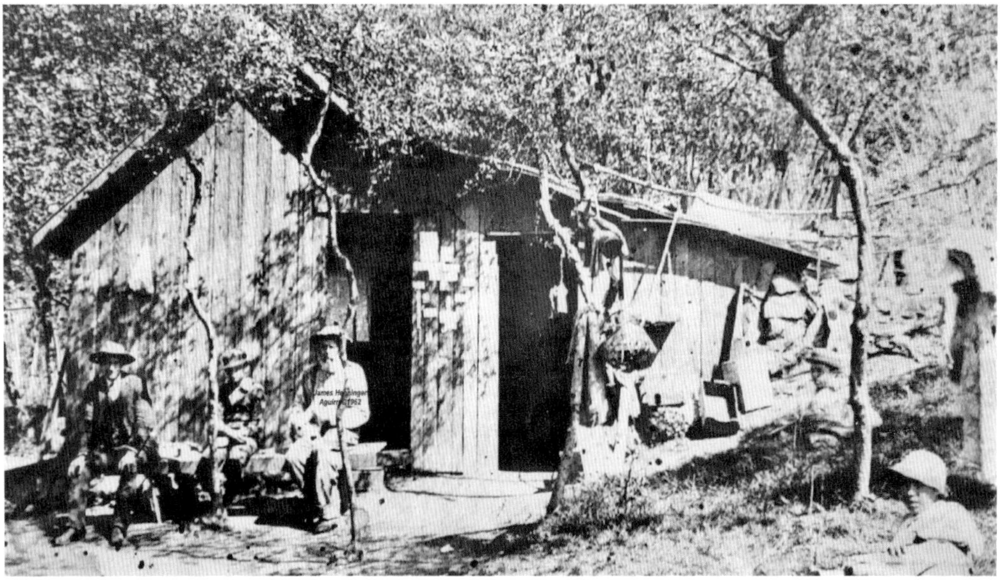

William Kimber Henninger (right) sits in front of his cabin at Henninger Flats in the San Gabriel Mountains in the 1880s. He was a pioneer and gold prospector who married a full-blooded Kumeyaay San Diego Mission Indian (Diegueño) named Teresa Serrano from Baja California. They had four daughters: Natividad, Louisa, Susana, and Josefa. Henninger purchased his homestead in the late 19th century; the land still bears the name Henninger Flats. (Courtesy of James Henninger Aguirre.)

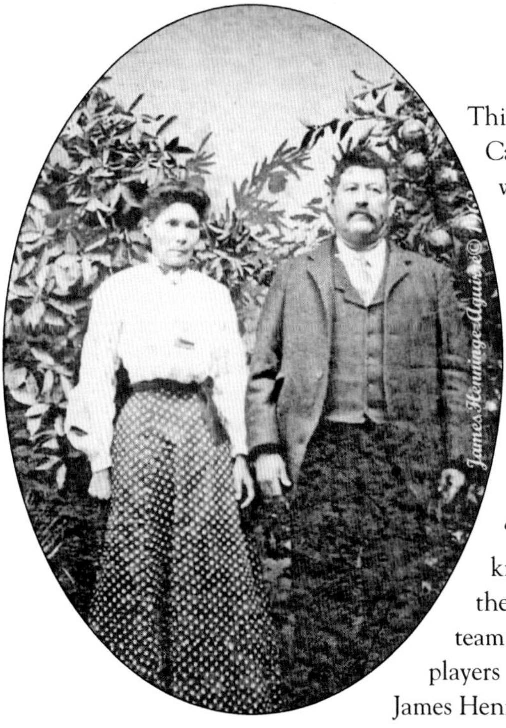

This picture of Louisa Emelia Henninger and David Carmen De La Ossa was taken in the 1890s. Louisa was the daughter of William Kimber Henninger, who owned Henninger Flats in the San Gabriel Mountains. David was the son of Vicente De La Ossa, who owned El Rancho de Los Encinos, now a state historic park in Encino, California. They had three children together: Elvira, Manuel, and Paul, who were born and raised in the city of San Gabriel. All three children were registered and enrolled with the federal government as San Diego Mission Indians "Diegueño." Manuel De La Ossa Henninger was known as "El Gato" (the cat) when he pitched for the San Gabriel S&S team in the early 1900s. The team was comprised of Mexican and Native American players born and raised in San Gabriel. (Courtesy of James Henninger Aguirre.)

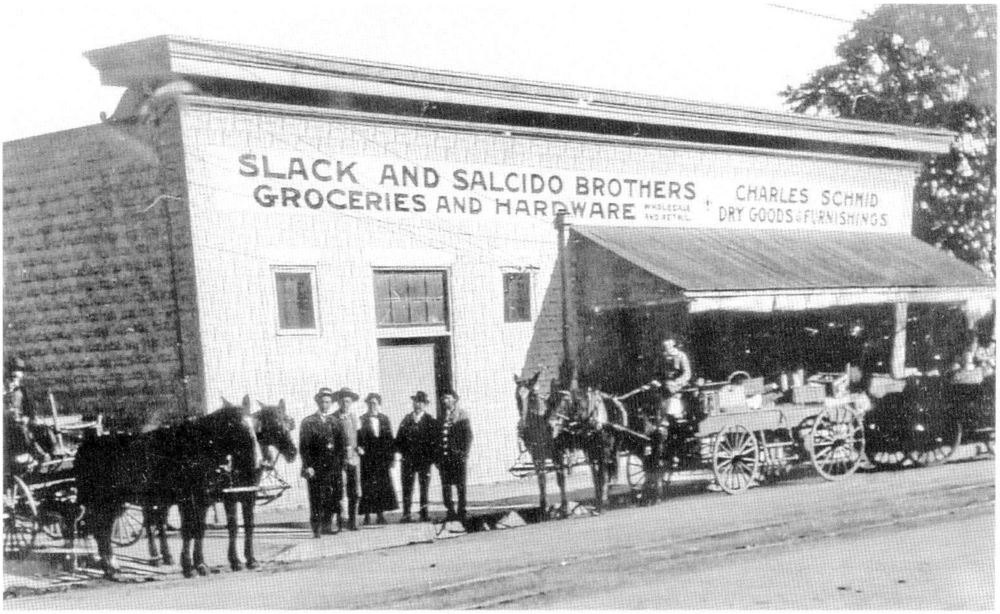

The Slack and Salcido Brothers groceries and hardware store is pictured on the northwest corner of Mission Drive and Carmelita Street in San Gabriel in the early 1900s. The store was owned by the city's first mayor, Alex J. Cuneo. The establishment sponsored many local baseball teams that played on a field on the corner of Mission Drive and Broadway. The San Gabriel teams displayed the big letters S&S on their jerseys. (Courtesy of James Henninger Aguirre.)

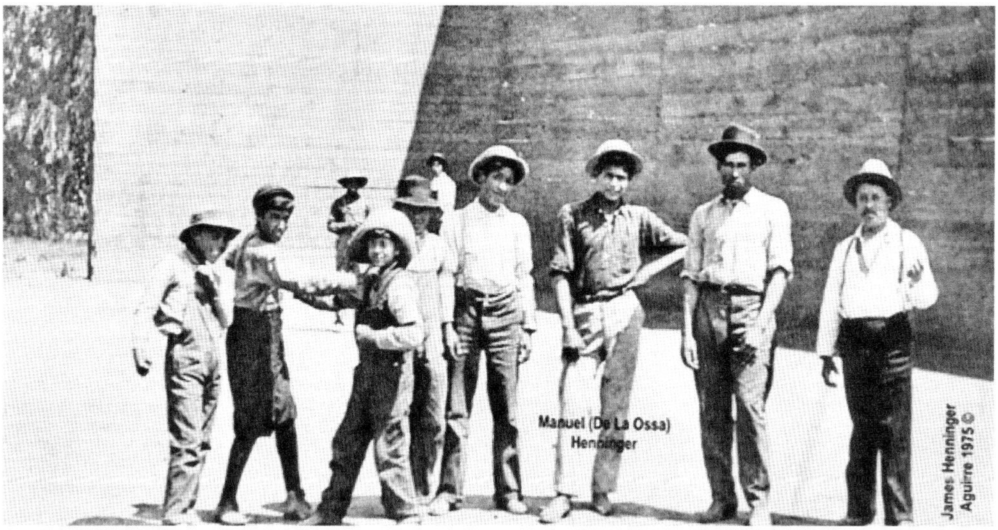

Most of these boys played on local baseball teams in the San Gabriel Valley. They also played handball (*rebote* in Spanish) on an outside court on the corner of Mission Drive and Del Mar Avenue in San Gabriel starting in the early 1900s. Manuel De La Ossa Henninger (sixth from left) was known as "El Gato" because of his foot and hand speed on the baseball diamond. He was the grandson of William Kimber Henninger, a famous pioneer who settled at Henninger Flats in the San Gabriel Mountains in the 1880s. (Courtesy of Billie Henninger Jeffredo.)

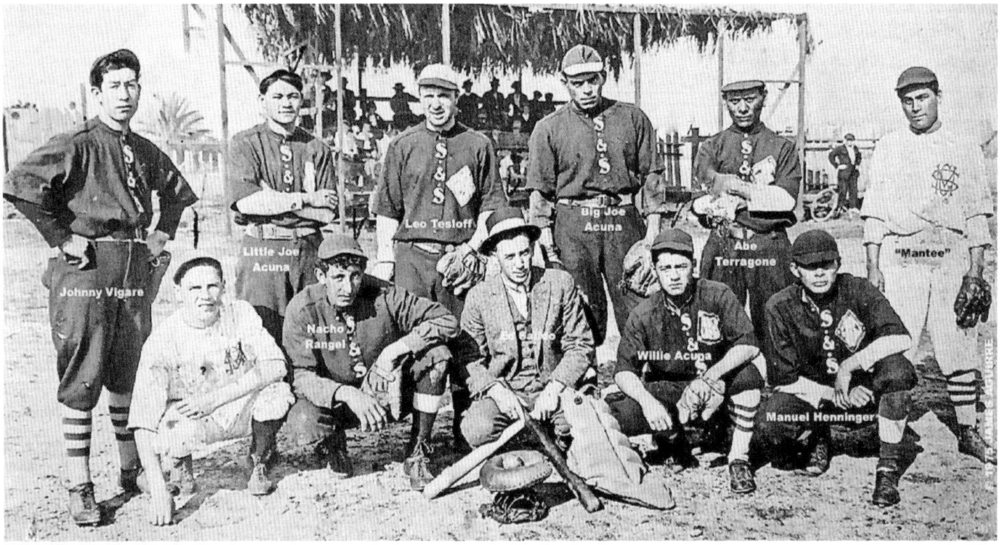

The 1915 San Gabriel baseball team was sponsored by Slack and Salcido Brothers, thus the S&S on their jerseys. The original field was on the corner of Mission Drive and Broadway, not far from the Mission Playhouse. It was home to many talented players from throughout the San Gabriel Valley. From left to right are (first row) unidentified, Nacho Rangel, Ed Salido, Willie Acuña, and Manuel "El Gato" Henninger; (second row) Johnny Vigare, "Little" Joe Acuña, Leo Tesloff, "Big" Joe Acuña, Abe Terragone, and unidentified. (Courtesy of James Henninger Aguirre.)

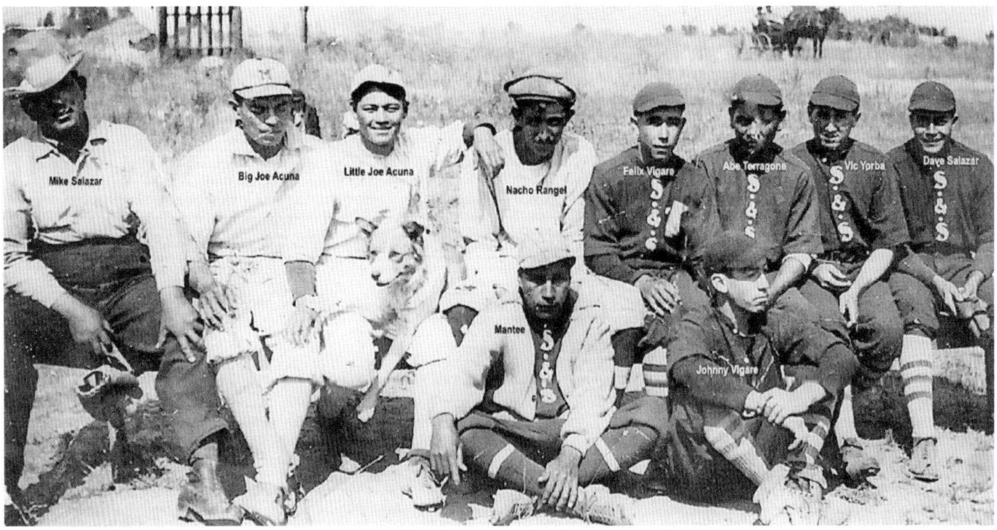

Members of the 1915 San Gabriel S&S team are, from left to right, (first row) unidentified and Johnny Vigare; (second row) manager Mike Salazar, "Big" Joe Acuña, "Little" Joe Acuña, Nacho Rangel, Félix Vigare, Abe Terragone, Vic Yorba, and Dave Salazar. Manager Mike Salazar owned the property at 238 South Mission Drive where he constructed a baseball diamond known as Salazar Park. He married a Gabrieleño Indian named Minnie Pérez Salazar. His brother Dave is the grandfather of major-leaguer Darrell Evans, who played for the Giants, Braves, and Tigers from 1968 through 1989. (Courtesy of Camila Alva López.)

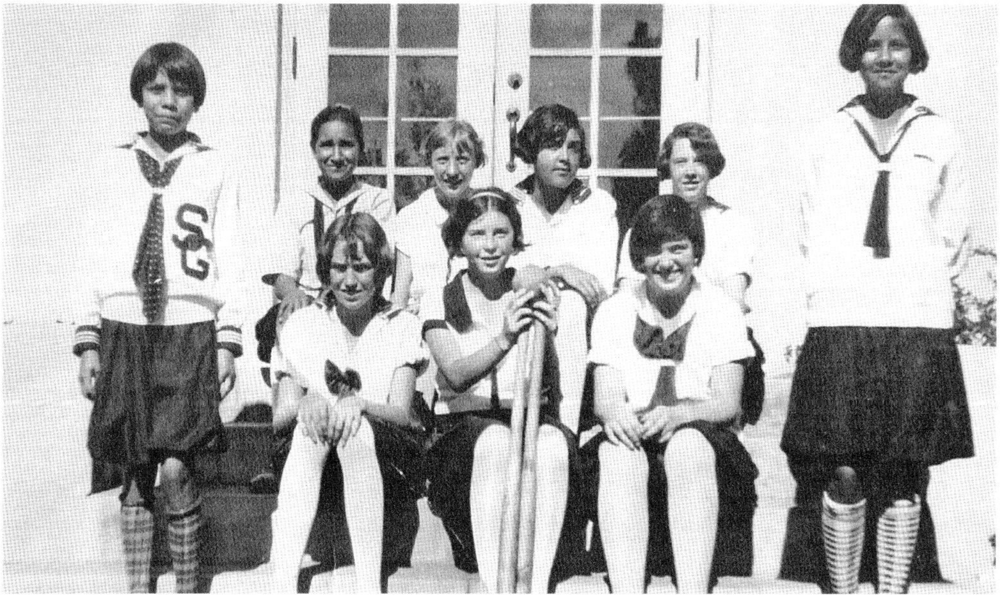

These 1920s San Gabriel girls were an outstanding softball team. From left to right are (first row) Grace Helen Reynolds, Mildred Newton, and Evelyn Oalenccia; (second row) Rudelia "Dee" Domínguez, Jean ?, Beatrice Salazar Alva, and Betty Lewis; (standing) Enid Téllez and Tillie Miller. Beatrice Salazar Alva was Mexican American and a descendant of the Gabrieleño-Tongva Band of Mission Indians. (Courtesy of Camila Alva López.)

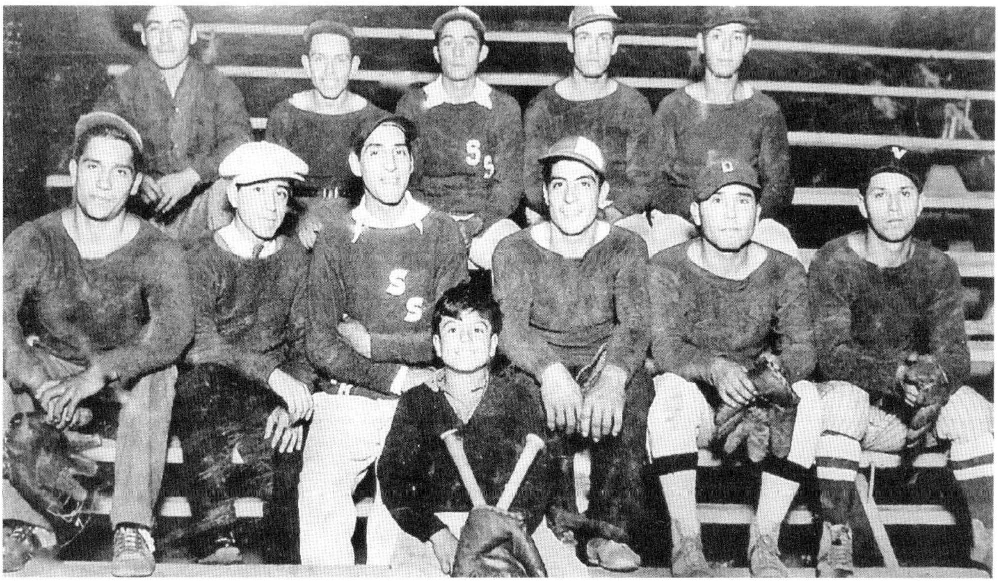

This 1920s San Gabriel team comprised many different racial and ethnic groups who played against traveling teams from other parts of Los Angeles County. Their local field was not far from the San Gabriel Mission. Johnny "Bear" Pérez (holding bats and glove in front) was the batboy, while his older brother Frank "Bear" Pérez (sitting to the right of Johnny) was an outstanding player. Tragically, Johnny was killed in action during World War II. (Courtesy of Bobby Domínguez.)

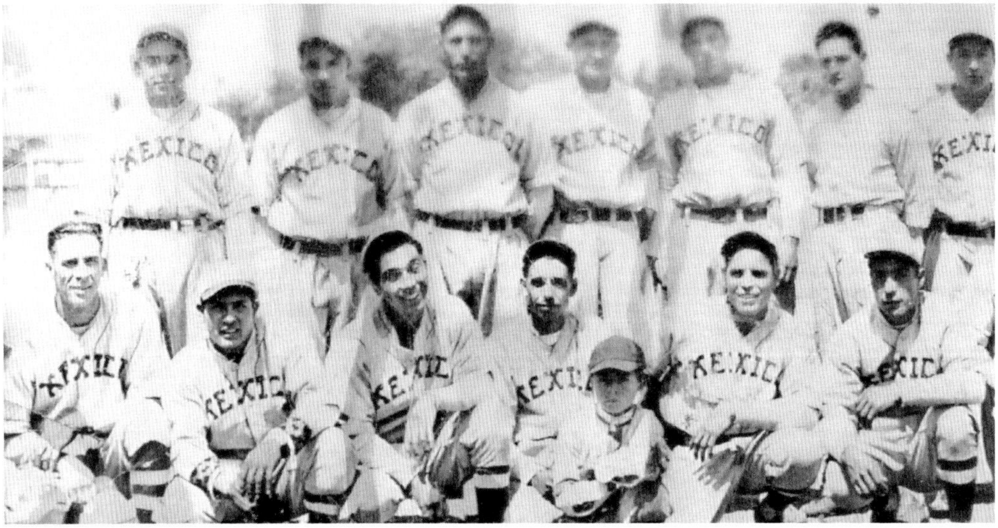

This rare picture shows the 1920s San Gabriel Xexico team. "Xexico" is another way that Mexico is spelled in some parts of the country. One of the most gifted players was Frank "Bear" Pérez (first row, far right), given his nickname because of his extremely large hands. He threw fast pitching left-handed. Frank was a proud Mexican American and a member of the Kizh tribe of the Gabrieleño Band of Mission Indians. (Courtesy of Louise Pérez Martínez.)

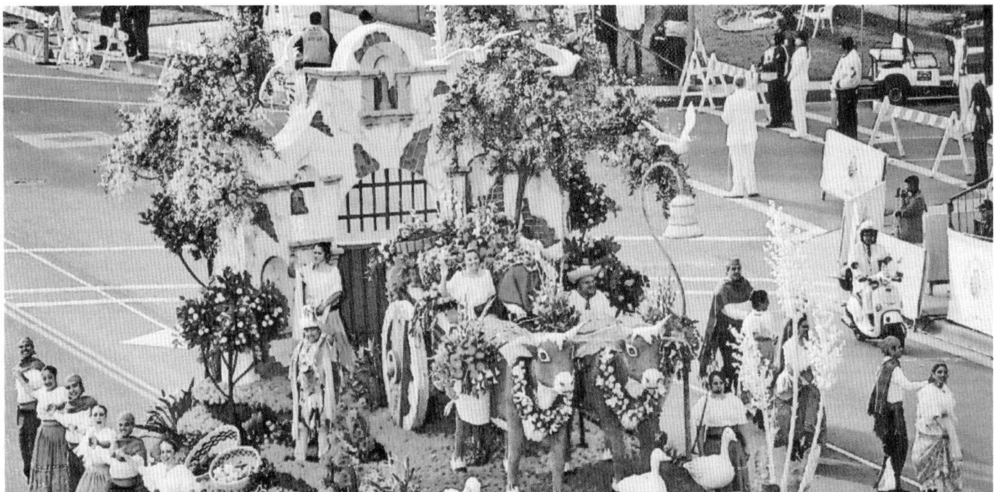

On January 1, 2013, San Gabriel sponsored a Rose Parade float to celebrate its city centennial. The designer was Charles Meier, and the float was awarded the Directors' Trophy. The float included iconic symbols of San Gabriel's history, including the grapevine, oxen, a bell representing El Camino Real, woven baskets filled with grapes and oranges, a tribute to the Gabrieleño-Tongva Band of Mission Indians, white doves, and geese. Folk dancers from Folkor Pasion Mexicana de Los Angeles danced alongside the float. Float riders, dressed in a diversity of attire, included Kevin Sawkins, Anthony Morales, Bruce Willems, Camila Alva López, Jacqueline Chai, and Kelly Ngo. (Courtesy of the *Pasadena Star News*.)

Beatrice Salazar Alva (1914–2010) became the first San Gabriel Mission Fiesta Queen in 1934. She married Henry Alva at the old San Gabriel Mission Church in 1936. They had four children: Camila, Rita, Anita, and Anthony. Beatrice attended Washington Elementary School in San Gabriel and graduated from Alhambra High School in 1931. She was an accomplished singer and pianist who starred in many plays in the 1930s with the Mission Opera Company including *The Mission Play* written by John Steven McGroarty. The 1933 San Gabriel Chamber monthly bulletin described Beatrice as the "Song Bird" of the San Gabriel Valley. She was a member of the San Gabriel Mission Choir from 1935 through 1980, a member of the Gabrielino Tongva Band of Mission Indians, and received the San Gabriel American G.I. Forum Outstanding Citizens' Award in 1964. (Courtesy of Camila Alva López.)

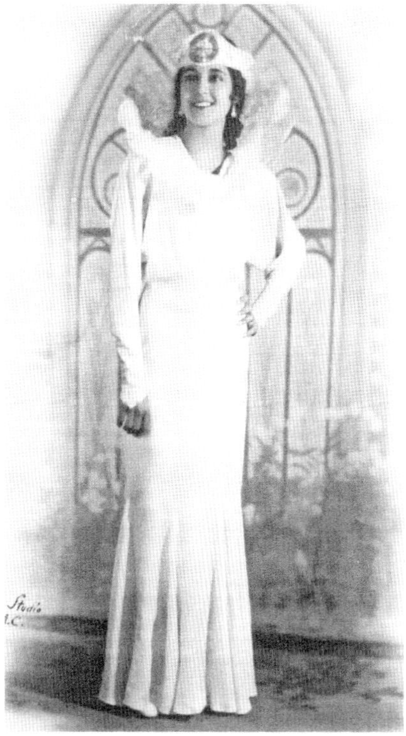

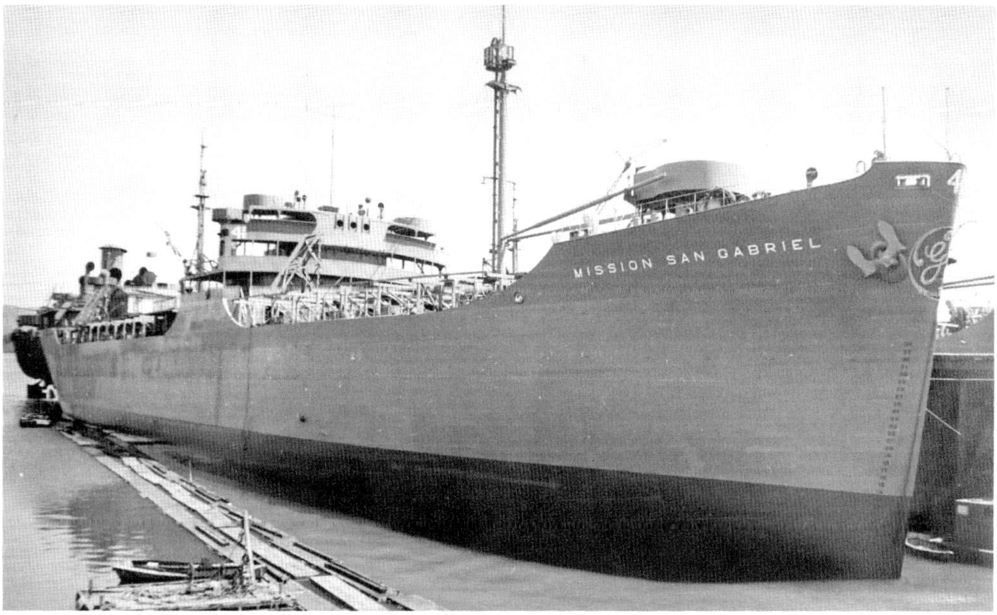

The tanker USS *Mission San Gabriel* was built for the US Maritime Commission during World War II. She is the only US Navy vessel named for the Mission San Gabriel Arcángel. She supplied oil to the US and Allied forces in the Pacific from 1944 until the end of the war. The ship also helped support US troops in Korea until 1954. Sadly, it was scrapped in 1983. (Courtesy of the San Gabriel Historical Association Museum archives.)

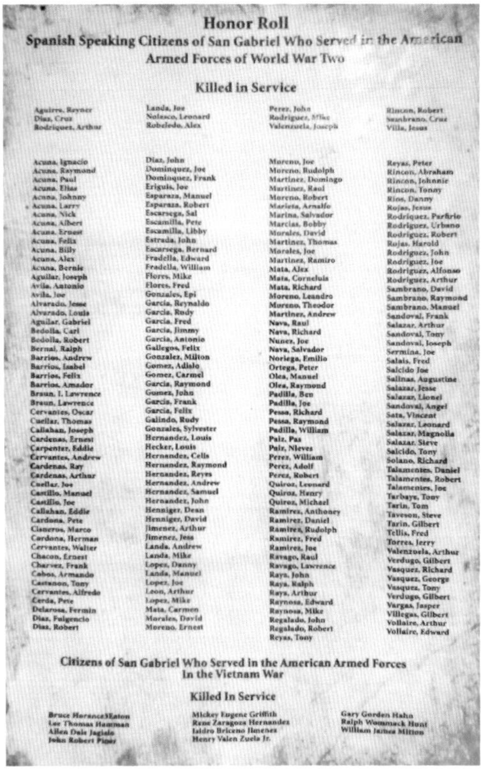

Honor Roll
Spanish Speaking Citizens of San Gabriel Who Served in the American Armed Forces of World War Two

Killed in Service

Aguirre, Reyner
Diaz, Cruz
Rodriquez, Arthur
Landa, Joe
Nolasco, Leonard
Robeledo, Alex
Perez, John
Rodriguez, Mike
Valenzuela, Joseph
Rincon, Robert
Sambrano, Cruz
Villa, Jesus

Acuna, Ignacio
Acuna, Raymond
Acuna, Paul
Acuna, Elias
Acuna, Johnny
Acuna, Larry
Acuna, Nick
Acuna, Albert
Acuna, Ernest
Acuna, Felix
Acuna, Billy
Acuna, Alex
Acuna, Bernie
Aguilar, Joseph
Avila, Antonio
Avila, Joe
Alvarado, Jesse
Alvarado, Louis
Aguilar, Gabriel
Bedolla, Carl
Bedolla, Robert
Bernal, Ralph
Barrios, Andrew
Barrios, Isabel
Barrios, Felix
Barrios, Amador
Braun, I. Lawrence
Braun, Lawrence
Cervanies, Oscar
Cuellar, Thomas
Callahan, Joseph
Cardenas, Ernest
Carpenter, Eddie
Cervantes, Andrew
Cardenas, Ray
Cardenas, Arthur
Cuellar, Joe
Castillo, Manuel
Castillo, Joe
Callahan, Eddie
Cardona, Pete
Cisneros, Marco
Cardona, Herman
Cervantes, Walter
Chacon, Ernest
Charvez, Frank
Cabos, Armando
Castanon, Tony
Cervantes, Alfredo
Cerda, Pete
Delarosa, Fermin
Diaz, Fulgencio
Diaz, Robert
Diaz, John
Dominquez, Joe
Dominquez, Frank
Eriguis, Joe
Esparaza, Manuel
Esparaza, Robert
Escarsega, Sal
Escamilla, Pete
Escamilla, Libby
Estrada, John
Escarsega, Bernard
Fradella, Edward
Fradella, William
Flores, Mike
Flores, Fred
Gonzales, Epi
Garcia, Reynaldo
Garcia, Rudy
Garcia, Fred
Garcia, Jimmy
Garcia, Antonio
Gallegos, Felix
Gonzalez, Milton
Gomez, Adlslo
Gomez, Carmel
Garcia, Raymond
Gomez, John
Garcia, Frank
Garcia, Felix
Galindo, Rudy
Gonzales, Sylvester
Hernandez, Louis
Hecker, Louis
Hernandez, Celis
Hernandez, Raymond
Hernandez, Reyes
Hernandez, Andrew
Hernandez, Samuel
Hernandez, John
Henniger, Dean
Henniger, David
Jimenez, Arthur
Jimenez, Jess
Landa, Andrew
Landa, Mike
Lopez, Danny
Landa, Manuel
Lopez, Joe
Leon, Arthur
Lopez, Mike
Mata, Carmen
Morales, David
Moreno, Ernest
Moreno, Joe
Moreno, Rudolph
Martinez, Domingo
Martinez, Raul
Moreno, Robert
Marieta, Arnalfo
Marina, Salvador
Marcias, Bobby
Morales, David
Martinez, Thomas
Morales, Joe
Martinez, Ramiro
Mata, Alex
Mata, Corneluis
Mata, Richard
Moreno, Leandro
Moreno, Theodor
Martinez, Andrew
Nava, Raul
Nava, Richard
Nunez, Joe
Nava, Salvador
Noriega, Emilio
Ortega, Peter
Olea, Manuel
Olea, Raymond
Padilla, Ben
Padilla, Joe
Pessa, Richard
Pessa, Raymond
Padilla, William
Paiz, Pas
Paiz, Nieves
Perez, William
Perez, Adolf
Perez, Robert
Quiroz, Leonard
Quiroz, Henry
Quiroz, Michael
Ramirez, Anthoney
Ramirez, Daniel
Ramirez, Rudolph
Ramirez, Fred
Ramirez, Joe
Ravago, Raul
Ravago, Lawrence
Raya, John
Raya, Ralph
Raya, Arthur
Raynosa, Edward
Raynosa, Mike
Regalado, John
Regalado, Robert
Reyas, Tony
Reyas, Peter
Rincon, Abraham
Rincon, Johnnie
Rincon, Tonny
Rios, Danny
Rojas, Jesus
Rodriquez, Parfirio
Rodriguez, Urbano
Rodriguez, Robert
Rojas, Harold
Rodriguez, John
Rodriguez, Joe
Rodriguez, Alfonso
Rodriguez, Arthur
Sambrano, David
Sambrano, Raymond
Sambrano, Manuel
Sandoval, Frank
Salazar, Arthur
Sandoval, Tony
Sandoval, Joseph
Sermina, Joe
Salais, Fred
Salcido Joe
Salinas, Augustine
Salazar, Jesse
Salazar, Lionel
Sandoval, Angel
Sata, Vincent
Salazar, Leonard
Salazar, Magnolia
Salazar, Steve
Salcido, Tony
Solano, Richard
Talamentes, Daniel
Talamentes, Robert
Talamentes, Joe
Tarbaye, Tony
Tarin, Tom
Taveson, Steve
Tarin, Gilbert
Tellis, Fred
Torres, Jerry
Valenzuela, Arthur
Verdugo, Gilbert
Vasquez, Richard
Vasquez, George
Vasquez, Tony
Verdugo, Gilbert
Vargas, Jasper
Villegas, Gilbert
Vollaire, Arthur
Vollaire, Edward

Citizens of San Gabriel Who Served in the American Armed Forces In the Vietnam War

Killed In Service

Bruce HoranceEaton
Lee Thomas Hamman
Allen Dale Jagialo
John Robert Piper
Mickey Eugene Griffith
Rene Zaragoza Hernandez
Isidro Briceno Jimenez
Henry Valen Zuela Jr.
Gary Gorden Hahn
Ralph Wommack Hunt
William James Milton

Mexican Americans in the city of San Gabriel have fought during wartime. In the 1950s, John W. Cokely, a former principal at Lincoln Elementary School, compiled a list of those who served in World War II. Friends and community members helped in compiling the roster. The list was lost for many years, but thanks to the herculean efforts of Art Hernández, it was rediscovered and offered to the Reyner Aguirre American Legion Post 748 in San Gabriel. The list includes over 300 Spanish surnames. (Courtesy of the San Gabriel Historical Association.)

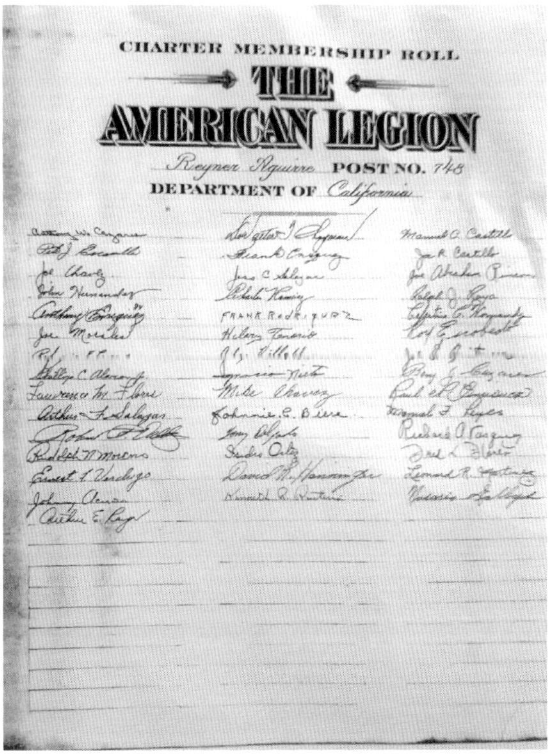

CHARTER MEMBERSHIP ROLL
THE
AMERICAN LEGION
Reyner Aguirre POST NO. 748
DEPARTMENT OF California

The Reyner Aguirre Post 748 was founded by Mexican American World War II veterans when they were denied membership by the local American Legion post. This form of discrimination was tragically commonplace throughout the country. In uniform response, Mexican American servicemen and servicewomen established their own posts. San Gabriel residents killed in action during World War II include Reyner Aguirre, Cruz Díaz, Joe Landa, Leonard Nolasco, John Pérez, Robert Regalado, Robert Reynoso, Salvador Reynoso, Robert Rincón, Alex Robeledo, Arthur Rodríguez, Mike Rodríguez, Cruz Sambrano, Joseph Valenzuela, Lupe Vásquez, and Jesús Villa. (Courtesy of the San Gabriel Historical Association.)

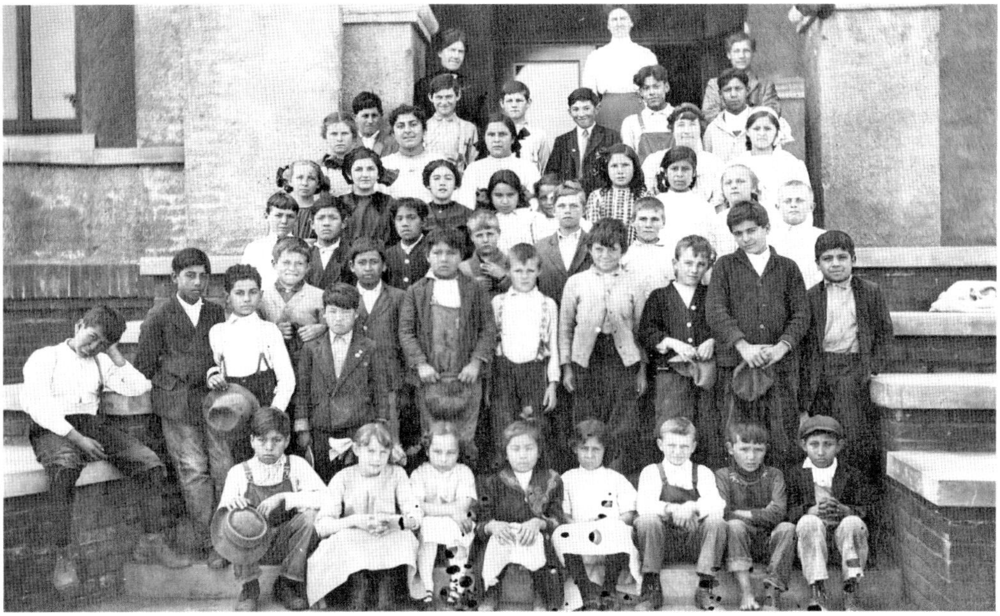

Lincoln School was built in 1912 in the Native/Mexican barrio of San Gabriel. Children from all ethnic backgrounds attended the school. It was torn down in 1935 and replaced by a modern four-story building. By the early 1950s, the school was becoming more segregated. White children living across the street from the school were sent to other schools in the district. Mexican parents became concerned and demanded that the school be closed and the school district integrated. The school was sold to the Los Angeles County School District in 1956. (Courtesy of the San Gabriel Historical Association Museum archives.)

Washington School was built in 1888 at the corner of Hermosa Drive and Shorb Street (now San Marino Avenue) in San Gabriel. It was considered one of the most ornate in Southern California. The bell in the school's tower could be heard all over the township of San Gabriel. A young George S. Patton rode his horse to school from his home near the Huntington Library. Patton later became a military hero during World War II. A larger school was built in 1923 and modernized in 1993. (Courtesy of the San Gabriel Historical Association Museum archives.)

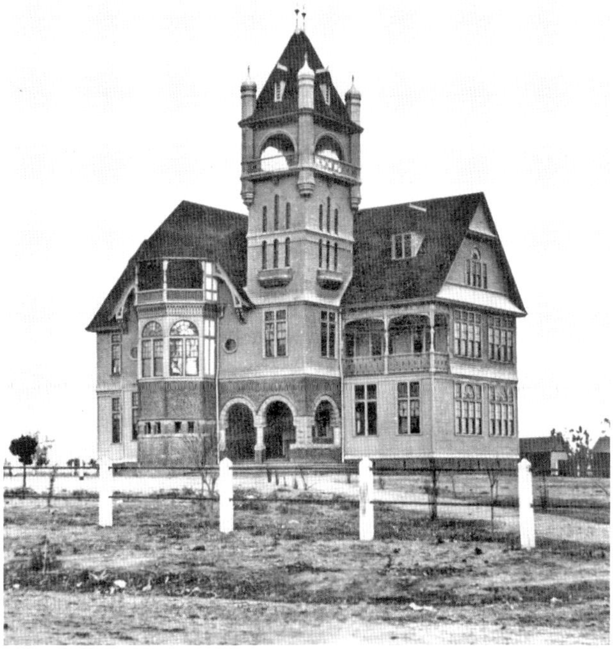

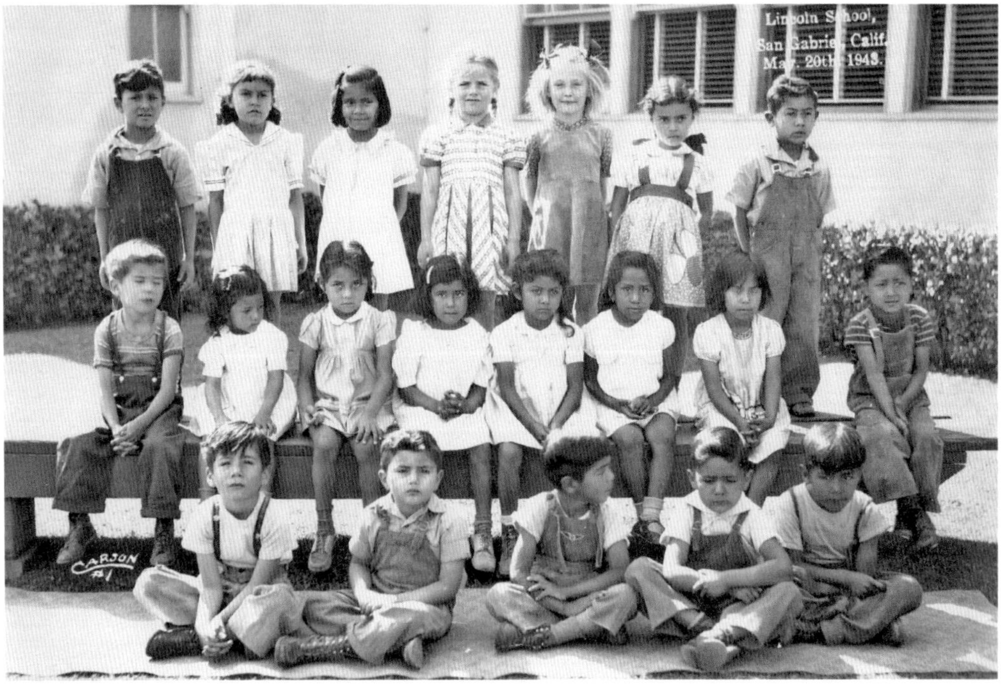

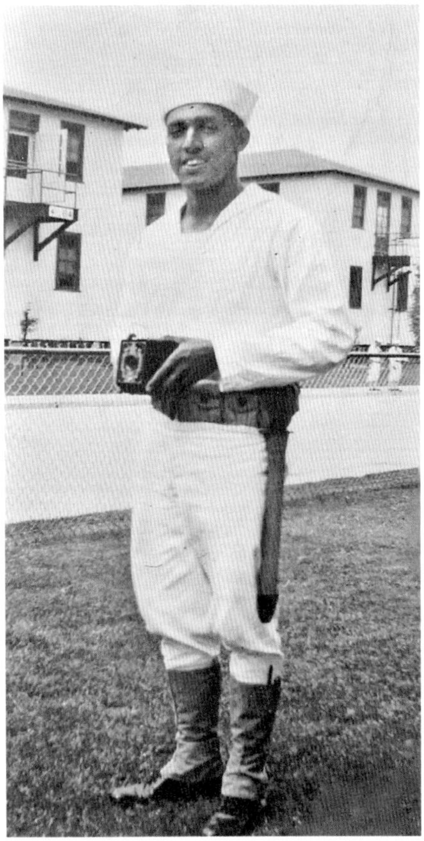

This is the 1942 Lincoln Elementary School graduating class. The school was built in the predominately Mexican American neighborhood in San Gabriel. Some of the students are ? Reynoso, Nacho Acuña, Ernie Hernández, Freddie Ramírez, ? Nieto, Albert Acuña, Frances Escobedo, Martha Chávez Guzmán, Everlyn Solano, Esther ?, Gloria Enríguez, Mary Díaz Barrios, Isabel Martínez, Delia Sánchez, ? Ramírez, Art Cobos, "Little" Joe Hernández, Fred Marquez, Peter Quintanar, and John Díaz. (Courtesy of Camila Alva López.)

Reyner "Nero" Aguirre was born in 1918 and raised in San Gabriel. He enlisted in the US Navy and was killed on the USS *Arizona* during the attack on Pearl Harbor on December 7, 1941. His name is fifth from the top in the first row on the USS Arizona Memorial. Reyner Aguirre American Legion Post 748 is named in his honor. The majority of the post members are Mexican Americans who have served in several wars since World War II. (Courtesy of Steve Salazar.)

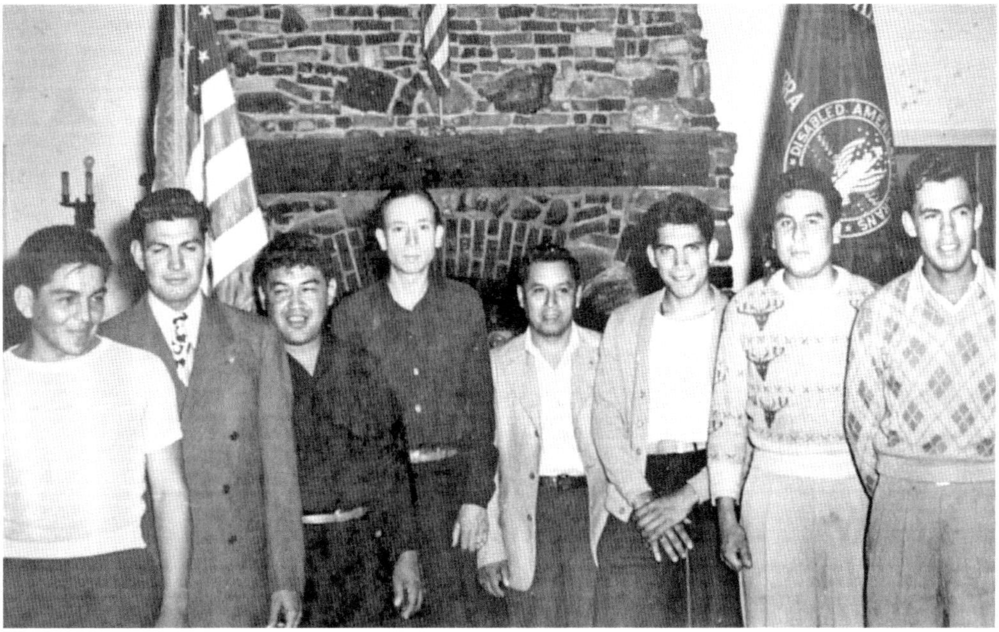

World War II veterans of Reyner Aguirre American Legion Post 748 are seen in the late 1940s. Nearly all of them were born and raised in San Gabriel and are from the original families who first settled in the city. Many played baseball and football on community and school teams. From left to right are Andrew Pérez, Dean Albert Henninger, Joe Robledo, Chubby Thompson, Johnny Miller, George García, Leo Quintar, and Tommy Martínez. (Courtesy of "Chief" Ernie Salas.)

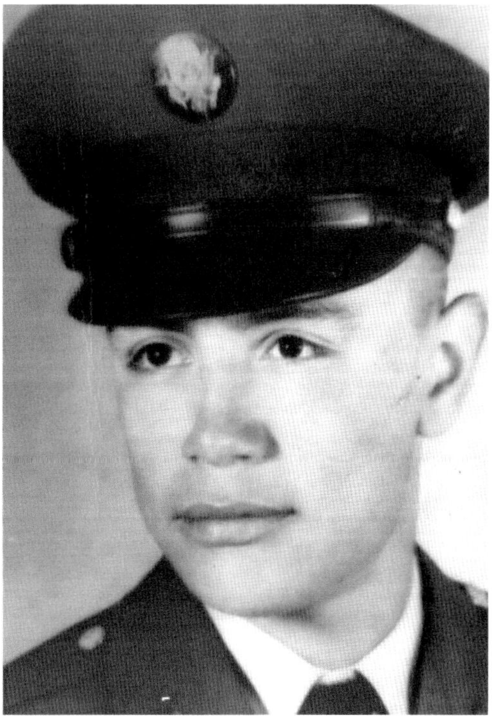

Dean David Henninger was born in 1943 in San Gabriel. His parents were David Raymond Henninger and Juanita Cortéz who had two other children, Lucille and Linda. The children attended San Gabriel Mission School and San Gabriel High School. In 1954, Dean played for the first-place San Gabriel little league Tigers, winners of 17 of 18 games, including playoffs and the American Minor League Championship game. Dean served three years in the Army from 1963 to 1966, graduating from Airborne school and serving two years in Germany. He later became a civilian truck driver. He married Corine Acuña in 1967 and raised three children, Lorrie, Michelle, and Dean. His family has played ball in the San Gabriel Valley for five decades. Dean passed away in 2013. (Courtesy of James Henninger Aguirre.)

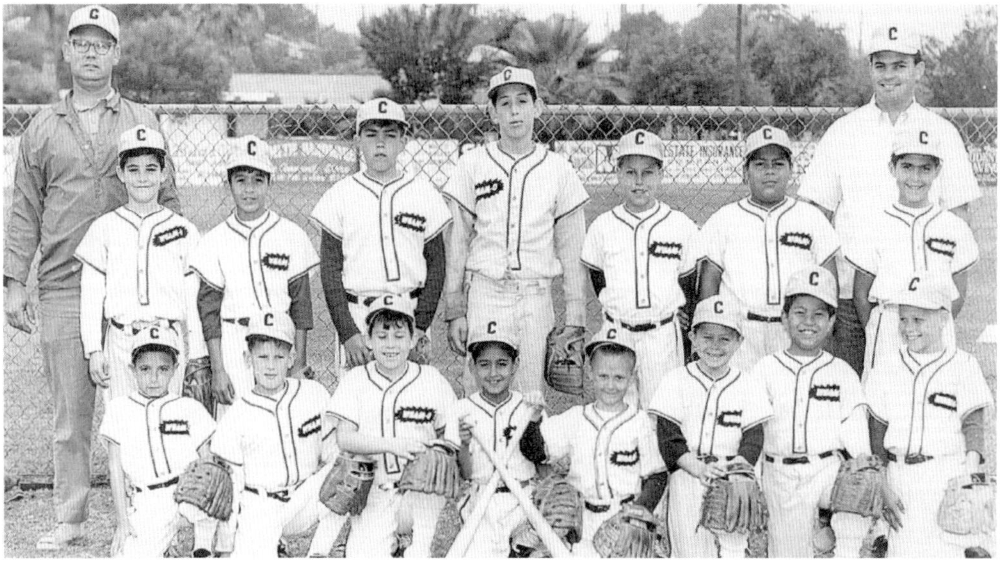

The San Gabriel little league Cubs played at Wells Park. The team was sponsored by the Wham-O toy manufacturing company, located at 835 East El Monte Street in San Gabriel. The company opened its doors in 1955. The San Gabriel little league gave many Mexican American boys the opportunity to play the game. John Ochoa (first row, third from left) was an outstanding starting pitcher for the Cubs. (Courtesy of John E. Ochoa.)

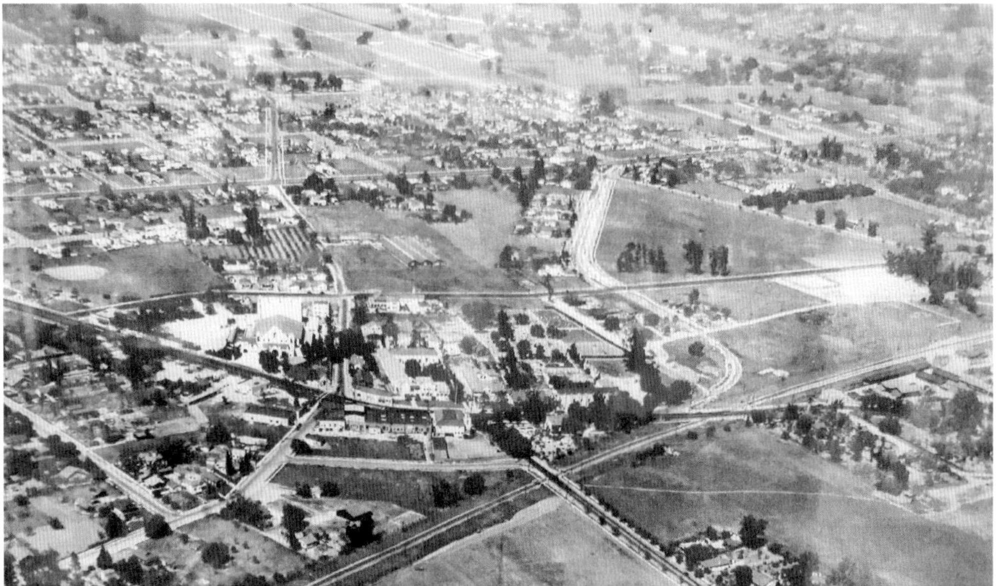

This 1933 aerial photograph shows the San Gabriel Mission District, the Mission Playhouse, and the surrounding neighborhood. The San Gabriel baseball diamond (left), known as Salazar Park, was constructed by manager Mike Salazar on South Mission Drive near Broadway. Several local teams and visiting teams from Mexico graced the field with their extraordinary play. (Courtesy of Camila Alva López.)

This poster promoted a 1928 game between the El Paso Shoe Store and Mission Bell Soaps teams in San Gabriel. The Los Angeles–based El Paso Shoe Store sponsored some of the best teams in Southern California during the 1920s and 1930s. Games were often publicized with posters on storefront windows, telephone poles, community centers, church halls, theater lobbies, factory lunchrooms, and barbershops. The first American citizen to come overland to San Gabriel was Jedediah Strong Smith, who led a group of trappers down from the Great Salt Lake and across the Mojave Desert, arriving at San Gabriel Mission in November of 1826. The first organized wagon train to San Gabriel brought William Workman, John Rowland, and Benjamin D. Wilson on November 5, 1852. That year, San Gabriel became one of the first townships in Los Angeles County; according to the 1860 census, the population was a mere 586. (Courtesy of the Orozco family and Richard J. Arnold.)

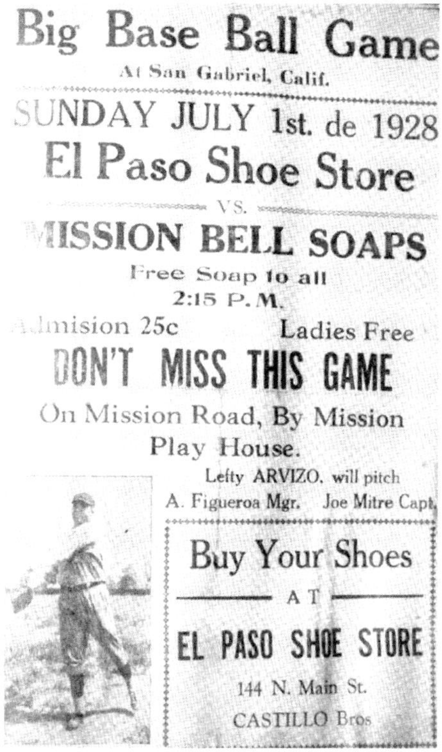

EL PASO SHOES WIN

The El Paso Shoe nine thumped the San Gabriel club, 12 to 2, yesterday. Score:

EL PASO SHOES	AB	H	O	A
Orosco,rf	6	3	1	1
Kat'ros,2b	5	1	3	0
Lima,3b	4	2	2	2
Speaker,ss	5	2	0	4
M.Lopez,cf	4	1	2	0
E.Lopez,1b	4	1	8	0
Rod'quez,p	3	2	0	0
Metro,c	5	2	10	2
Ramirez,lf	5	0	1	0
Totals	41	14	29	9

SAN GABRIEL	AB	H	O	A
Thorne,3b	4	0	1	0
Diaz,c	4	2	7	2
Gonzales,lf	4	0	1	0
Perez,ss	3	1	1	2
Gradias,1b	4	1	11	1
M'All'er,2b	3	1	3	1
Manzer,rf	4	3	1	0
Molina,cf	4	0	2	0
Puter,p	1	1	0	1
Ryan,p	1	0	0	2
Vidales,lf	1	0	0	0
Totals	33	9	27	9

SCORE BY INNINGS

El Paso Shoes......	4	0	2	1	5	0	0	0	0	—12
Base hits	4	0	3	2	4	0	0	0	1	—14
San Gabriel	0	1	0	0	0	0	0	1	0	— 2
Base hits	0	2	1	1	1	0	1	1	2	— 9

SUMMARY

Errors—Speaker, Perez. Innings pitched —By Rodriguez, 9; Luter, 3 1-3; Ryan, 2 2-3; Cerez, 3. Credit victory to Rodriquez. Charge defeat to Puter. Struck out—By Rodriquez, 8; Perez, 4. Hit by pitched ball—Speaker. Stolen bases—Orozco, Ramirez. Three-base hit—Orozco. Time of game—2h.

Major newspapers in Los Angeles and throughout the San Gabriel Valley ran daily baseball stories, game summaries, side notes, box scores, and photographs, especially on the powerhouse teams like the El Paso Shoe Store, Carmelita Provisions Company, and several San Gabriel teams. This is a box score from a 1920s game between the El Paso Shoe Store and a San Gabriel team. Fans purchased newspapers to keep abreast of their favorite players and teams. During this time, some families actually kept scrapbooks of newspaper clippings highlighting members of their families and neighborhood teams. A few of these remarkable scrapbooks have survived to the present day and provide a glimpse of the golden age of Mexican American baseball in the San Gabriel Valley. (Courtesy of the Orozco family.)

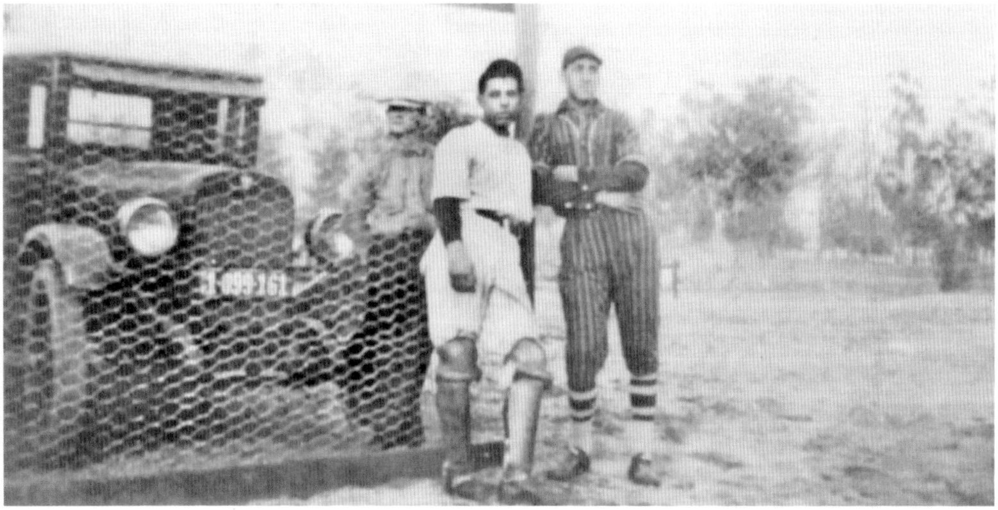

Andrés Díaz (left) and Joe Barreras pose before a game. The car and well-dressed man behind the fence indicate that wealthy and influential people attended games, contrary to the notion that Mexican American baseball only attracted working-class fans. For Mexican American women ballplayers, the game was a social counterbalance to the strict cultural roles defined for them. Many players also devoted their lives to the unrelenting struggle for social justice. (Courtesy of Margaret Sosa.)

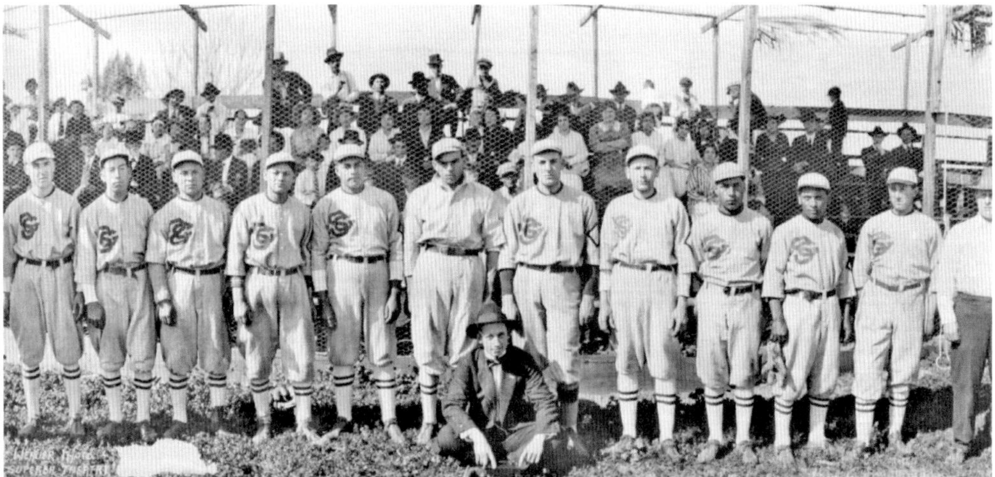

This 1917 San Gabriel Aztecs team was sponsored by Killinger Brothers. Mexican American teams were sponsored by local merchants who saw value in having these teams promote their businesses. In many cases, several businesses would collectively sponsor Mexican American teams. That is why many teams were called the Merchants. In order to attract the best players, merchants often enticed players with free food, gas, and of course, beer. Wealthier merchants purchased the uniforms, equipment, and transportation for road games. It was not uncommon for the best Mexican American players to play on more than one team. (Courtesy of James Henninger Aguirre.)

District 18 little league baseball for the state of California encompasses several leagues in the San Gabriel Valley, including Alhambra, El Monte, Rosemead, San Gabriel, South El Monte, South Pasadena, Sunnyslope, and Temple City. This 1966 award for sportsmanship recognizes district administrator Roy A. Praisler. The San Gabriel Valley, like so many other regions in California, has reflected the various patterns of immigration during the past century, including players with cultural roots in Europe, Latin America, Asia, and the Middle East. (Courtesy of the San Gabriel Historical Association.)

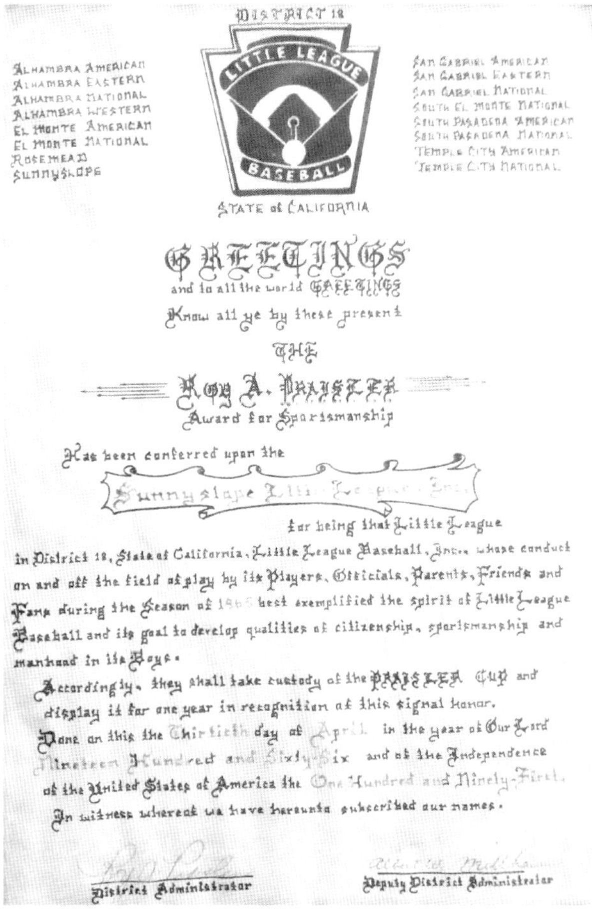

DISTRICT 18

Alhambra American
Alhambra Eastern
Alhambra National
Alhambra Western
El Monte American
El Monte National
Rosemead
Sunnyslope

LITTLE LEAGUE BASEBALL

San Gabriel American
San Gabriel Eastern
San Gabriel National
South El Monte National
South Pasadena American
South Pasadena National
Temple City American
Temple City National

STATE of CALIFORNIA

GREETINGS
and to all the world GREETINGS
Know all ye by these present
THE
Roy A. Praisler
Award for Sportsmanship

Has been conferred upon the
Sunnyslope Li[illegible]
for being that Little League
in District 18, State of California, Little League Baseball, Inc., whose conduct on and off the field of play by its Players, Officials, Parents, Friends and Fans during the Season of 1965 best exemplified the spirit of Little League Baseball and its goal to develop qualities of citizenship, sportsmanship and manhood in its Boys.

Accordingly, they shall take custody of the PRAISLER CUP and display it for one year in recognition of this signal honor.

Done on this the Thirtieth day of April in the year of Our Lord Nineteen Hundred and Sixty-Six and of the Independence of the United States of America the One Hundred and Ninety-First.

In witness whereof we have hereunto subscribed our names.

District Administrator

Deputy District Administrator

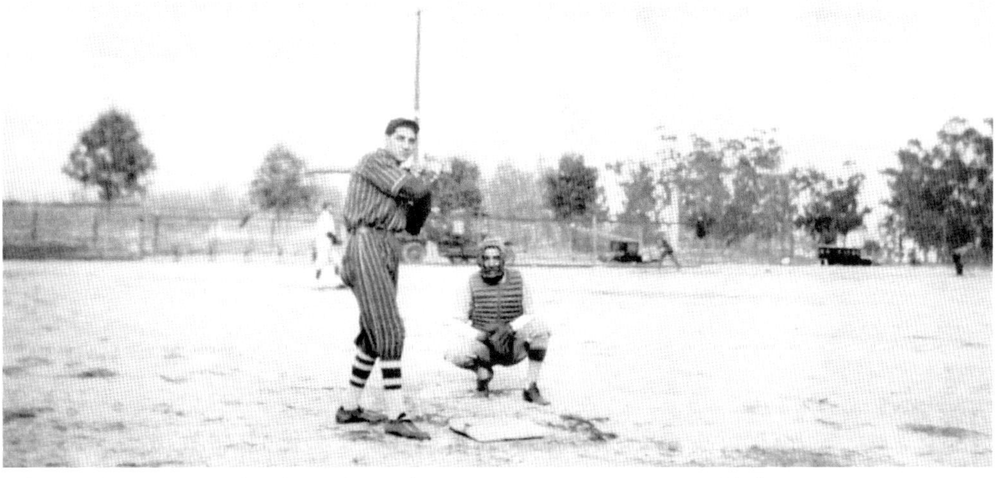

After California gained independence from Mexico, Gov. Pio Pico sold the 21 missions in 1846. Pres. James Buchanan returned the missions to the Catholic Church in 1859. Mexican Americans often played baseball near their local mission. Here, players Andrés Díaz (left) and Joe Barreras pose before a game with the Gosney Stars. (Courtesy of Margaret Sosa and Richard J. Arnold.)

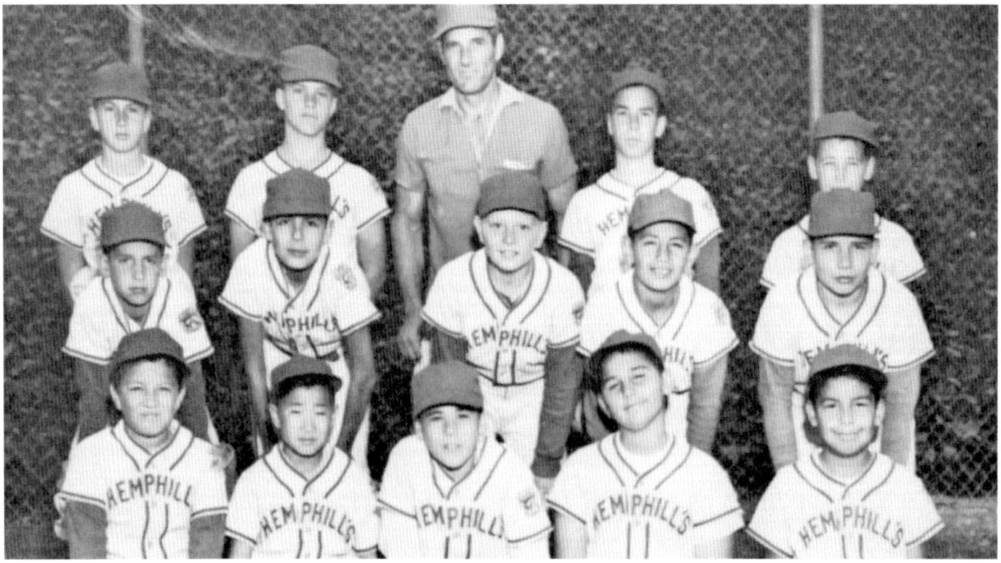

The San Gabriel Eastern little league Stride Rites were the champions in 1962. From left to right are (first row) John Gómez, Glen Ito, Larry Johnson, Tom Miali, and Raoul Martínez; (second row) Bob Hardman, Anthony Alva, Jacky Kuehfuss, John Adams, and Edward Rodríguez; (third row) Michael Ciaglia, Brad La Verne, coach Bob La Verne, Lawrence Ricci, and Robert Kaczmarek. Manager Bob Martínez and Mike Greene are not pictured. (Courtesy of the San Gabriel Historical Association Museum archives.)

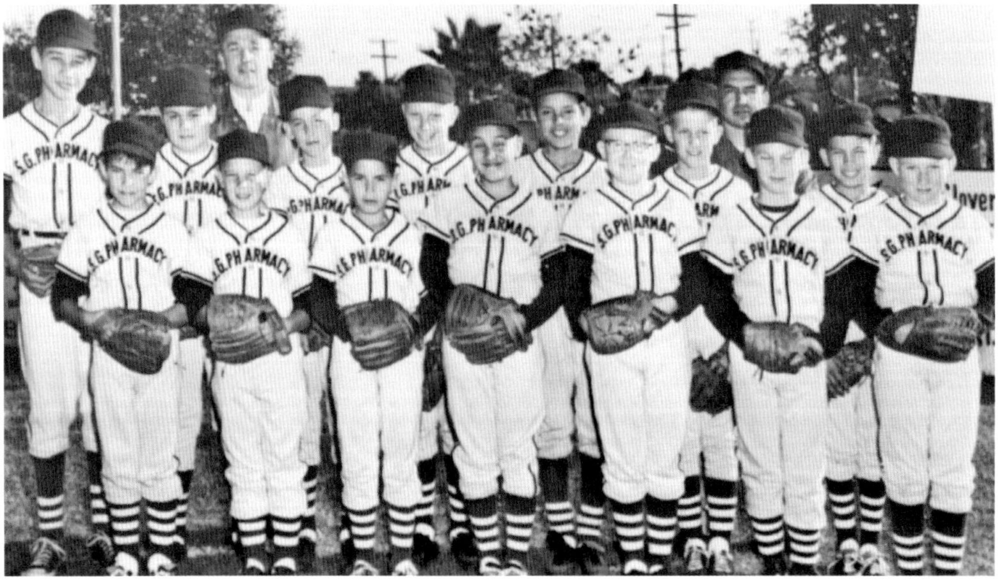

The 1963 San Gabriel little league Colts were sponsored by S.G. Pharmacy. From left to right are (first row) Russell Dion, Mitchell Herdman, Mike Catelli, Rick Raya, Don Pollard, Tom Nelson, and John McInvale; (second row) Edward Águilar, Ronnie Luján, Robbie Herdman, Tifin Bush, Ed Del Palacio, Tony Marley, and Marion Acuña; (third row) manager Bob Herdman and coach Art Raya. (Courtesy of the San Gabriel Historical Association Museum archives.)

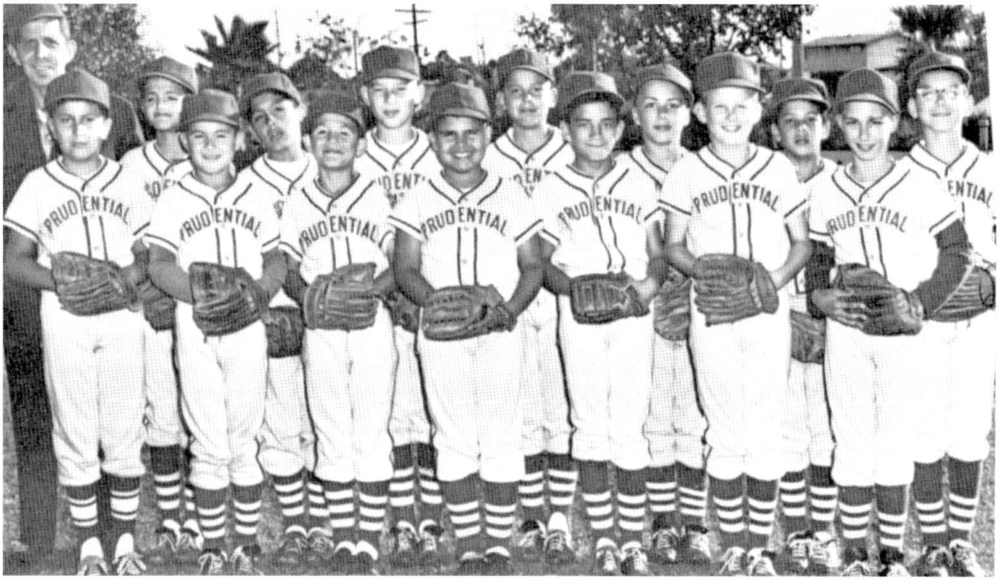

The 1963 San Gabriel little league Savers were sponsored by the Prudential Company. From left to right are (first row) Anthony García, Michael Poblano, Arthur Andrade, Leonard Díaz, Richard Castillo, Gary Franzen, and Bryron Banks; (second row) manager Jess Jiménez, Richard Esparza, Richard Valenzuela, Mike Rodríguez, Frank Rodríguez, Bruce Banks, Bob Espalin, and Tom Blomo. (Courtesy of the San Gabriel Historical Association.)

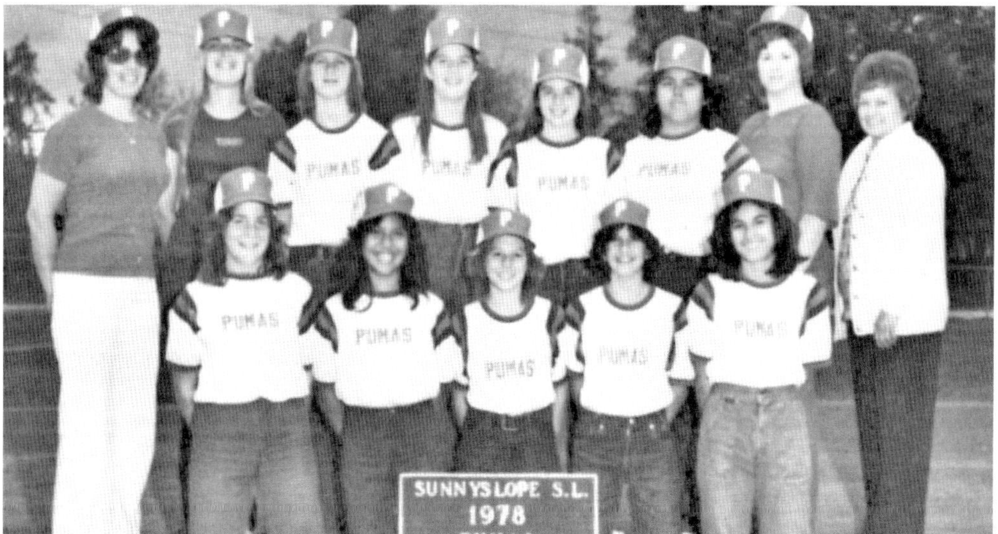

The 1978 San Gabriel Pumas softball team played against several rivals, including the Eagles, Condors, Mustangs, Jaguars, Panthers, and Cougars. From left to right are (first row) Kathy Palmer, Denise Marquéz, Deanna Bracci, Cheri López, and Michelle Guzmán; (second row) Kathy Johnson, Donna Raef, Mary Geer, and Rhonda Guzmán. Also included are manager Claudia Johnson, business manager Betty Geer, and coaches Terry Raef and Vicky López. Michele Basta and Carrie Spaulding are not pictured. (Courtesy of San Gabriel Historical Association Museum archives.)

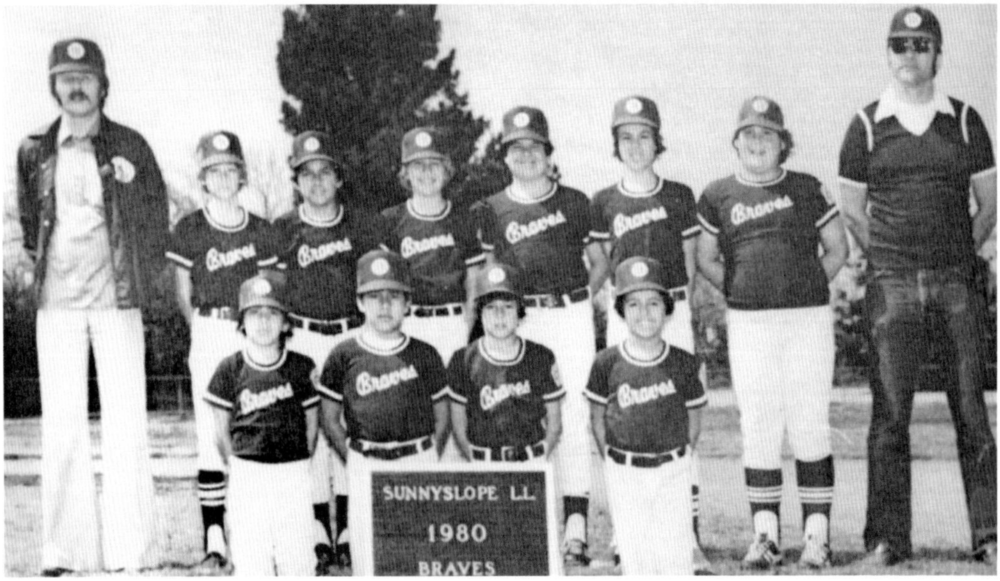

The 1980 Sunnyslope little league Braves played in San Gabriel. Players from left to right are (first row) Arthur Castro, Camillo Suárez, Aaron Ruíz, and Peter Nava; (second row) Gus Hooper, Paul Ramírez, Mike Johnson, Paul Rubio, George Hardash, and Mike Muscato. (Courtesy of the San Gabriel Historical Association Museum archives.)

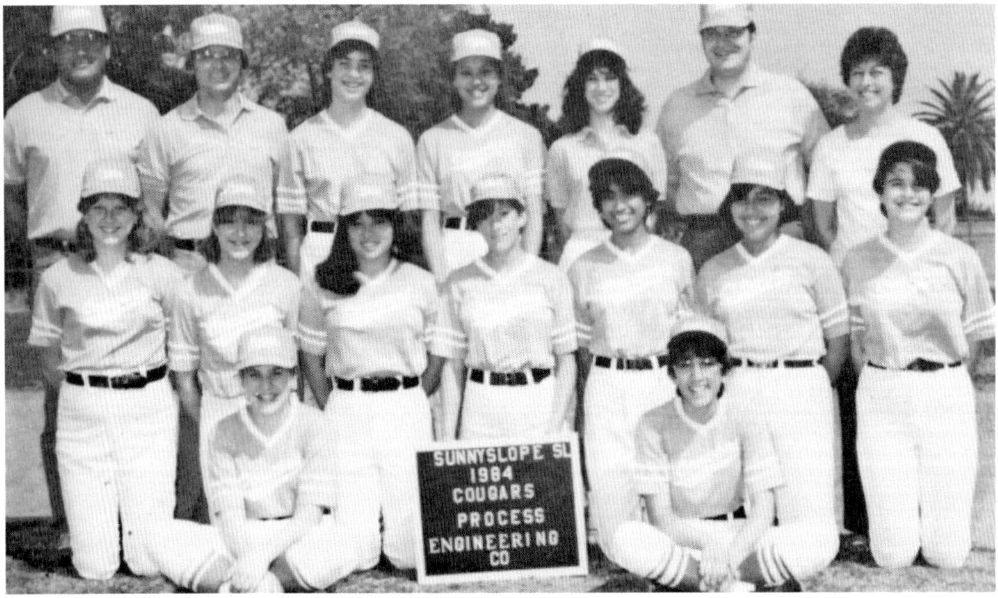

The 1984 Sunnyslope little league Cougars played softball in San Gabriel. From left to right are (first row) Jennifer Giambelluca and Christi Montes; (second row) Michelle James, Amy Lewis, Kim Rodríguez, Carolyn Basulto, Rosie Reyes, Erika Quintana, and Annelies Evans; (third row) Mona Soto and Dioni Rovello. Also included are manager Rei James, business manager Judy Hand, coaches Russ Giabelluca and Charlie Soto, and assistant coach Natalie Willer. (Courtesy of the San Gabriel Historical Association Museum archives.)

Hank John Aguirre (1931–1994), nicknamed "the Tall Mexican" due to his height, was born in Azusa, California, to Joseph Aguirre and Jenny Alva. In his youth, he worked at his father's business, the Aguirre Market in San Gabriel. He pitched in the major leagues for 16 years, including for the Los Angeles Dodgers in 1968 and the Chicago Cubs from 1969 to 1970. After retirement, Aguirre became a successful businessman and founder of Mexican Industries in Detroit. He passed away in 1994 and is survived by his former wife, Barbara; their four children, Rance, Pamela, Robin, and Jill; and his widow, Tina. He is buried at the San Gabriel Mission Cemetery. (Courtesy of James Henninger Aguirre.)

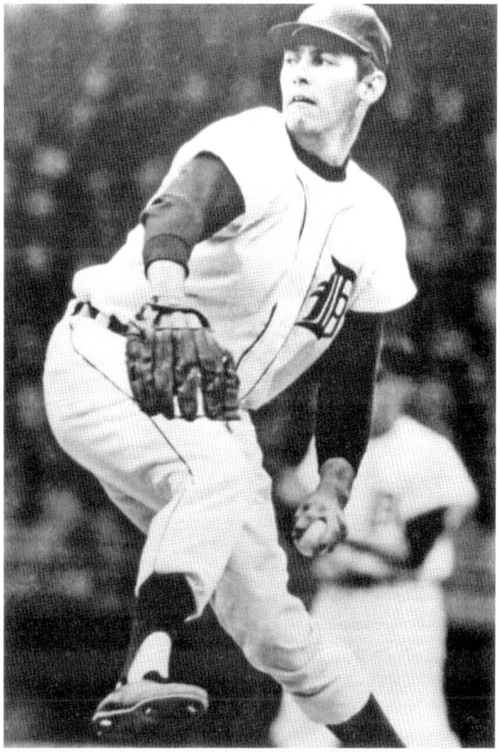

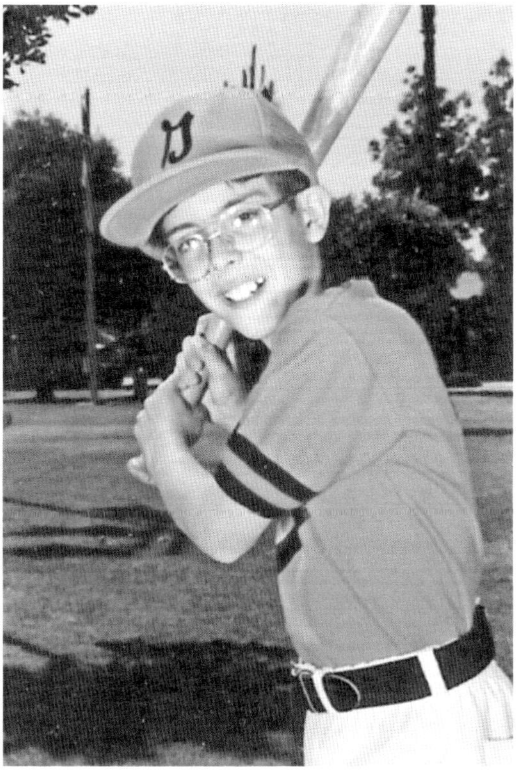

Born in Boyle Heights in East Los Angeles, where Japanese American doctors who had been interned during World War II helped deliver him and save his life, Paul Cole Padilla was raised by his Pilgrim-Scottish-Irish American mother, Margaret, and Chicano father, Fred, in San Gabriel. The only son of schoolteachers, he is a proud graduate of San Gabriel public schools (Coolidge and Jefferson), Don Bosco Technical Institute (Materials Science) and UCLA (Chicanx Studies). From 1987 to 1991, he played little league in San Gabriel. An educator and activist, Paul is considering entering public service to contribute more to his community and country. (Courtesy of Paul Cole Padilla.)

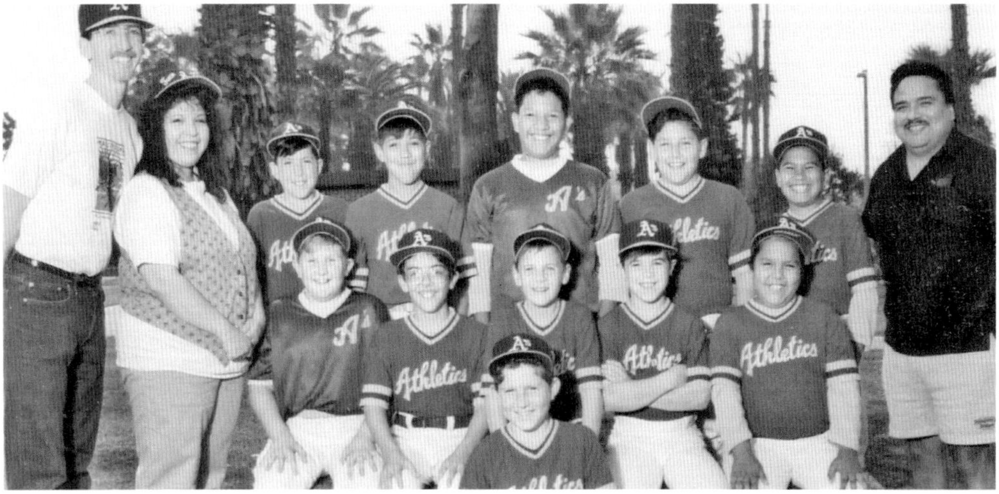

The 1990 San Gabriel little league Athletics (majors level) included Paul Cole Padilla (seated, glasses). Like all teams in the majors, the A's played at Vincent Lugo Park, formerly Municipal Park and Wells Park, which was rechristened in 1988 in honor of San Gabriel's longtime parks supervisor, a member of the Los Angeles region's historic Lugo family. Behind the baseball diamond lies La Laguna (the lagoon), a legendary playground full of giant mythical and real sea creatures brought to life by noted Mexican American artist Benjamin Domínguez in 1965. The playground is affectionately known as "Dinosaur" or "Monster" Park. (Courtesy of Paul Cole Padilla.)

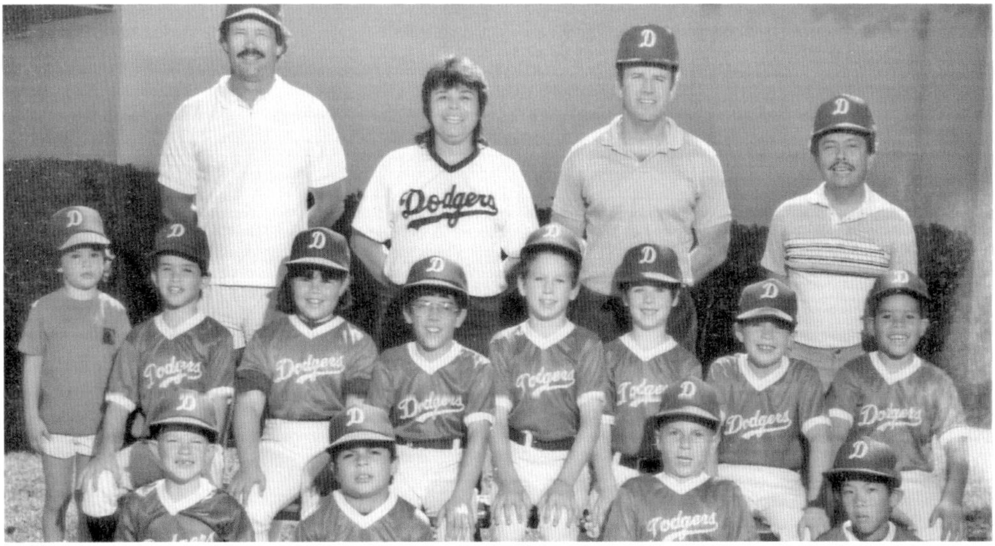

The 1988 Dodgers were not just Major League Baseball's World Series champions, they were also a fun San Gabriel little league team that featured ballplayers Napoleón Quezada (first row, second from left), Paul Cole Padilla (second row, third player from left), and R.C. Cardiel (second row, far right). The coaches included Andrea Cardiel (second from left) and Fred Padilla (Paul's father, far right). Games were played at McKinley Elementary School's diamond, where all T-ball, instructional, and minors-level games were played in San Gabriel's little league. (Courtesy of Paul Cole Padilla.)

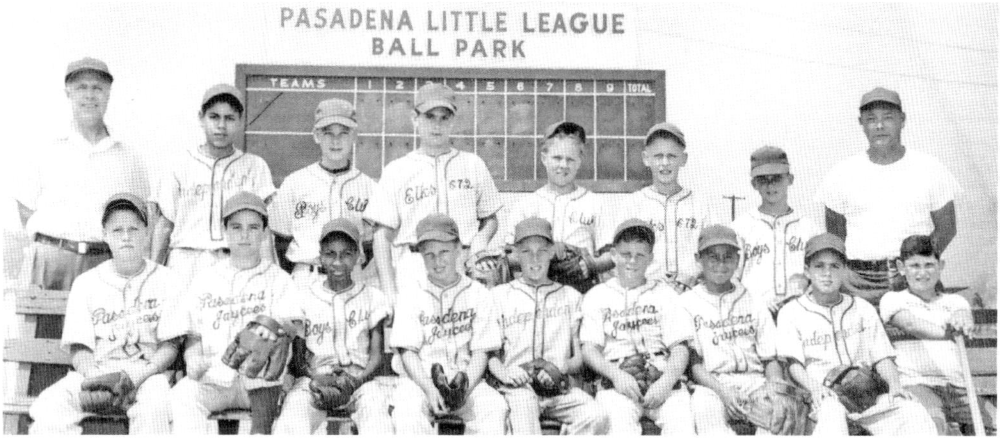

Carlos Salazar's family has a long and rich baseball history in the San Gabriel Valley dating to the 1920s. His uncle Mike built a baseball field at South Mission Drive and Broadway near the San Gabriel Playhouse in the late 1920s. Carlos's father, Dave, was one of the biggest baseball stars in California, Arizona, New Mexico, and Mexico. The Salazar family is related to another legendary baseball family, the Orozcos. Carlos (second row, second from left) is seen in 1952 with the West Pasadena little league All Stars. (Courtesy of Carlos Salazar.)

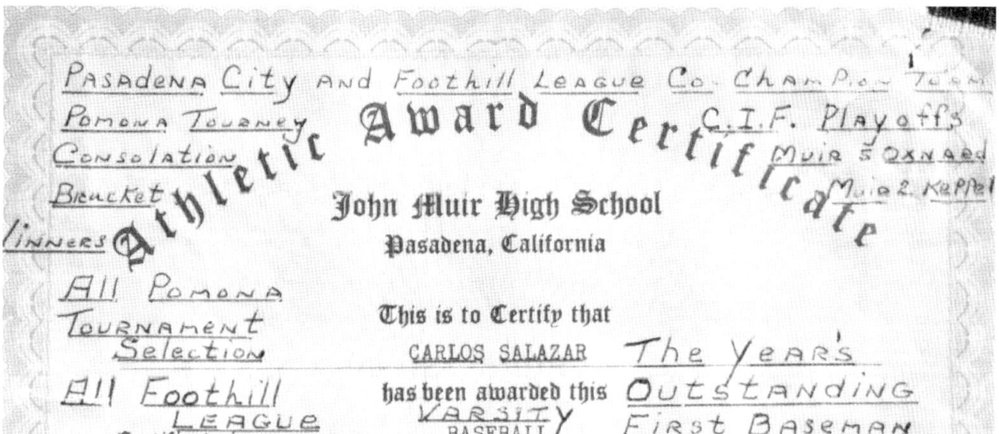

Pasadena City and Foothill League Co. Champion Team
Pomona Tourney Consolation Bracket Winners
C.I.F. Playoffs Muir 5 Oxnard Muir 2 Keppel

Athletic Award Certificate

John Muir High School
Pasadena, California

This is to Certify that
CARLOS SALAZAR
has been awarded this
Certificate in VARSITY BASEBALL
for the season of NINETEEN HUNDRED AND FIFTY-SEVEN

The Year's Outstanding First Baseman

All Pomona Tournament Selection
All Foothill League

Ed. J. Lawrenson — Director
Don Shoup — Coach

355 Batting Average

Carlos Salazar was an outstanding ballplayer at John Muir High School and at Pasadena City College. His two older sisters, Eleanor and Margaret, played softball for Muir Tech and for Carl's Shoes, the Pasadena Ramblers, and professionally. His brother, David, had a great career, including military ball while stationed in Japan. Carlos and David extended their baseball careers by becoming umpires and often umpired the same game. Carlos and David are related to Camila Alva López of San Gabriel. The Salazar and Alva families are spread throughout the San Gabriel Valley. (Courtesy of Carlos Salazar.)

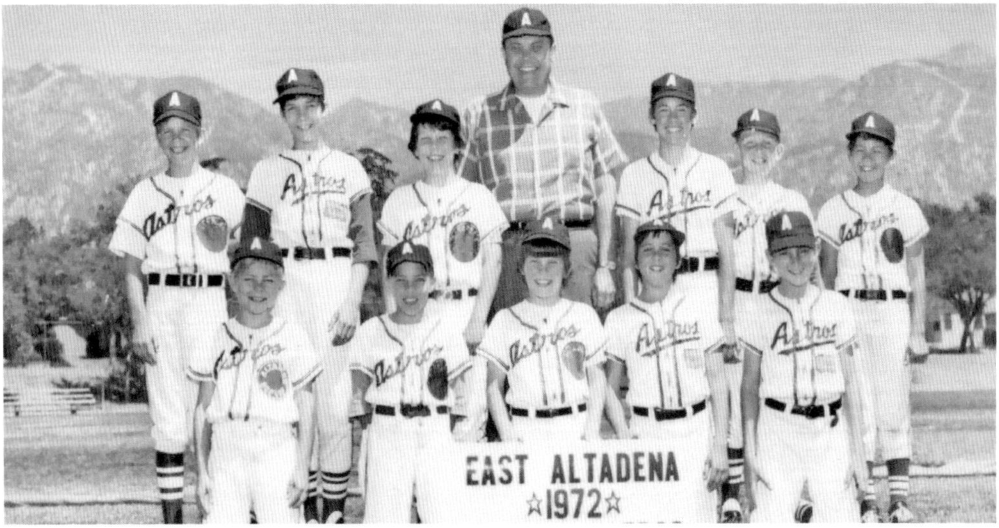

Greg Salazar (second row, far right) played for the 1972 East Altadena Astros. He played four years of little league, two years with the Pasadena Pony League (coached by his cousins Kenneth and Bernie Peralta), and one year of Babe Ruth League. Sadly, he blew out his knee swinging a bat, and ended his playing days. Greg comes from several generations of ballplayers. His father, Carlos, had a remarkable career in youth, high school, college, and community ball, and later was an outstanding umpire. Greg's grandfather Dave and great uncle Mike had distinguished baseball careers throughout California, especially in the San Gabriel Valley. (Courtesy of Carlos Salazar.)

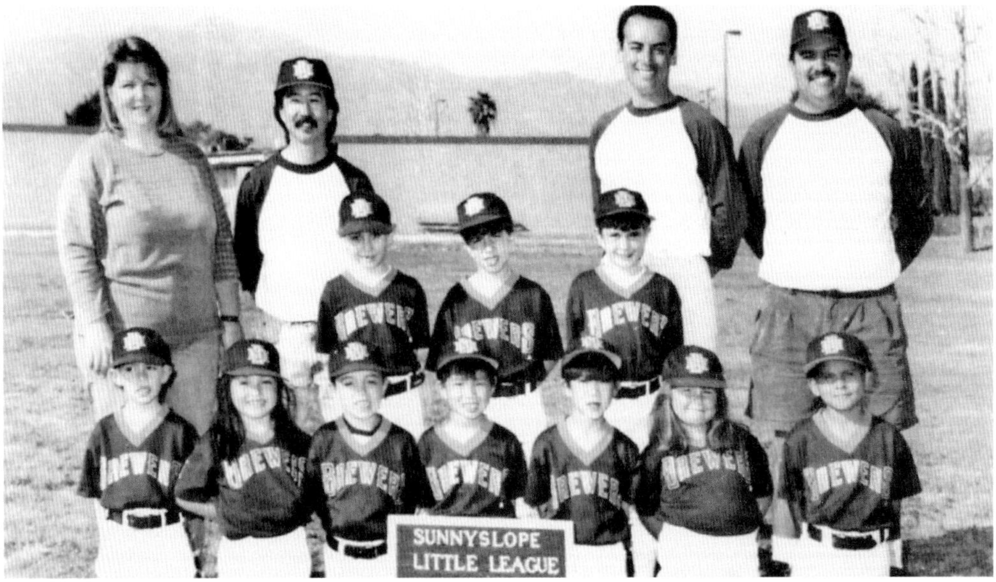

The 1996 Sunnyslope little league Brewers played T-ball in San Gabriel. The T-ball commissioner was Steve Soto. From left to right are (first row) Aaron De La Rosa, Valerie Pérez, Johnny Escobedo Jr., Daniel Chen, Shawn Yoshida, Samantha Streit, and Venancio Pérez; (second row) Jimmy Delgadillo, Andrew Águilar, and Danny Bryant; (third row) parents and coaches Debbie Streit, Glenn Yoshida, John Escobedo, and unidentified. (Courtesy of the San Gabriel Historical Association.)

2

SAN GABRIEL VALLEY

The indigenous people of the Los Angeles Basin occupied the San Gabriel Valley for about 12,000 years. The tribal name for these original people was Kizh, meaning "house." After the arrival of the Spanish in the 1760s, especially the Catholic Church and the military, a series of missions were constructed throughout California. Franciscan priest and friar Junipero Serra spread the Christian faith and renamed the Kizh peoples the San Gabriel Mission Indians or Gabrieleños after the mission. The original San Gabriel Mission was erected about 1771 in the Kizh village of Shevannga or Siba. The Spanish referred to this land as Potrero Chico ("small pasture land"), which was comprised of willows, tule, and brush, which they used to make their homes.

Floodwaters destroyed the first mission, and a second one was built on higher ground in the Kizh village of Toviscangna. Most of the indigenous people were forced to provide slave labor, resulting in many dying from physical exhaustion and illness. The Spanish established other missions and towns in native villages. After centuries of colonization and intermarriage in both California and Mexico, the majority of indigenous people today are Catholics, speak Spanish, and have Spanish surnames. These are the origins and roots of thousands of Mexican Americans in the San Gabriel Valley. Names of cities and streets reflect this reality: San Gabriel, Alhambra, Montebello, Monterey Park, El Monte, La Puente, Pico Rivera, and Sierra Madre.

The Mexican American population is now the majority in the San Gabriel Valley. Its participation and contribution to sports in this region is deep and remarkable, dating back over a century. Generations of men, women, and children have played baseball and softball in little league, high school, college, summer and winter leagues, industrial teams, church leagues, the military, women's clubs, semiprofessional leagues, minor leagues, and the major leagues. The game teaches the value of teamwork and fair play. It also shows that regardless of race, color, creed, class, gender, physical ability, or age, on the playing field, everyone is equal and has the opportunity to succeed or fail. Baseball and softball diamonds in the San Gabriel Valley are truly fields of dreams.

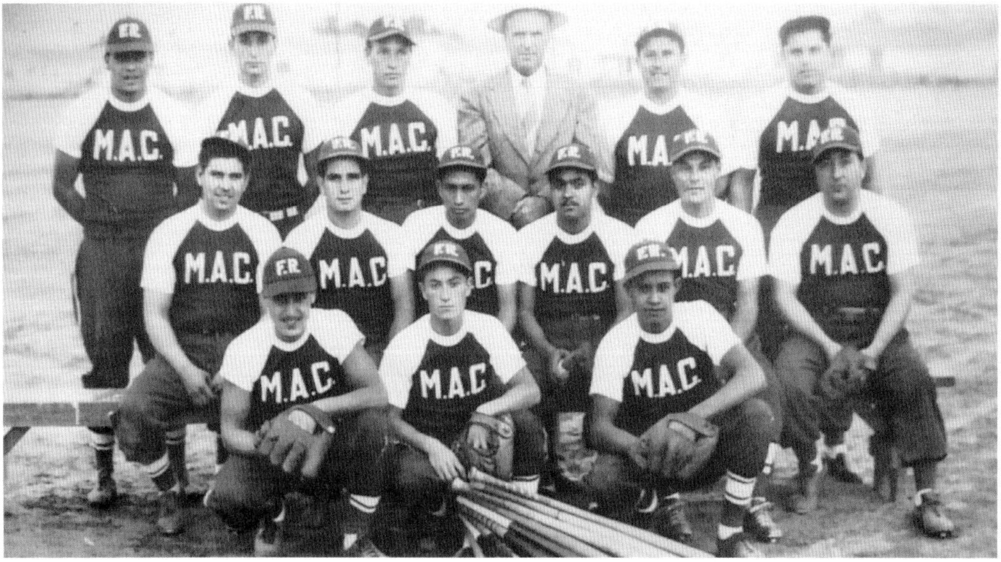

The 1948 Mexican Athletic Club softball team is seen at Memorial Park in Azusa, California. The team was sponsored by the Foothill Ranch Citrus Packing House. All the players were first-generation Mexican Americans and residents of Azusa, and most had served in the US armed forces. From left to right are (first row) Tony Arias, Oscar Aguirre, and Frank Yrigoyen; (second row) Lino Arriaga, Bobby Álvarez, Hank Toledo, Al Rocha, Jesse Bracamontes, and Herman Domínguez; (third row) Sal Luévanos, Tony Ortiz, unidentified, team owner Art Moráles, Tony García, and Pete González. (Courtesy of Bobby Pedroza.)

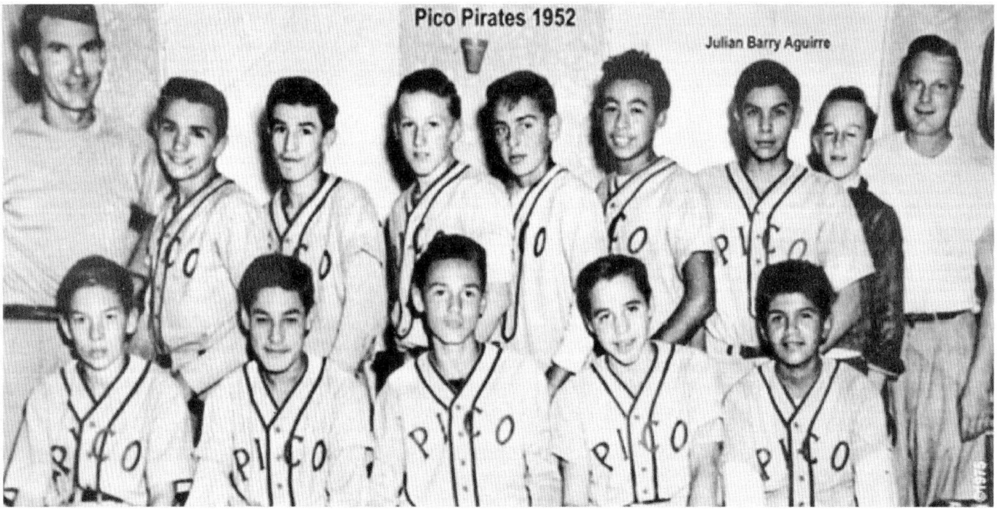

The 1952 little league Pirates played in Pico Rivera. From left to right are (first row) Ronald Barlass, Art Lagunas, Joe Hunt, Dick Constable, and David Olagüe; (second row) coach Art Barlass, Frank Colantuano, Bob Lagunas, Barton Kirk, Carl Clayton, David Salazar, Julian Barry Aguirre, Mike Hamlin, and coach Harris O. Hogenson. Aguirre was born and raised in Pico Rivera and was one of the team's outstanding players, along with childhood friends Art and Bob Lagunas. (Courtesy of James Henninger Aguirre.)

Julian Barry Aguirre and Lucille Henninger Aguirre were married in 1961. They had four children, named Danny, James, Brian, and Jannine. The Aguirre and Henninger families have been playing ball in the San Gabriel Valley for over 100 years. Julian played in the 1950s for the Pico Rivera Pirates. His family were Yaqui, who originally came from Sonora, Mexico, and settled in Pico Rivera, California, in the 1850s. Julian's two brothers, Telesfor and Bernard, served in the armed forces during World War II. Lucille was born in San Gabriel and attended San Gabriel Mission School and San Gabriel High School. Her father, David, served in the Army during World War II and later retired as a police officer with the Los Angeles Police Department. Lucille still lives on the original property in San Gabriel that her family purchased in 1899. (Courtesy of James Henninger Aguirre.)

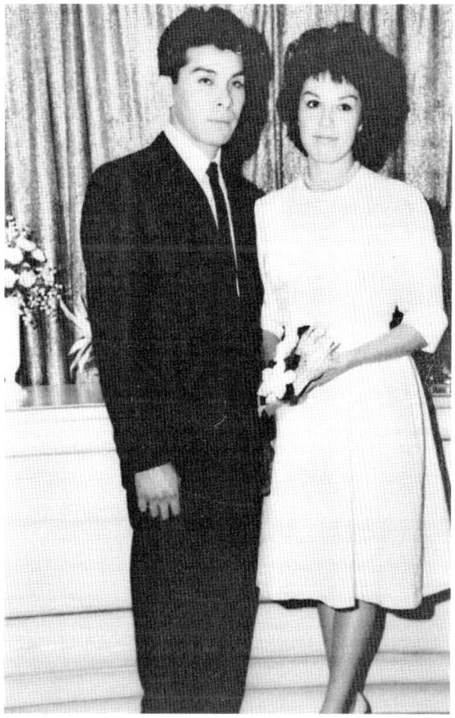

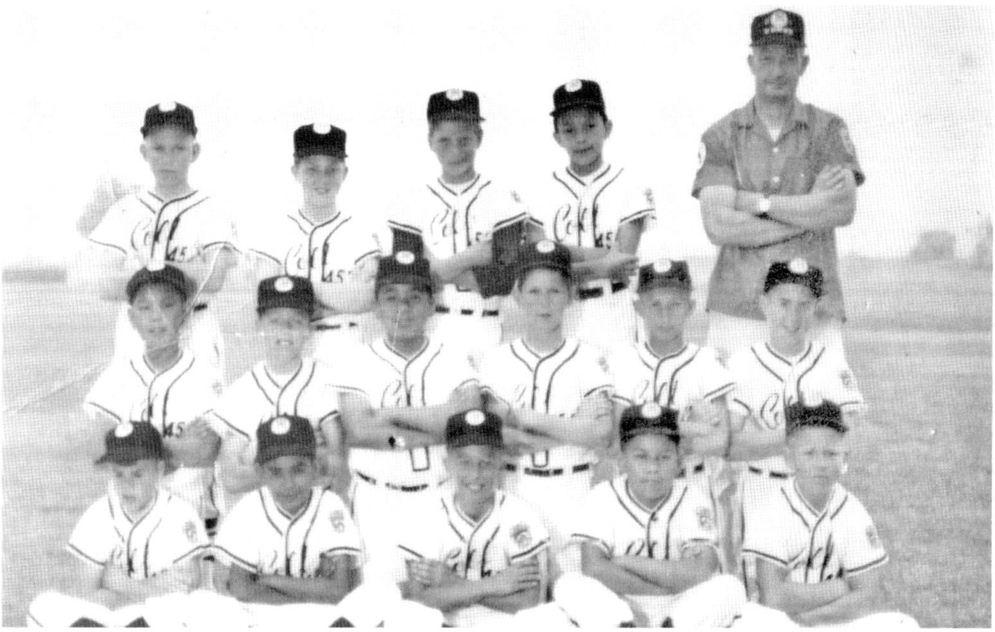

The 1964 Major Division little league Colt 45s played in La Puente. The baseball field was at La Puente Park on the corner of Hacienda Boulevard and Temple Avenue. Henry "Hank" Pedregón (first row, second from right) was a standout outfielder and one of four Mexican Americans on the team. Pedregón also played outfield for the Workman High School Lobos from 1968 through 1971. (Courtesy of Lucy Vera Pedregón.)

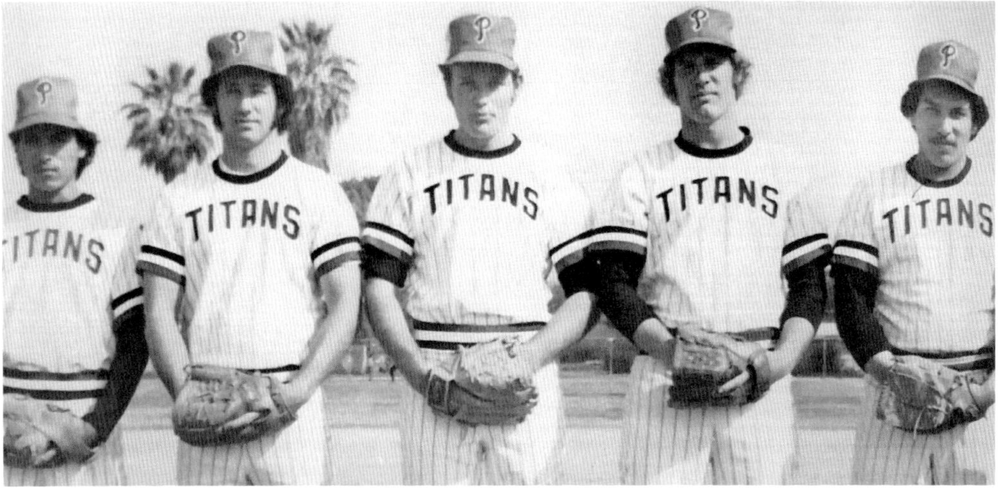

The 1977 Pioneer High School Titans baseball team in Whittier included, from left to right, Victor Montenegro, Steve Valencia, Dennis Aikey, Jeffery Larmore, and Mario Cuevas. Montenegro was an outstanding second baseman and leftfielder, helping his team make the California Interscholastic Federation playoffs in the Whitmont League. After graduating from high school in 1977, Montenegro enlisted in the US Marine Corps. Coach Anthony González (not pictured) later became the athletic director at Pioneer. (Courtesy of Victor Montenegro.)

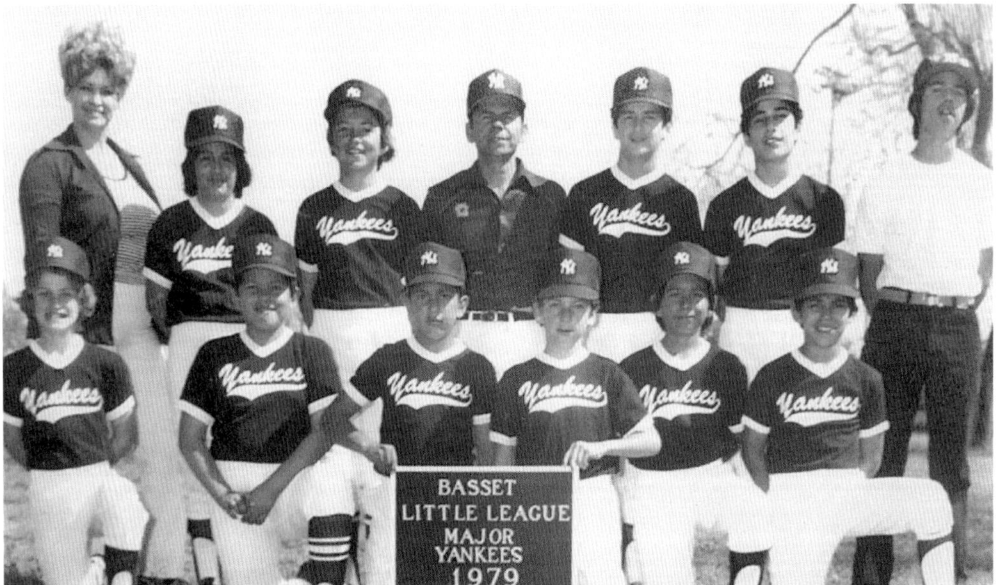

The 1979 little league Yankees played at Shyre Park in Bassett, California. The team won the championship that year under the leadership of manager Simón Martínez Sr. (second row, center) and coach Simón Martínez Jr. (second row, far right). Manuel Martínez (first row, second from right) pitched and played shortstop. Manuel learned the basic fundamentals of the game and leadership skills from his father, Simón Jr., whom he referred to as Mr. Martínez or Coach Martínez. (Courtesy of Manuel Martínez.)

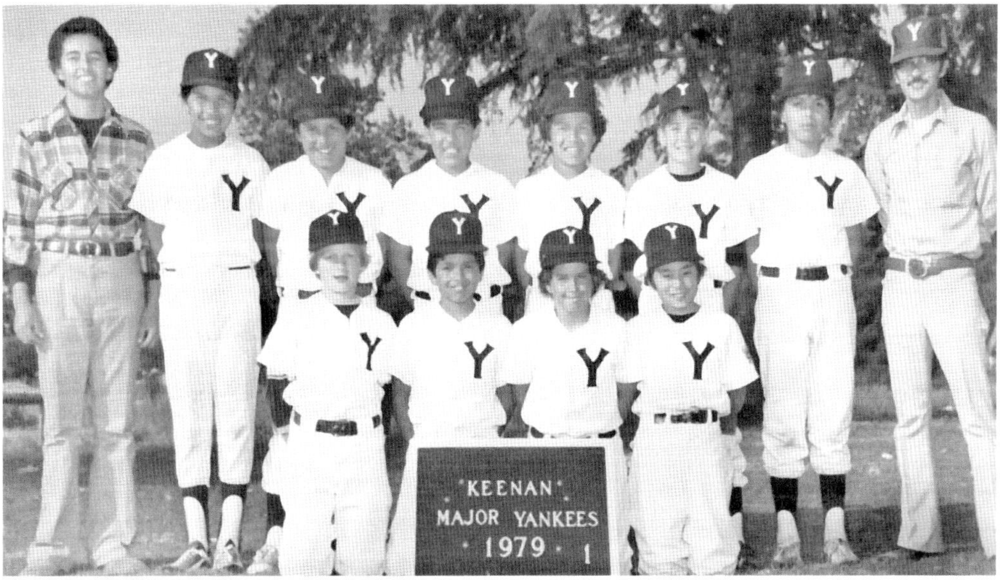

The 1979 Keenan little league Yankees played home games in La Puente. From left to right are (first row) Kelly Segal, Ray Ramírez, James King, and Steven Akiyoshi; (second row) coach Orlando González, Raúl Mendoza, Robbie Fergoso, Mario Félix, Ernie Ceyela, Sam Manning, James Henninger Aguirre, and coach Chris Akiyoshi. Aguirre was the number-one draft pick as a pitcher and catcher for the Yankees that year. (Courtesy of James Henninger Aguirre.)

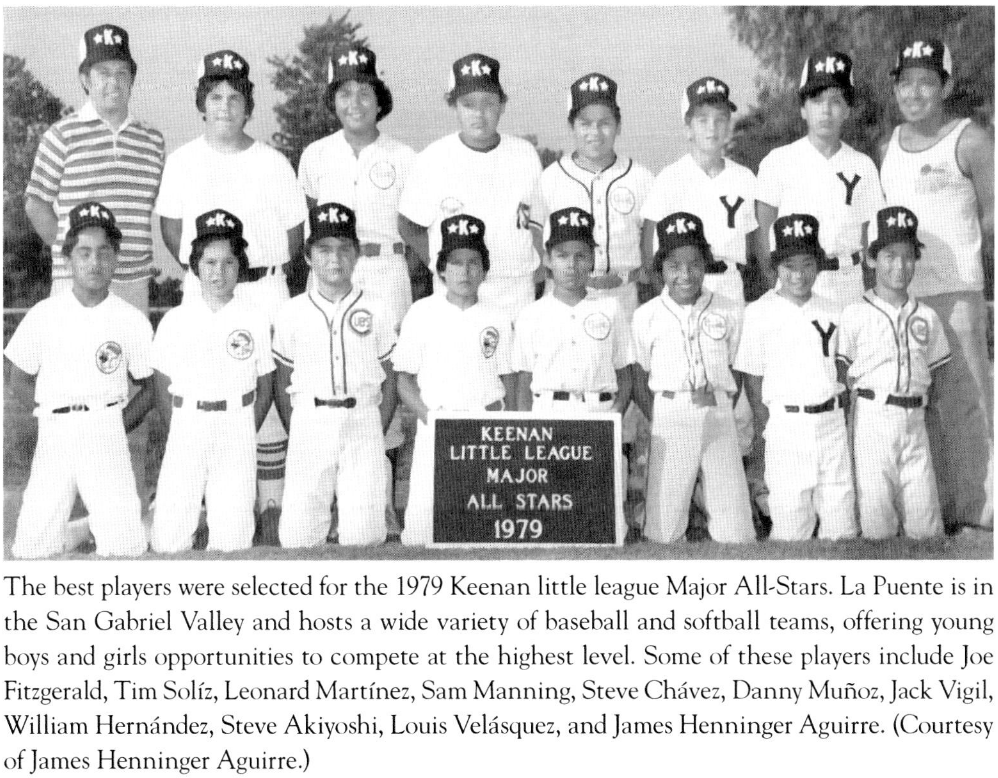

The best players were selected for the 1979 Keenan little league Major All-Stars. La Puente is in the San Gabriel Valley and hosts a wide variety of baseball and softball teams, offering young boys and girls opportunities to compete at the highest level. Some of these players include Joe Fitzgerald, Tim Solíz, Leonard Martínez, Sam Manning, Steve Chávez, Danny Muñoz, Jack Vigil, William Hernández, Steve Akiyoshi, Louis Velásquez, and James Henninger Aguirre. (Courtesy of James Henninger Aguirre.)

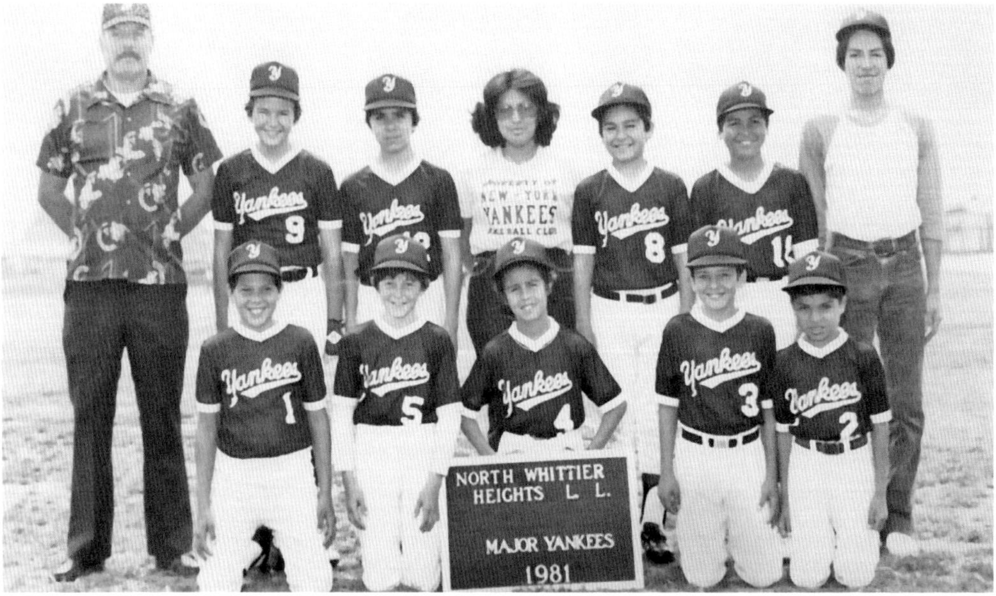

The North Whittier Heights little league Yankees played in Avocado Heights. Their field was at Don Julian Elementary School. Brian Aguirre (second row, third from left) was a hard-throwing pitcher and speedy outfielder. He joined the US Army in 1988 and is a career military police officer, a staff sergeant, and a combat veteran of Operation Iraqi Freedom. (Courtesy of Brian Aguirre.)

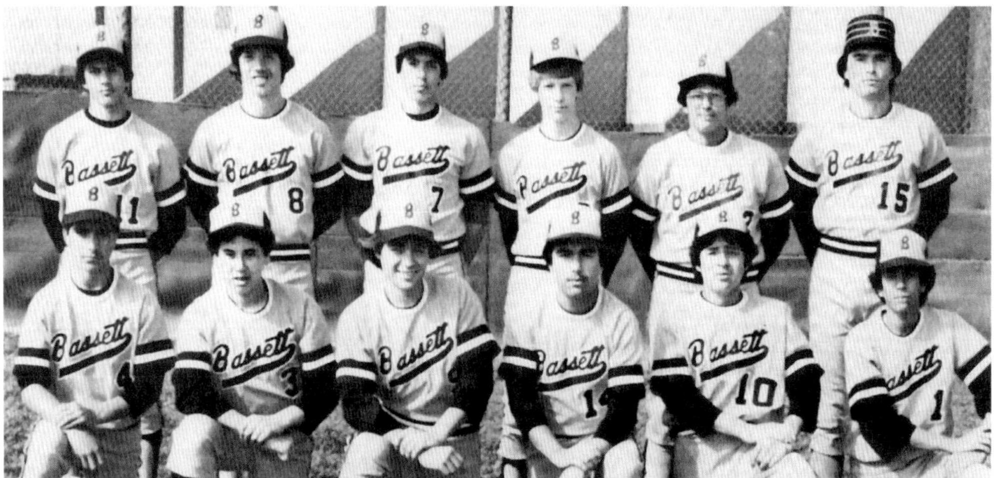

The 1983 Bassett High School Olympians junior varsity team played in Bassett. From left to right are (first row) Luceo Pérez, Joel Gonzáles, Jack Vigil, Jesse Cabuto, Pedro Arguesta, and Sammy Sosa; (second row) Román Gardea, Dean Ramos, James Henninger Aguirre, Walter Cullen, Jesse Badillo, and coach Willie Rubalcava. Aguirre was a hard-throwing pitcher with outstanding control, and he often traveled with the varsity team as an outfielder when he was not scheduled to pitch with the junior varsity club. (Courtesy of James Henninger Aguirre.)

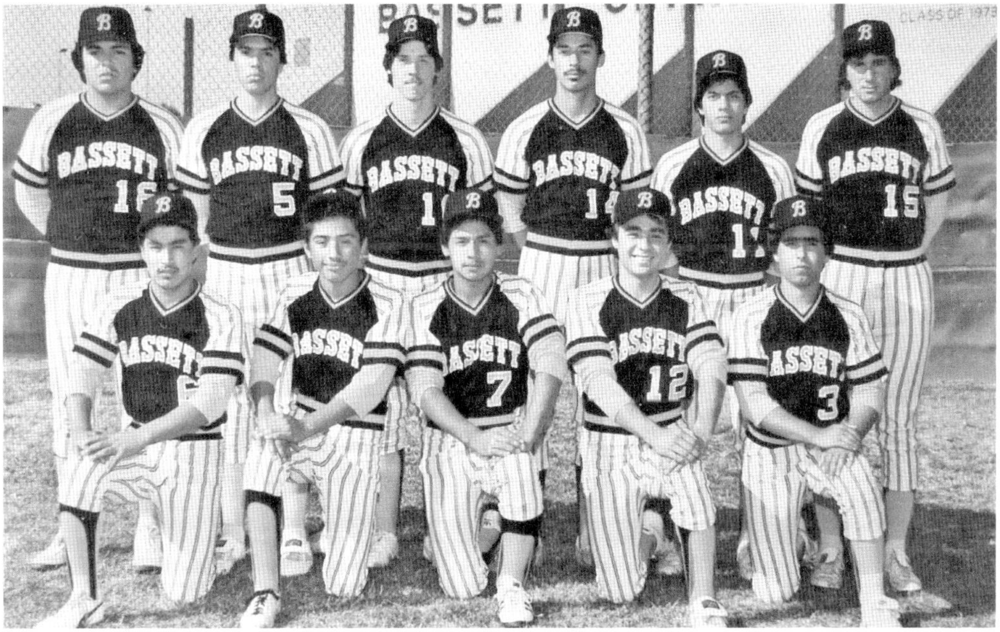

The 1984 Bassett High School Olympians varsity team was very competitive. From left to right are (first row) Steve Chávez, William Hernández, Martin Martínez, Jack Vigil, and Manuel Martínez; (second row) Eddie Hidalgo, James Henninger Aguirre, Dean Ramos, Andy Lucero, Román Gardea, and coach Nicholas Jannis. Aguirre had a flaming fastball and was highlighted in the local newspaper, the *Highlander*, on three different occasions. (Courtesy of James Henninger Aguirre.)

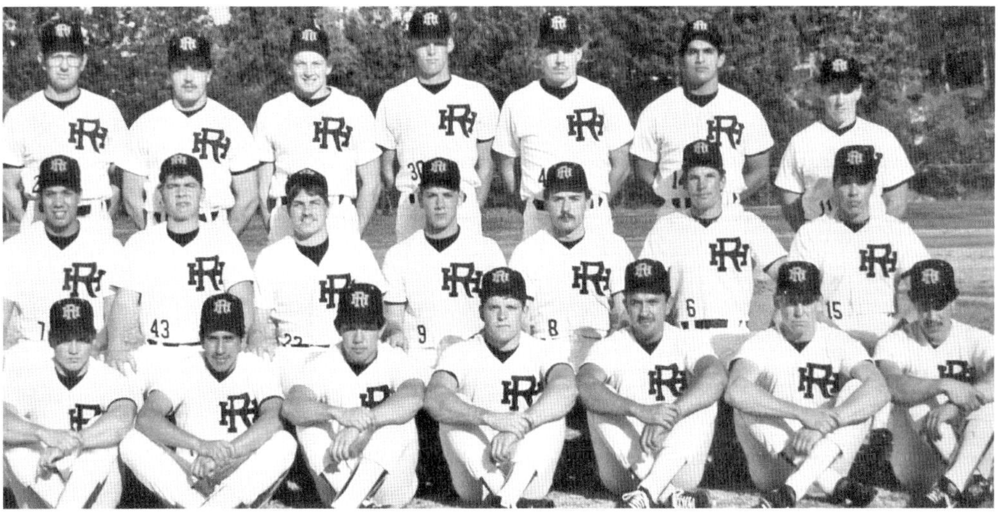

Rio Hondo Community College is located in Whittier and is named after a nearby river. The 1985 Rio Hondo Roadrunners are, from left to right, (first row) Craig Tippings, Dan Elias, David Hazama, Kyle Borland, Steve Muñoz, Rod Rainey, and Rudy Martínez; (second row) Kiki García, Tim Crow, Tim Jiménez, Ray Paschket, Tim McKinney, Tom Lorenz, and James Henninger Aguirre; (third row) coach Jerry Schlegelmilch, Ralph Acosta, Bill Faulkner, Chris Freitag, Darren Nadolski, Anthony Corona, and coach Dan Roddy. (Courtesy of James Henninger Aguirre.)

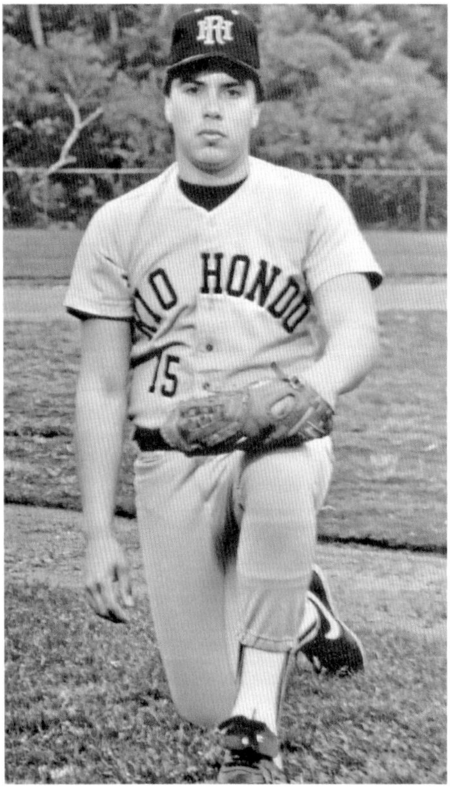

James Henninger Aguirre was born in San Gabriel in 1966. His family has been playing baseball and softball in the region for over 100 years. In 1986, at 19 years of age, he was known as "Big Jim" due to his muscular build and intimidating fastball. The previous year, he was a starting pitcher as a walk-on for the Rio Hondo Community College Roadrunners, the only starting pitcher on the team not recruited. (Courtesy of James Henninger Aguirre.)

The 1988 Lucky Charms softball team played in the Bobby Sox League in Pico Rivera. The team played at Rio Vista Park and consisted of Mexican American players and coaches. Jessica Martínez (first row, third from right) was a five-year-old standout who later played for St. Paul High School. The coaches were Raúl and Teresa Camacho and Richard Senteno (the first three adults at left in the second row, from left to right). Gracie Senteno (standing far right) was the team mom. (Courtesy of Jessica Martínez.)

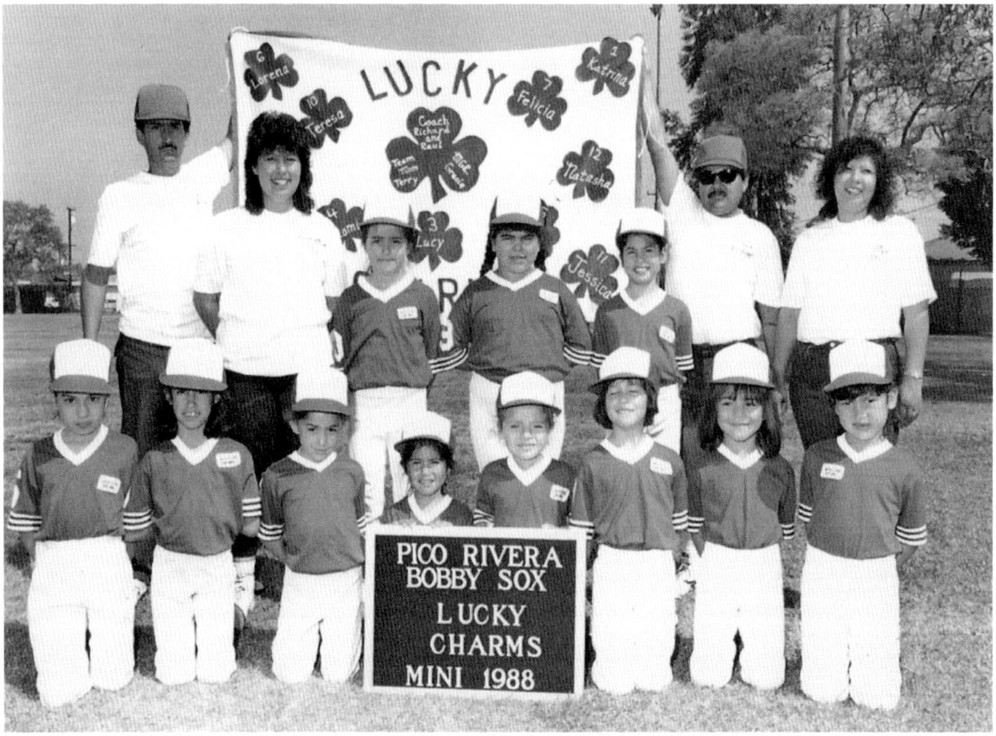

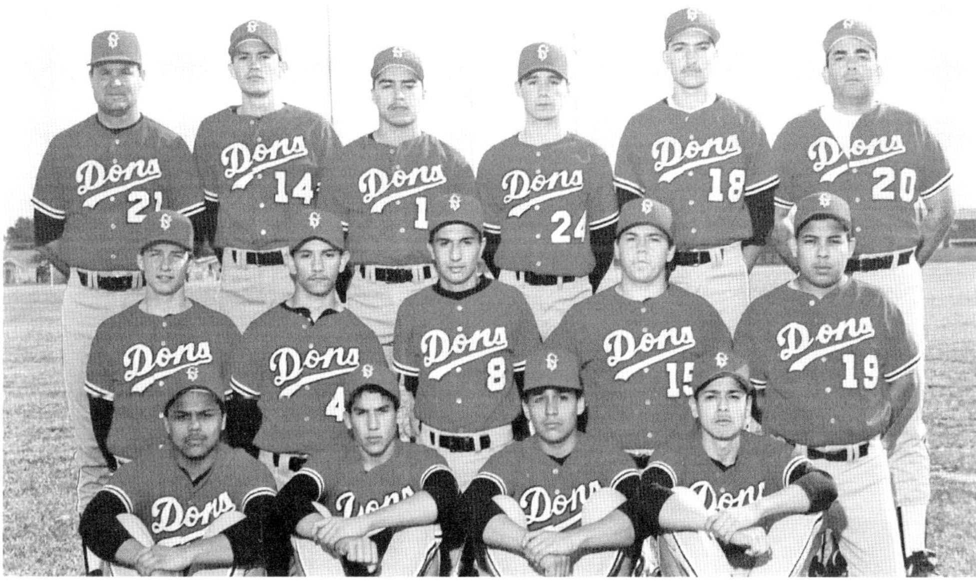

The 1992 Sierra Vista High School Dons varsity team played in Baldwin Park. The Dons were co-champions of the Mountain View League with the best record heading into the California Interscholastic Federation (CIF) playoffs. Davey Escobedo (second row, center) was the starting shortstop on this predominantly Mexican American team. He played two years on the varsity club and was selected Second Team All-League. This was the first time in the school history that the team finished in first place. (Courtesy of Davey Escobedo.)

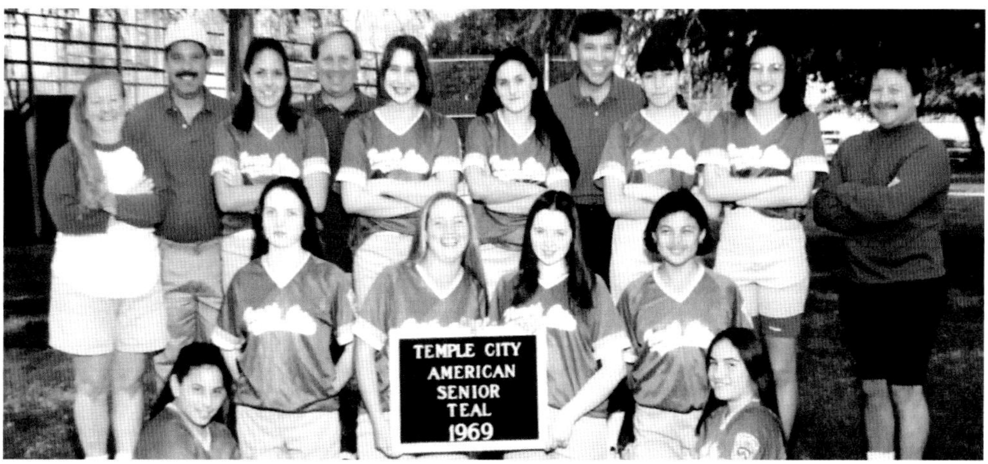

Jacquelyn Arenas (first row, seated, far right) is the eldest daughter of Jack and Dolores Arenas. She attended San Gabriel Mission Grammar School and played softball, volleyball, and basketball. She graduated from San Gabriel Mission as valedictorian and athlete of the year in 1997. Arenas started playing T-ball with San Gabriel little league and softball with Sunnyslope little league. She attended Maranatha High School in Sierra Madre, excelling in softball and volleyball; she was awarded Scholar-Athlete of the Year and graduated with honors in 2001. She graduated from Loyola Marymount University in 2005. She and her husband, Ben, and three children, Shelby, Isaac, and Julian, reside in Livermore, California. (Courtesy of Jack Arenas.)

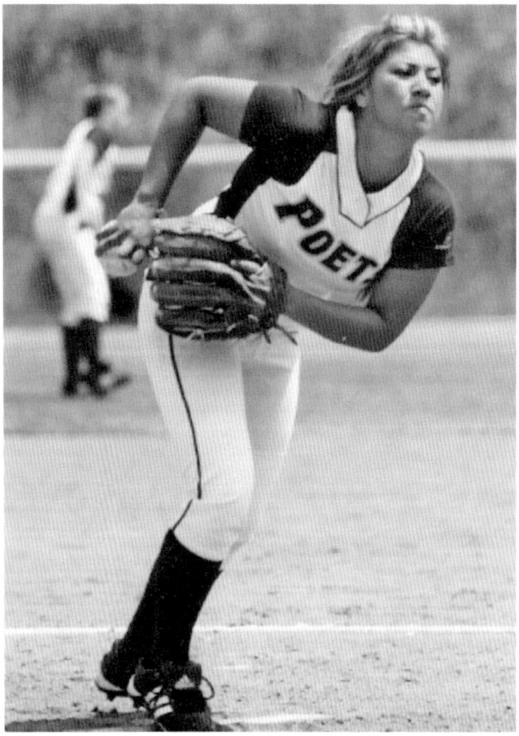

Deena Arenas is the second oldest daughter of Jack and Dolores Arenas. She attended San Gabriel Mission Grammar School and San Gabriel Christian Junior High. She started playing softball at the age of eight. She graduated from Walnut High School in 2004 as an honor student and a four-year starter for the varsity softball team. She went on to play softball at Whittier College, graduating in 2008, and continued her graduate studies at the University of Southern California. She graduated with a doctor of chiropractic degree and resides in Livermore, California, with her husband, Demitris, and their son, Nicholas James. (Courtesy of Jack Arenas.)

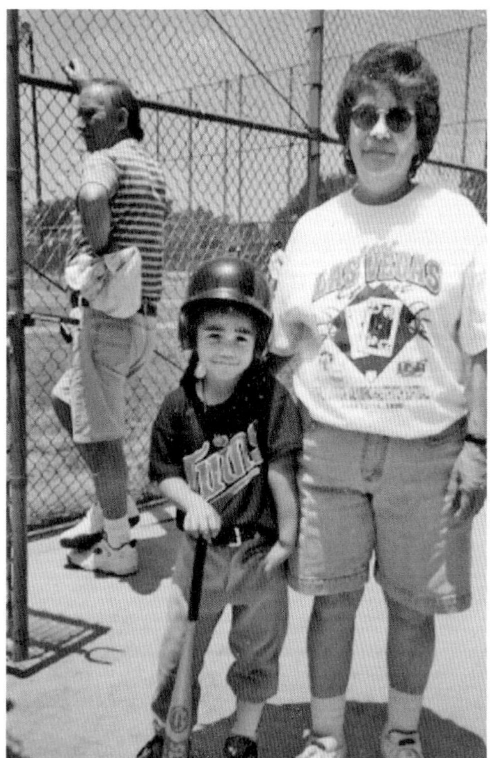

Delilah is the youngest daughter of Jack and Delores Arenas. She attended San Gabriel Christian Junior High and started playing T-ball at the age of five in Temple City, as well as travel ball with the San Dimas Cobras. She graduated from Walnut High School in 2010 and was selected All-CIF in volleyball and first-team all-league in softball for three years. Delilah attended California State University at Fullerton from 2010 to 2012, and resides with her partner Jesse and five-year-old son Dominic. She is seen here with her aunt Sally Arenas. Delilah's father, Jack, worked in the recording industry for the past 43 years, 30 years with Sony and 13 years with Capitol Records. He lives in Los Angeles and has four grown children, Jacquelyn, Deena, Joaquin, and Delilah, and seven grandchildren, Shelby, Lauren, Isaac, Dominic, Julian, Nicholas, and Valentino. (Courtesy of Jack Arenas.)

Joaquin "Jay" Arenas attended San Gabriel Mission Grammar School and San Gabriel Christian Junior High. He played T-ball at Sunnyslope little league in San Gabriel, little league and Pop Warner football in Temple City, and Pony baseball in Arcadia. Jay attended Bosco Tech and played junior varsity football and baseball. He played baseball at Walnut High School and graduated in 2005. He is finishing his bachelor's degree at Mount Sierra College in Monrovia, California, and resides in Los Angeles with his partner, Angie, daughter Lauren, and son Valentino. (Courtesy of Jack Arenas.)

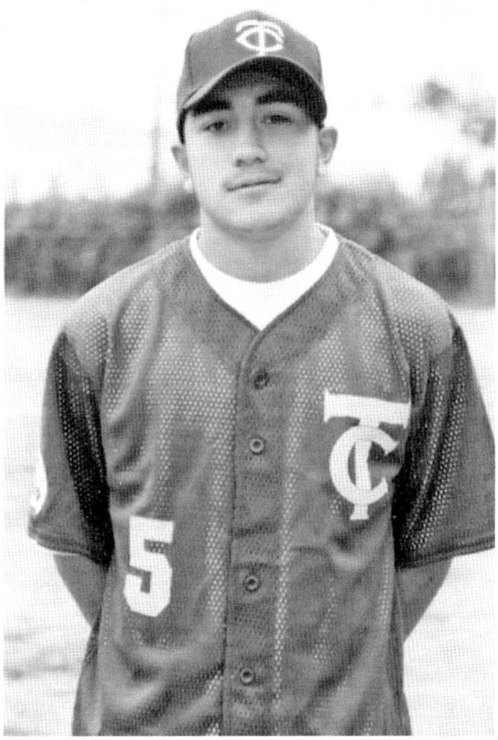

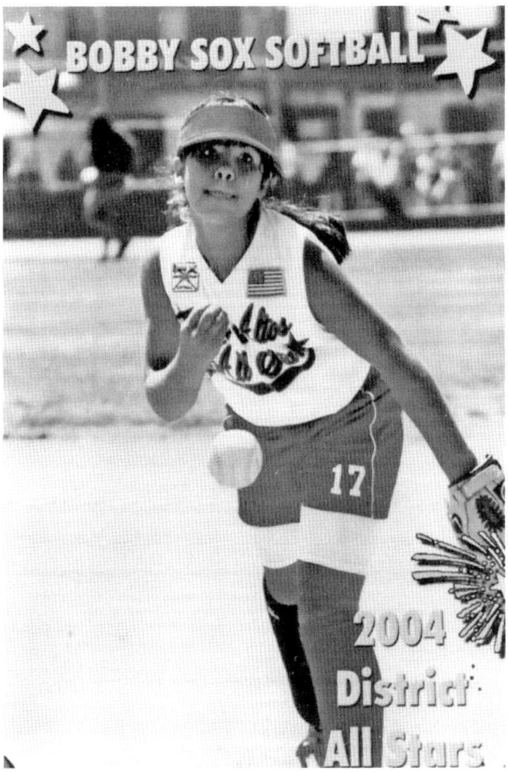

Eris Pérez played for the Blue Angels, Black Widows, Vipers, Punishers, Southern California Bombers, Lakewood Ladies, Strike Force, and Adrenaline. She made several all-star teams and played four years of varsity for the Milliken High School Rams and the Long Beach City College Vikings. Her father, Hiram, coached three of her teams, while her mom, Cynthia, helped host tournaments, worked the snack bar, and helped maintain the fields. In high school, Eris was the only freshman on the varsity team and was captain in her senior year. She is in the Long Beach City College nursing program. (Courtesy of Eris Peréz.)

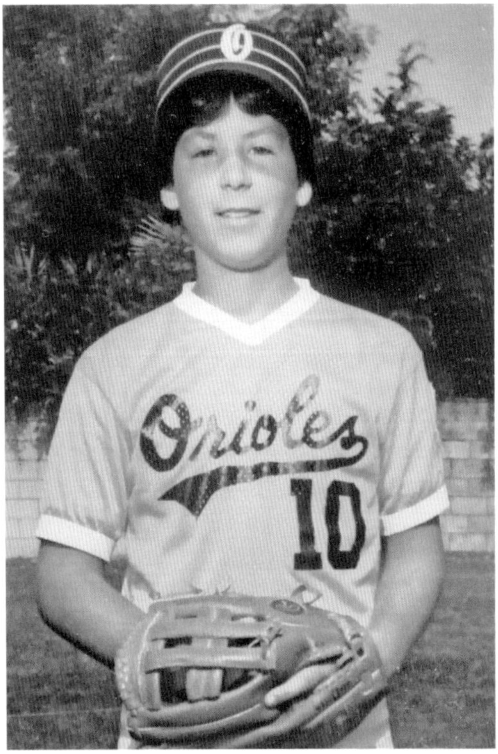

Ralph Van Dyke began playing baseball at 10 in El Monte. He played with the Lambert little league, Lambert Senior League, Arcadia Pony League, and at Arroyo High School. He played several positions, including pitcher, catcher, and third base. In one game, he struck out 14 batters. Van Dyke's high school team won the championship for four consecutive years, from 1984 to 1987. His father, George, played baseball and football at Polytechnic High School in Los Angeles during the 1950s. Ralph's mother, Maria Holguín Van Dyke, was born in El Paso, Texas. (Courtesy of George and Maria Van Dyke.)

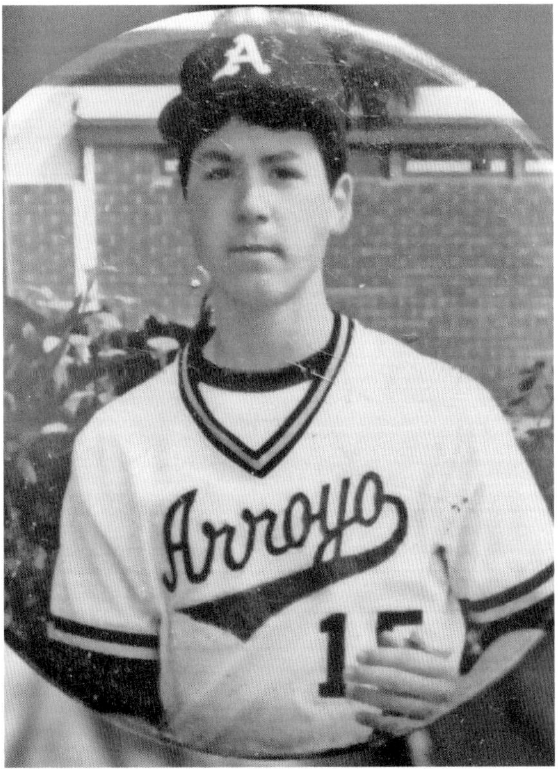

Ralph Van Dyke was an outstanding baseball player from youth ball to the high school varsity team at Arroyo High School in El Monte. He played on the 1987 traveling US team, competing against England, Holland, Italy, and Switzerland, with the USA winning all of the games on the tour. Van Dyke played baseball briefly at California State University at Pomona. He married Sherry Ware, and they live in Pocatello, Idaho, with their four children, who played baseball and softball. Ralph is a sheriff and continues to play senior ball as of 2018. (Courtesy of George and Maria Van Dyke.)

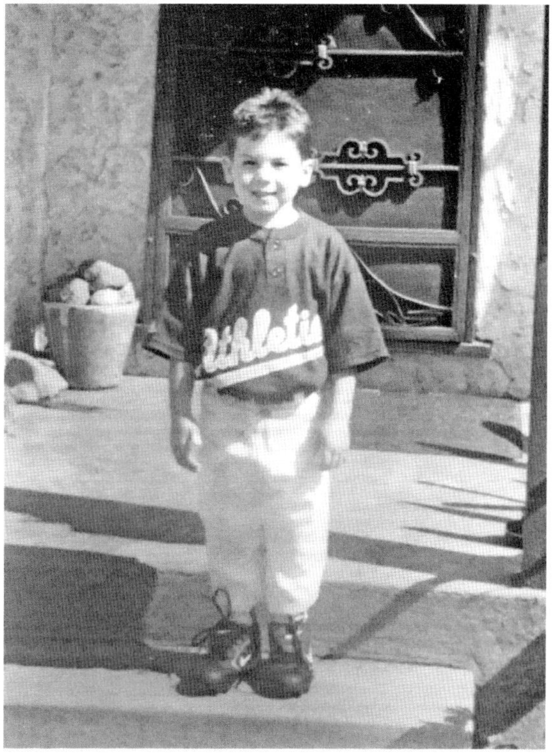

Eric Ralph Van Dyke was born in 1998 and raised in El Monte. He followed in his father, Ralph's, footsteps playing little league at Lambert Park in El Monte. He was a left-handed pitcher and played both the infield and outfield. His family moved to Pocatello, where he joined the little league and played only one more season, even though he won the Most Valuable Player award. His grandfather George Van Dyke was an outstanding football and baseball player at Polytechnic High School in Los Angeles. (Courtesy of the Van Dyke family.)

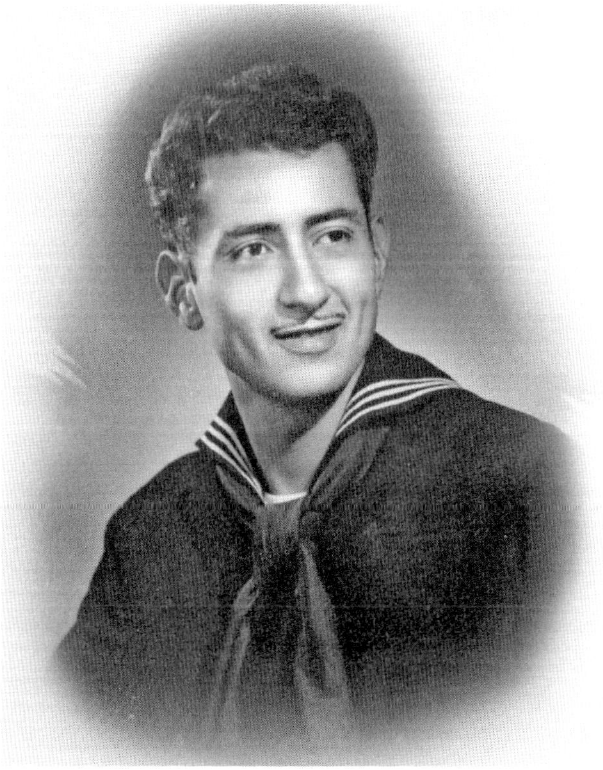

Manuel González was born in 1931 and raised in La Verne. The family moved nearby to Claremont when Manuel was in high school. He played basketball, football, softball, and baseball. He enlisted in the Navy in 1953 and played baseball in the service. His son Anthony was born in 1951, and daughter Christina was born in 1954. Both children attended Holy Name of Mary in San Dimas and graduated from Bonita High School. Anthony received his master's degree from the University of La Verne. Christina found a job at Mount San Antonio Community College and later earned an associate of arts degree in liberal studies there. (Courtesy of Anthony González.)

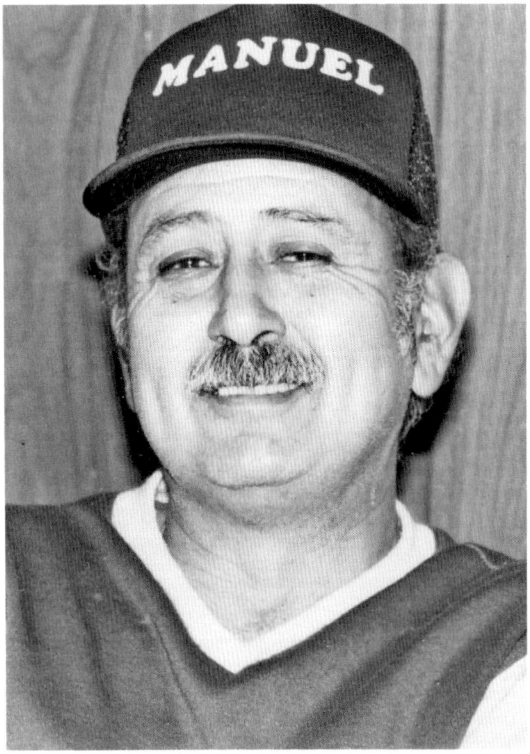

Manuel González enlisted in the Navy in 1948 and eventually was shipped to Pearl Harbor. His ship, the *Tausigg*, was sent to the northern part of Japan. During this time, the fleet was part of atomic bomb testing exercises. The crews were instructed to turn their backs as the bomb was detonated. Once the blast was completed, they were told it was fine to turn and look at the plume of smoke that mushroomed higher and higher. González said it was a sight to see. His love of baseball began in his younger years in elementary school and later high school. He especially loved pitching slow pitch. He played softball for the Southern Pipe and Casting Company in Irwindale in 1965 and played on softball leagues in several local cities and for the Pomona Lancers in the 1960s. (Courtesy of Christina González Magoni.)

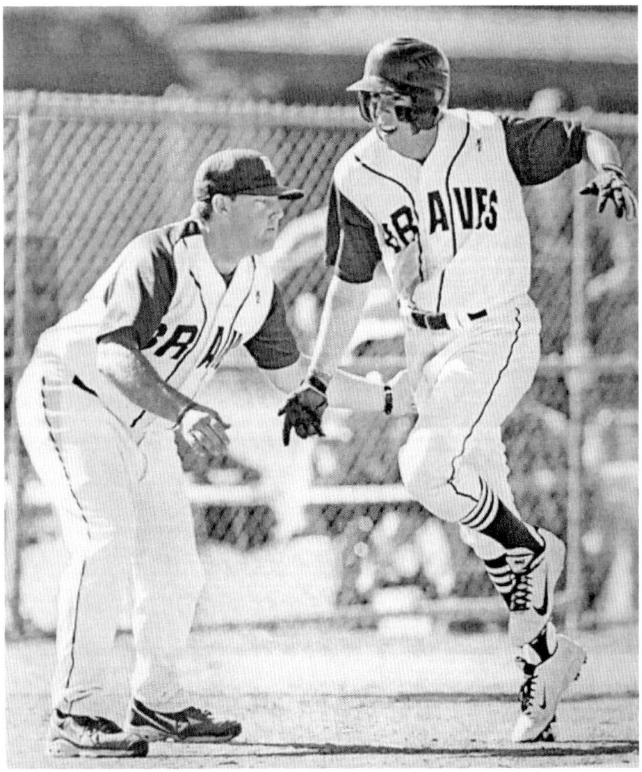

Senior right-fielder Ryan Cruz and coach Joe Laski celebrate a huge three-run home run in the bottom of the fifth inning, giving the Baldwin Park Braves a 4-2 lead in 2013 against El Rancho; the Braves lost the game when El Rancho scored three runs in the last two innings, earning a trip to the CIF championship game. This was the first baseball team in over 20 years at Baldwin Park High School to reach a CIF semifinal game. The Braves' playoff run included wins over Century, La Serna, and La Sierra. (Courtesy of Joe Laski.)

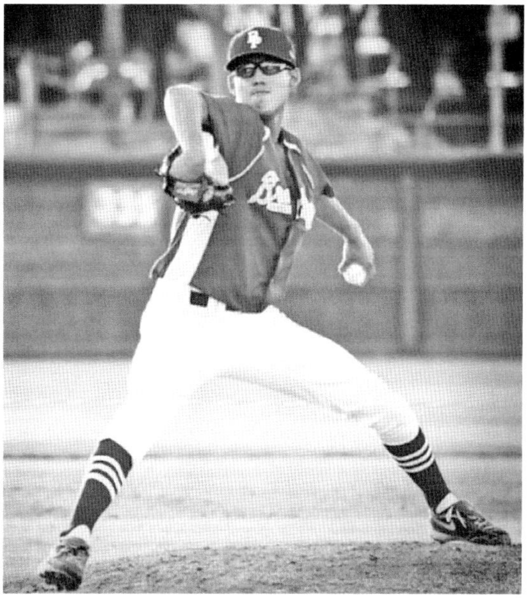

Left-handed pitcher Bernardo Flores was a four-year varsity starter, and team captain for two seasons at Baldwin Park High School. He went on to three successful seasons at the University of Southern California, drawing scouts with his 95-mile-per-hour fastball. He was drafted in 2016 by the Chicago White Sox, playing minor-league ball with their Winston-Salem club, and earned remarkable accolades as an All-Star and rising prospect. In the off season, Flores still lives in Baldwin Park, works with the current high school players, and donates equipment to the baseball program. In June 2018, he was promoted to the AA Birmingham Barons. (Courtesy of Joe Laski.)

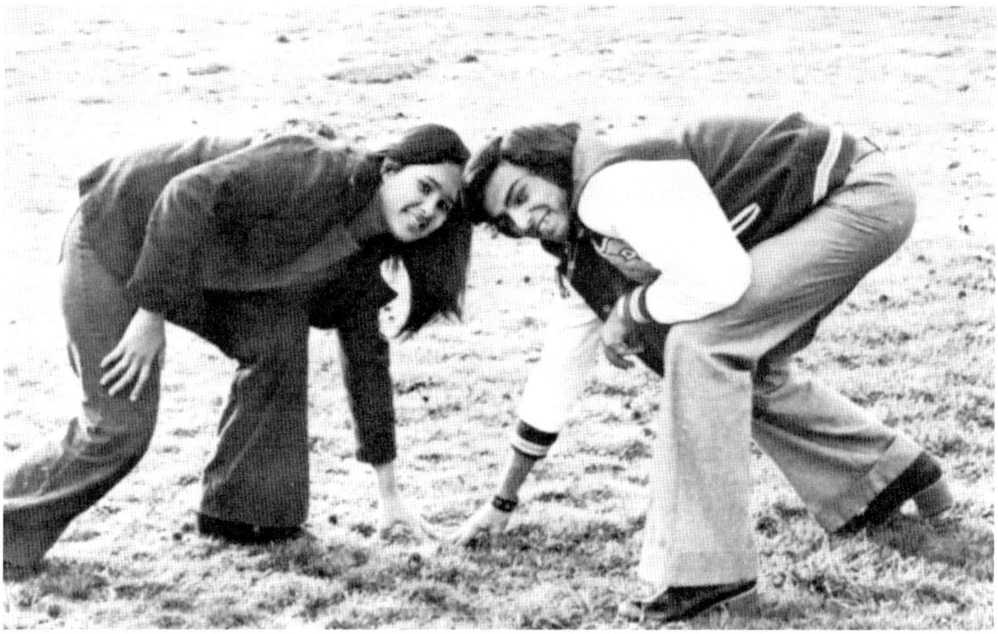

Isabel Sherrill (left) is the daughter of John and Mary Robles. She was born in East Los Angeles and raised in Baldwin Park. Her father and uncles, Tom and Louie Robles, were outstanding athletes in boxing, baseball, and football. John was a Golden Gloves contender in 1947 and Louie won the Golden Gloves in 1937. Isabel swam, took up martial arts, and was named the youngest brown belt west of the Mississippi by *Jiu-Jitsu Magazine*. Isabel played softball, volleyball, and basketball at St. John Church, and was named Baldwin Park High School's Most Athletic Female in 1974. She is seen here with Clifford Orosco. (Courtesy of Isabel Sherrill.)

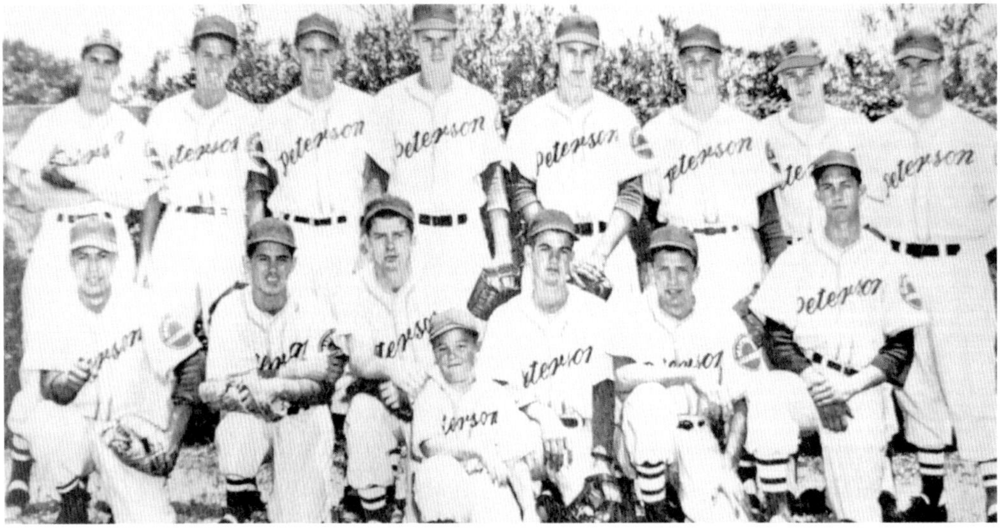

Adolph García (first row, far left) played for the 1953 Maywood All-Stars. He played football and baseball at Lincoln High School in East Los Angeles and youth ball on the Pico Rivera Golden State little league travel club as a catcher, and made this Peterson squad as the only Mexican American. García played military ball in Colorado Springs with the 7th Army, Battery B, 45th Field Artillery Battalion. He was then transferred to Fort Bliss, Texas, with the Operations Intelligence Division. His unit was deployed to Germany, where he played catcher and outfielder for the base team, the Rams. (Courtesy of Steve Gewecke.)

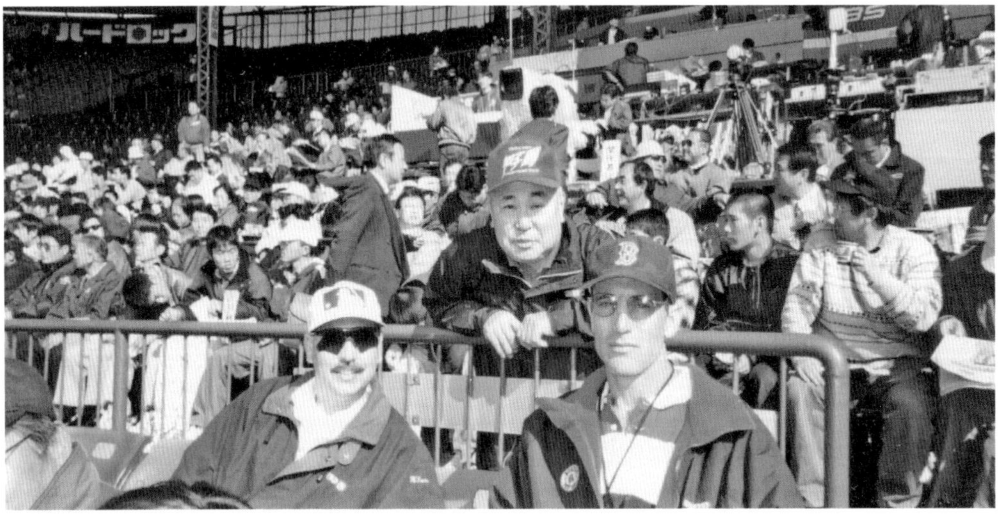

Mark R. García played youth football and basketball at All Saints Elementary school, travel ball with the Golden State Baseball League, baseball at Bishop Amat High School and Pasadena City College, and for a development team in Australia. He eventually became a major league scout for the Brewers and worked in international operations with the Angels and Red Sox. He is seen here (left) seated next to Red Sox scout Lee Sigman at the world famous Koshien High School Baseball Tournament in Osaka, Japan, at Hanshin Stadium. Over 50,000 people attended the games. (Courtesy of Mark R. García.)

The García brothers, from left to right, Mark, Steven, and Greg, grew up in the northeast section of Los Angeles known as El Sereno. They played all sports at All Saints Catholic Church, but their passion was baseball. Mark and Greg participated in the El Sereno Golden State little league, while Steven was the batboy. All three played sports at Bishop Amat High School in the east San Gabriel Valley, Mark baseball, Greg football, and Steven basketball. All three attended Pasadena City College, where Mark played baseball. (Courtesy of Mark García.)

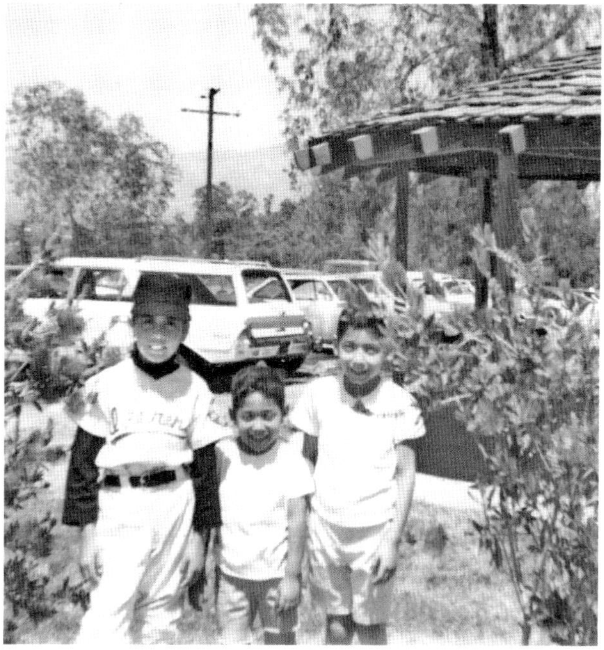

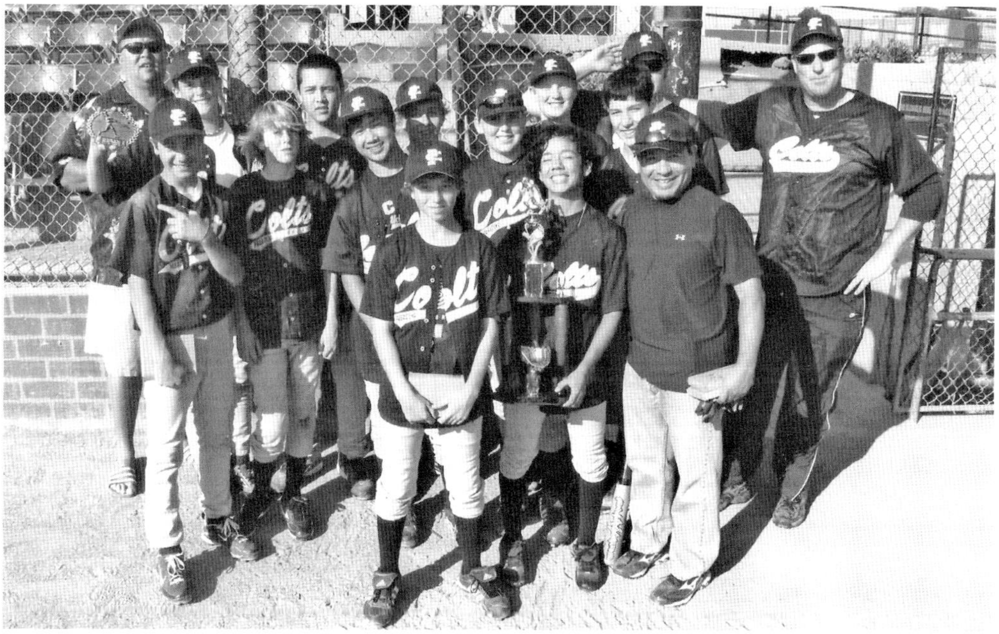

Matthew Morales (holding trophy) is seen with his Colts team in Arcadia in 2008. Morales was born at the Huntington Hospital in Pasadena. He played in the Arcadia National little league for seven years as a pitcher and sometimes catcher. He played four years at Arcadia High School (2009–2013). His maternal grandmother, Juana Lozano Dominguez, was born in El Paso. She was the valedictorian at Austin High School in 1944 and worked at William Beaumont Army Medical Center in El Paso during and immediately after World War II. Her parents were from Zacatecas, Mexico. (Courtesy of Bob and Diane Morales.)

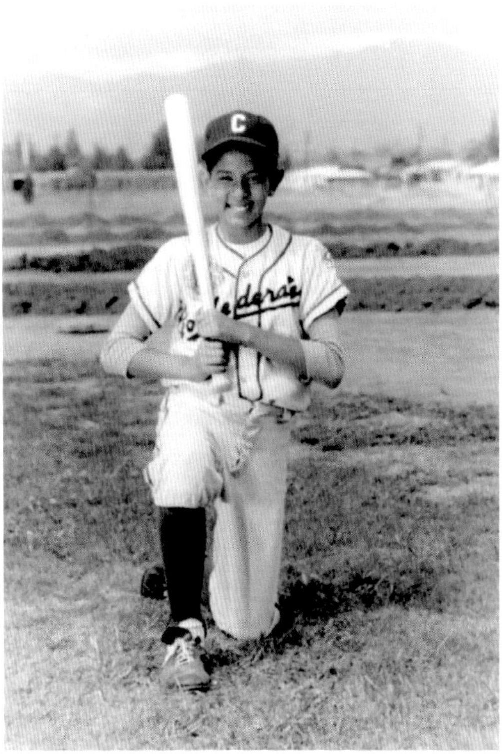

David Saul Rodríguez was born in El Paso, Texas, in 1951. His father, Alfredo, moved the family to South San Gabriel to pursue steady construction work. David and his brother Ruben played softball at Garvey Park in Rosemead. David played outfield and second base. It was during this time that his father took him to see his first Dodgers game at the Los Angeles Memorial Coliseum. David pitched in little league, making the all-star team. He also played Pop Warner football for the Rosemead Rebels. David received a trophy for his scholastic and athletic achievements and was class valedictorian at Garvey Junior High School. In high school, he played basketball, baseball, and football. He became a teacher in Boyle Heights and Paramount and a software engineer with Hughes Aircraft. He attributes his success to his father. (Courtesy of David Saul Rodríguez.)

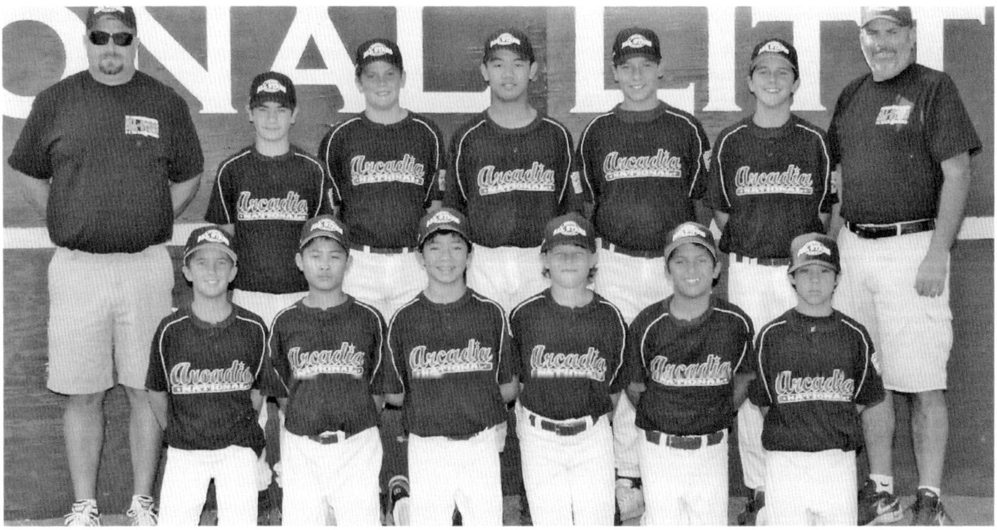

Matthew Morales (first row, third from left) was a member of the Arcadia All-Stars in 2008. Following his graduation from Cal Poly Pomona, he completed the emergency medical technician (EMT) course first in his class. His maternal grandfather, Manuel Joseph Domínguez, was born in Los Angeles in 1926. Manuel's parents were from Mexico and Arizona. He attended St. Mary's Elementary School and two years at Cathedral High School. He joined the Army in 1944 and was stationed at Fort Bliss in El Paso. He met his future wife, Juana, at a dance in Los Angeles in 1950. He completed his high school education in 1955. (Courtesy of Bob and Diane Morales.)

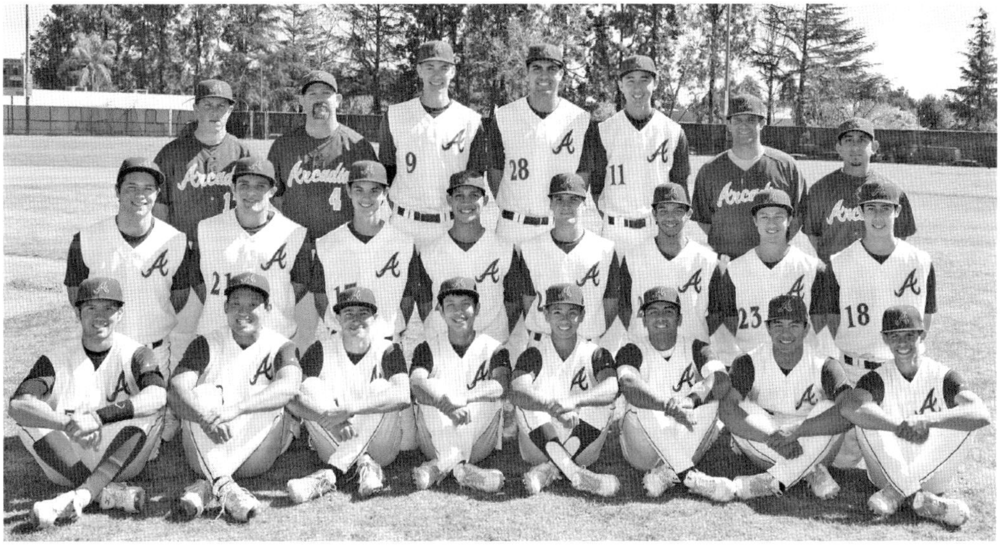

Matthew Morales played on the Arcadia High School team from 2009 to 2013. His career goal is to work as a physician assistant in a sports medicine office. His sister Andrea played softball for the Arcadia Softball Association for six years, at Arcadia High School for two years, and as a catcher at Glendale Community College for two years. She works as a licensed hair and makeup stylist in Arcadia. Matthew's paternal grandmother, Margaret Agnes Vargas Morales, was born in 1931 in Los Angeles. She graduated from Bishop Conaty High School in 1949 and later worked as a medical secretary at LAC-USC Hospital. (Courtesy of Diane and Bob Morales.)

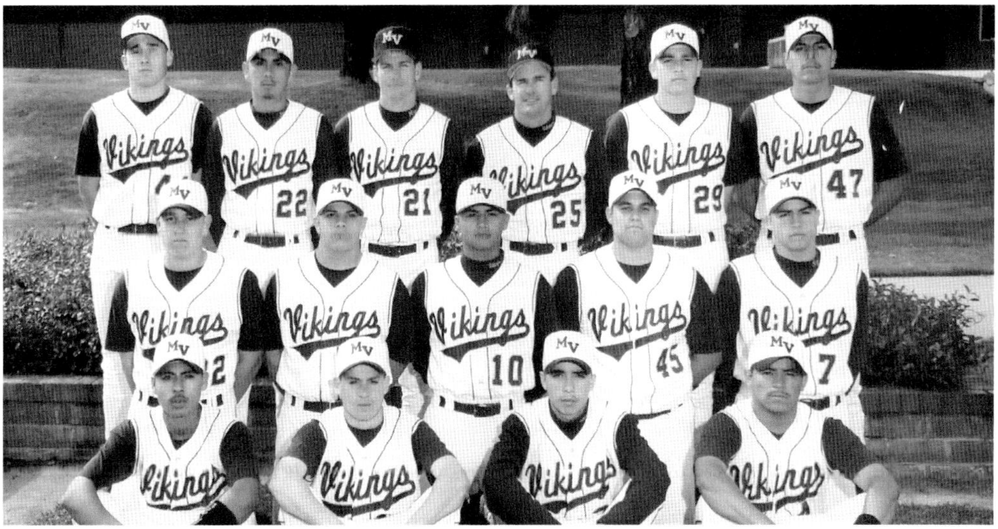

The 1995 Mountain View High School Vikings from El Monte had an outstanding season, winning 20 games, making the CIF Division 4 semifinals, and winning the Montebello Tournament. From left to right are (first row) Joe Reyes, Gabriel Trujillo, Ronnie López, and José Sánchez; (second row) Charles Flores, Bruce González, Gary Oliverea, Jerry Rochin, and José Salcido; (third row) Scott Arrendano, Mike Pinedo, assistant coach Steve Gewecke, head coach Dan Henley, Eddie Ruezca, and Sal Juárez. Alfred Orozco and Ulises Borrago are not pictured. (Courtesy of Steve Gewecke.)

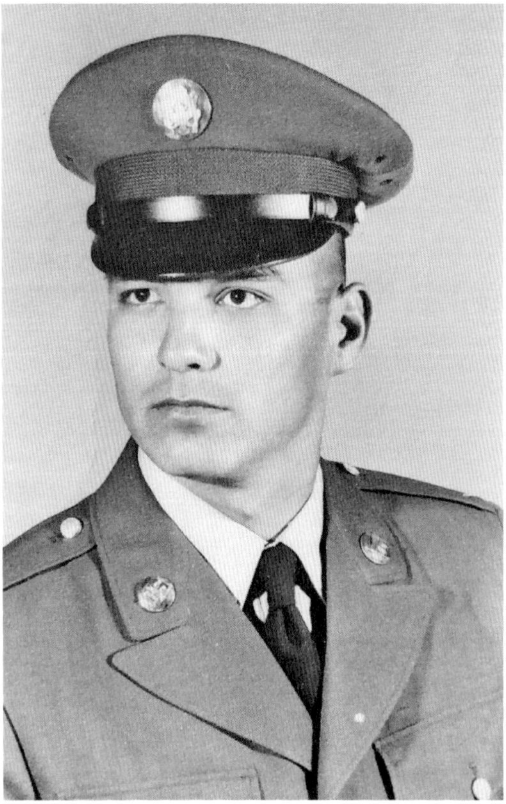

Alfredo Hernández graduated from Franklin High School in Eagle Rock. He was drafted in 1965, doing his basic training at Fort Ord, California, in advanced infantry training, and was stationed in Mainz, Germany, with the 8th Infantry Division, 1st Airborne Brigade. He played briefly on the base softball team. His father, Amado Sr., was drafted in World War II, leaving his wife and nine children to serve in the South Pacific. Alfredo's older brother Enríque "KiKi" served in Berlin, while brother Robert joined the Army with the 82nd Airborne Division. Amado Jr. was the only brother to join the Marine Corps. (Courtesy of Alfredo Hernández.)

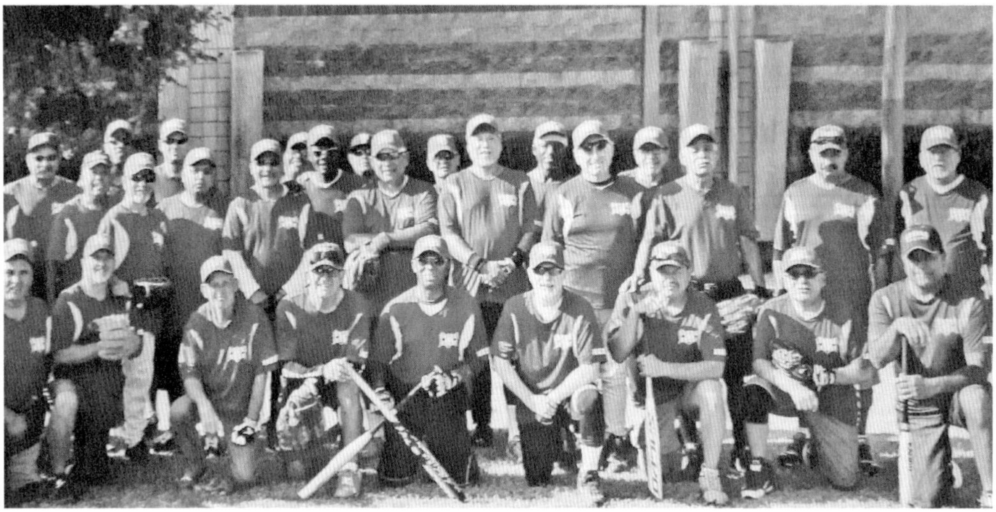

Alfredo Hernández (second row, far right) was born in El Paso in 1941. The family moved to San Dimas, California; his father, Amado Sr., had a sister living there. While his father picked oranges, Alfredo's brother Robert made bats out of tree branches and used oranges as balls with his siblings. After his military service, Alfredo formed a family touch football team, and after his retirement from Lucent Technology in 1999, he started playing senior ball at Cameron Park in West Covina and with the Big League of Dreams. (Courtesy of Alfredo Hernández.)

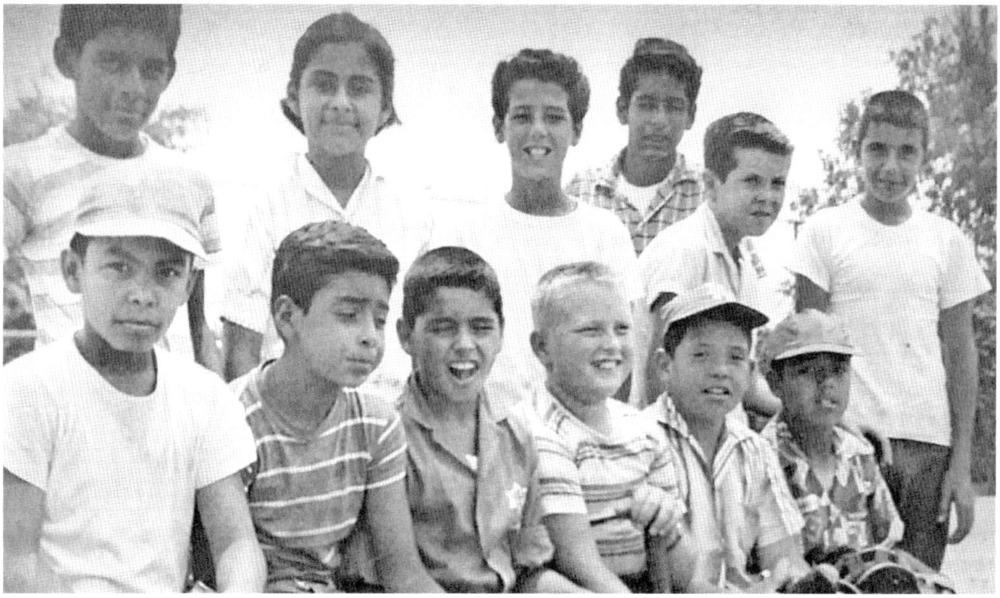

Linda Gutíerrez Hernández (second row, second from left) played ball at Loreto Street School against other local teams, including El Sereno and Los Angeles. Loreto Street School did not have uniforms but had a great team and lots of fun and won games. Linda was the first girl on the team in 1957. Other boys' teams started to include girls as well. From left to right are (first row) Daniel Martínez, Daniel Solís, Gabby ?, Craig ?, Daniel Gutíerrez, and Victor ?; (second row) Joe Solís, Linda Gutíerrez, Larry ?, coach Richard Solís, Larry Jones, and Frankie ?. Linda later moved to Chino. (Courtesy of Linda Hernández.)

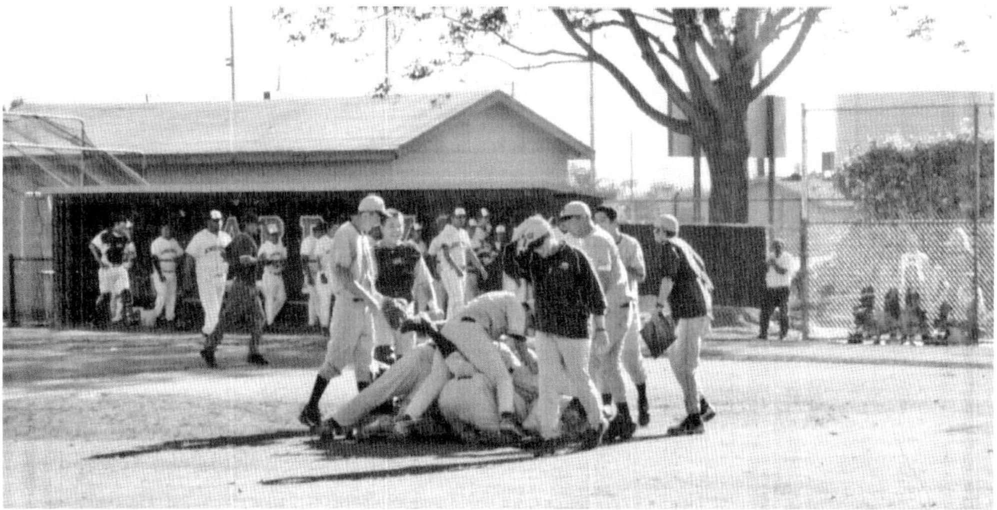

The Gabrielino High School Eagles are seen celebrating in an old-fashioned dogpile after winning the school's first Mission Valley League title in 2007. The high school, located in San Gabriel, shut out host Arroyo High School 1-0. Winning pitcher Angel Cabral was mobbed by his teammates. Eagles coach Joe Laski said that Cabral was the ultimate competitor, always wanting to win, even in table tennis. (Courtesy of Joe Laski.)

Cabral leads Eagles to first league crown

BY FRED J. ROBLEDO
STAFF WRITER

EL MONTE — In what has truly been the year of the pitcher with standouts like Pasadena Poly's Robbie Rasmussen, Monrovia's Eddie McKiernan and Alhambra's Noe Ramirez, it would be foolish to not mention Gabrielino High School's Angel Cabral.

All the junior did on Wednesday was toss his fourth straight complete-game shutout and drive in the game-winning run to help the Eagles earn a 1-0 victory over host Arroyo, and with it the school's first Mission Valley League title in history.

Cabral ran his scoreless innings streak to 29 and has not allowed an earned run in 36 innings to improve to 7-1.

Not bad for a 5-foot-8 right-hander with a so-so fastball, but with a heart as big as they come.

The Eagles improved to 17-6 and 11-3 in beating the Knights (9-10, 8-6) after losing their first two meetings against them.

"He's the ultimate competitor in everything he does," Eagles coach Joe Laski said of Cabral. "Whether he's on the mound or playing table tennis, he wants to beat you every time.

"He doesn't have the big fastball or best stuff around. But when it comes to hitting spots and wanting it more than other guys, he's the one."

Cabral scattered five hits and battled out of a huge jam in the fourth inning when the Knights loaded the bases with one out.

But Cabral got Arroyo's Miguel Barrios to fly out to short right, and then got Chris Armijo to ground out to first to end the threat.

If that wasn't enough, Cabral helped himself in the sixth inning with one out and Ricky Pokorny on second by knocking a single up the middle to score Pokorny for the game's only run.

"This is the type of team we want to be," Laski said. "Pitchers that throw strikes, players that make routine plays, and make the tough plays when you need them. That's us."

Cabral, mobbed by his teammates afterward, admits he doesn't have the natural abilities of other top hurlers, but that hasn't stopped him from becoming a dominant pitcher.

He has allowed only five earned runs in 52 innings.

"I throw every kind of pitch," Cabral said. "You name it and I throw it, because the name of the game is keeping hitters off balance. I love to throw the sinker and slider because most teams are fastball-hitting teams.

"But I don't have this streak without my teammates, because I put it in play and they get it done."

fred.robledo@sgvn.com
(626) 962-8811, Ext. 4485

Coach Joe Laski is in his 16th year as a high school baseball coach in 2018, his first as the pitching coach and assistant varsity coach at Los Altos High School in the San Gabriel Valley. A 1996 graduate of El Toro High School, Laski played briefly at Grossmont and Orange Coast Community Colleges. He has coached at Baldwin Park, Gabrielino, Rancho Cucamonga, Whittier, and Los Alamitos High Schools. At Gabrielino High School, he coached his team to four consecutive Mission Valley championships (2007–2010). He has an incredible family with fiancée Cecilia and children Brylyn, Tomás, and Marcos. (Courtesy of Joe Laski.)

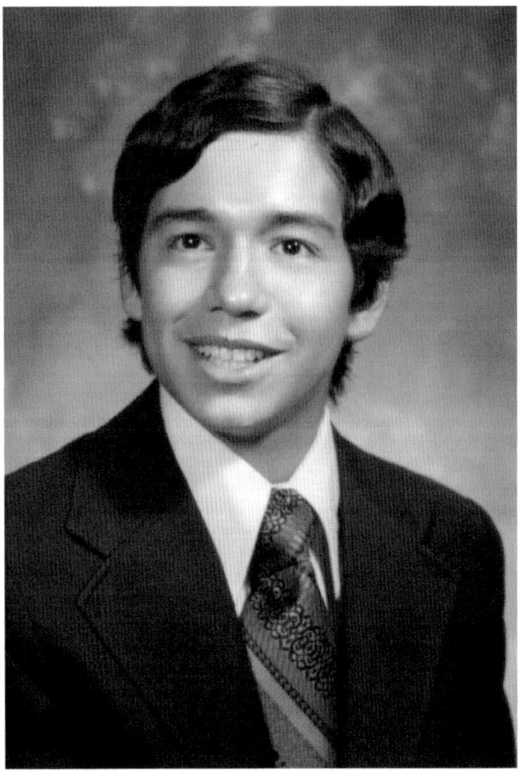

Bob Morales was born in 1955 and is the eldest of five boys raised in the El Sereno area of Los Angeles. He and his brothers, Michael, Freddie, Mark, and John, all played baseball, football, and basketball during their elementary school years and all graduated from Loyola High School in Los Angeles. Bob coached his son, Matthew, during his little league years and was the unofficial team photographer for the Arcadia High School baseball team from 2009 to 2013, the four years that Matthew played ball at Arcadia. Bob's father, Fred Morales, was born in Los Angeles in 1930 and graduated from Fremont High School. Fred's parents, Florence and Ubaldo, were from Mexico. Fred served overseas during the Korean War in the US Air Force, and retired from the City of Los Angeles Community Redevelopment Agency. (Courtesy of Bob Morales.)

3

Alhambra, Monterey Park, and Montebello

Alhambra's roots begin with the San Gabriel Mission, founded in 1771. The land that would later become Alhambra was part of a 300,000-acre land grant given to Manuel Nieto by the Spanish. These lands were transferred to the United States after the Mexican-American War. A wealthy developer, Benjamin Davis Wilson, married Ramona Yorba, daughter of Bernardo Yorba, who owned the land that would eventually be known as Alhambra. Yorba named the land after a book his daughter Ruth was reading, Washington Irving's *Tales of the Alhambra*—the Alhambra is a palace in Granada, Spain. There is a Pyrenees Castle, and the high school mascots are the Moors and Aztecs. Ramona Convent Secondary School opened in 1889, and Alhambra High School opened its doors in 1898, five years before the city became incorporated. Alhambra has experienced waves of immigration—Italians in the 1950s, Mexicans in the 1960s, and Chinese in the 1980s.

Monterey Park, neighbor to Alhambra, has the largest concentration of Chinese Americans of any city in the United States. Following the Civil War, an Italian, Alessandro Repetto, purchased 5,000 acres of the Rancho San Antonio and built his ranch house where Garfield Avenue crosses the Pomona Freeway. Richard Garvey also purchased land but had to sell portions because of debts. In 1906, the first subdivision in the area was known as Ramona Acres, inspired by the novel *Ramona*, which the developer's daughter had read. In 1920, a large area along the south edge of the city broke away and became the city of Montebello.

Before the arrival of the Spanish, Montebello (Spanish and Italian for "beautiful mountain"), was populated by the Gabrieleño-Tongva. By 1870, most of the native population in Alhambra, Monterey Park, and Montebello had been killed off by European diseases. The current city of Montebello is comprised of land grants from Rancho San Antonio, Rancho La Merced, and Rancho Paso de Bartolo. The Juan Matias Sanchez Adobe, built in 1844, still stands in East Montebello. Japanese American farmers, who lost their property during the World War II internment, populated South Montebello. Standard Oil Company discovered oil in Montebello in 1916. Montebello High School's teams are the Oilers.

Today, most of the players, coaches, team moms, and board members in the area are Mexican American.

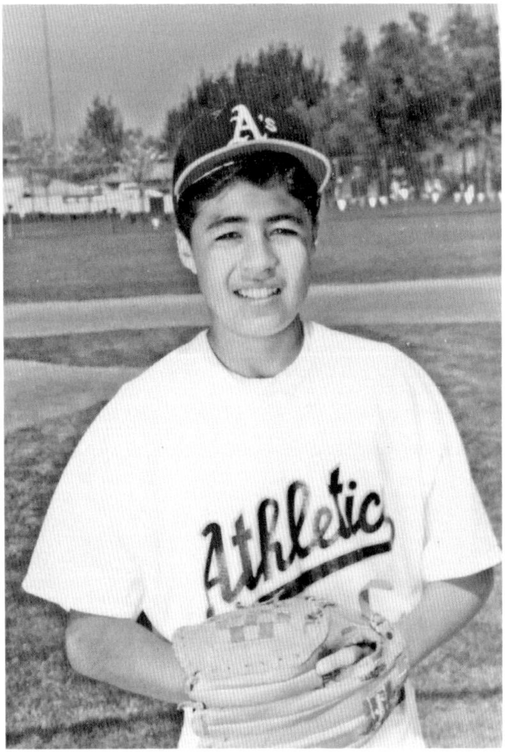

John Talamantes was born in 1978 at Kaiser Hospital in Hollywood. He was an outstanding little league player at Granada Park in Alhambra, where he pitched on several all-star teams. He also played basketball at St. Thomas More Catholic School and for years was an excellent youth tennis player throughout Southern California, winning several championships. John played with the American Youth Soccer Organization (AYSO) No. 60 at Almansor Park. He was a hard-throwing pitcher for the Alhambra High School Moors. He still resides in Alhambra and is currently a security guard for Commerce Casino. (Courtesy of Teresa M. Santillán.)

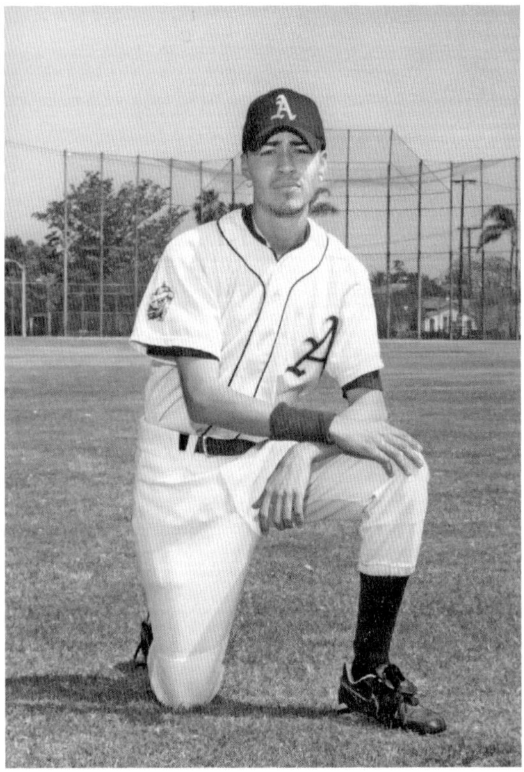

John Talamantes attended St. Thomas More Catholic School, Margarita Elementary School, and Alhambra High School. He was an outstanding all-around athlete, playing baseball, basketball, soccer, and tennis. As a young boy during the 1980s and 1990s, he traveled with his parents all over the country, watching major-league baseball games in Boston, New York, Atlanta, Houston, Oakland, Seattle, San Francisco, Denver, Chicago, Pittsburgh, and Baltimore. He was five days short of seeing Cal Ripken break Lou Gehrig's consecutive game record in 1995. (Courtesy of Teresa M. Santillán.)

Román Mejía was born at the San Gabriel Valley Medical Center in 1997 less than one mile from the San Gabriel Mission. Mejía played several years of Alhambra little league baseball at Granada Park. He was an excellent hitter, a fast runner, and demonstrated very good defensive skills on the diamond. He made several all-star teams. At St. Thomas More Catholic School, he played basketball and was in the Chess Club for years. One season, the basketball team won the league championship under the coaching of Nick Pérez. Mejía graduated from Cathedral High School, only a couple of blocks away from his favorite place, Dodger Stadium. He currently attends Pasadena City College where he is majoring in business. (Courtesy of Dianne Sánchez.)

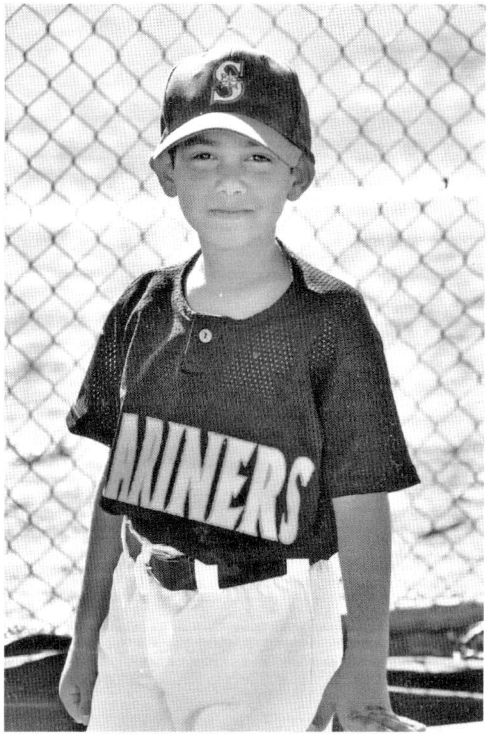

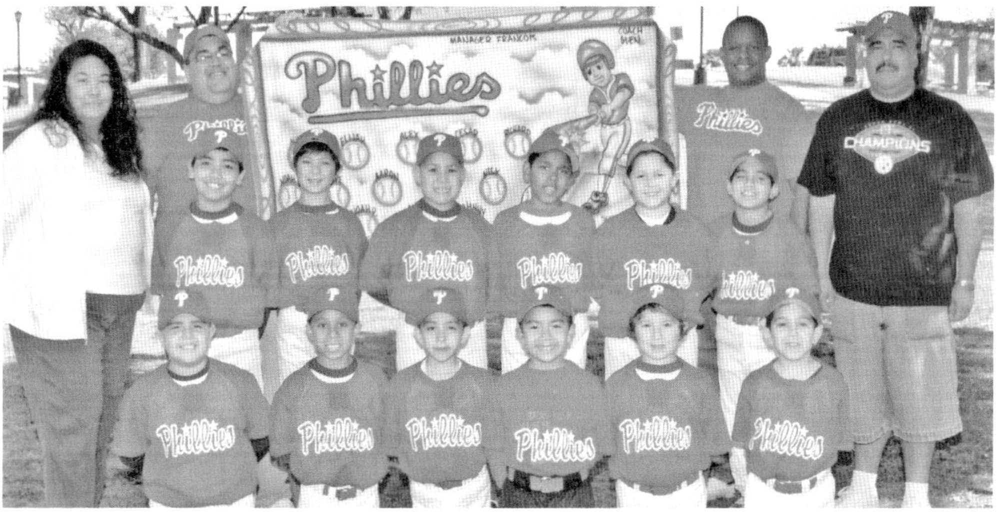

Román Mejía (second row, last player on right) played several sports before high school, including baseball, flag football, soccer, basketball, and hockey. He played ice hockey for many years in Orange County as a goalie. He attended his first Los Angeles Kings game at the old Forum in Inglewood at the age of one in 1998. He attended the only two California hockey games played outdoors so far, at Dodger Stadium (Kings versus Ducks) and Levi Stadium (Kings versus Sharks), the National Hockey League All-Star Game at the Staples Center in 2017, and two Stanley Cup Finals games in 2012 and 2014. In 2017, he fulfilled another dream by attending a game at Lambeau Field in Green Bay, watching his Packers defeat the Chicago Bears. (Courtesy of Dianne Sánchez.)

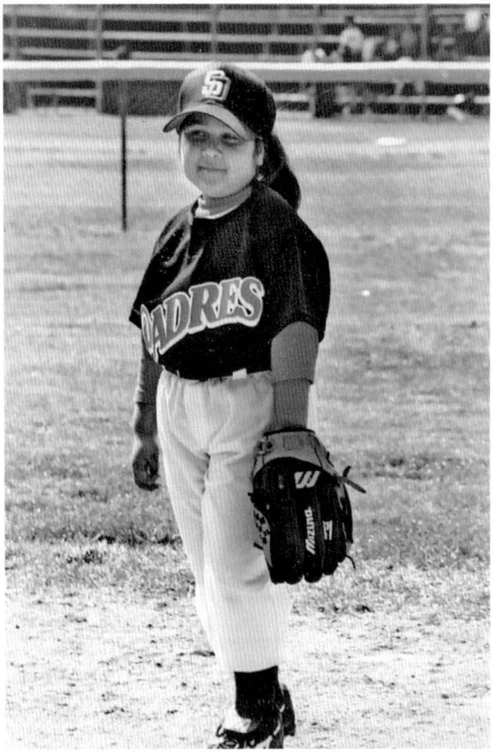

Rhiannon Mejía was born in 1997 at San Gabriel Valley Hospital. She played Alhambra little league at Granada Park from T-ball to majors, making several all-star games as a pitcher and at first base. She also played basketball at St. Thomas More Catholic School and six years of soccer with AYSO No. 60 at Almansor Park. She also played volleyball at Assumption Catholic School. She graduated from Sacred Heart of Jesus High School in Lincoln Heights, where she played varsity softball for three years, serving as co-captain in her senior year. She has attended every Dodgers opening game since she was born. She currently attends California State University at Los Angeles majoring in business. (Courtesy of Dianne Sánchez.)

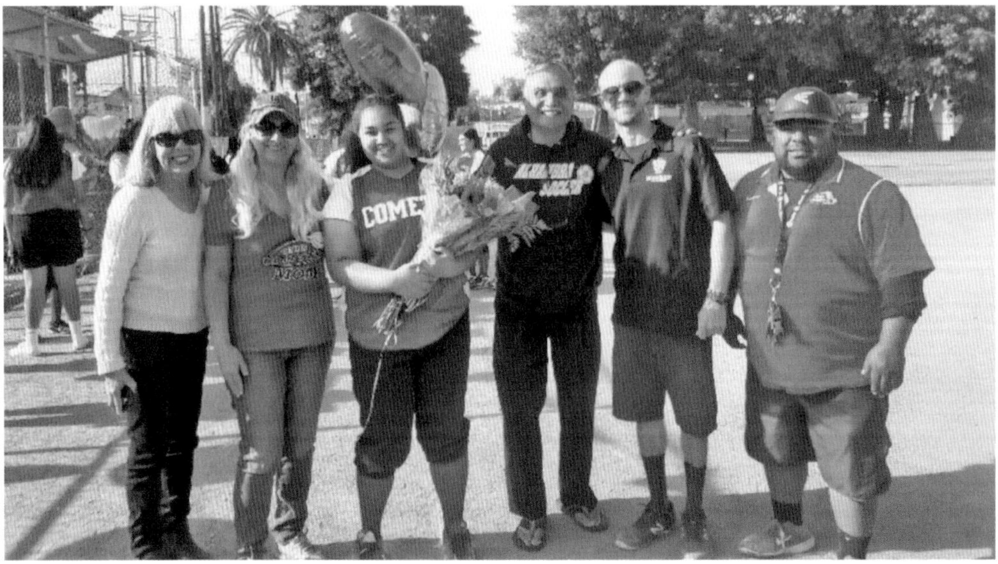

Rhiannon Mejía started playing T-ball at the age of four with the Alhambra American little league at Granada Park. Her first team was the Cubs, and she played first base. She insisted at that age that someone pitch to her rather than placing the ball on the tee. She played on several teams and made the all-star team nearly every season. She is seen here in 2017 in her last high school game. From left to right are Teresa M. Santillán, Dianne Sánchez, Rhiannon, Richard A. Santillán, and coaches Grant Kinman and Joseph Salazar. (Courtesy of Richard A. Santillán.)

Dianne Sánchez was born at Kaiser Hospital in Hollywood. She attended Farmdale Elementary School in El Sereno and Margarita Middle School and graduated from Alhambra High School in 1985. At Margarita, she was student body president, cheerleader, and second base on the softball team. She received her associate of arts degree from Pasadena City College and a bachelor's degree in broadcast journalism from Cal State–Los Angeles. Sánchez was an intern at KTLA Channel 5 working with Ray Gonzáles and has worked in the news department for 26 years as planning editor. She is the corecipient of six Emmy Awards for best news broadcast, morning broadcast, and major stories. (Courtesy of Dianne Sánchez.)

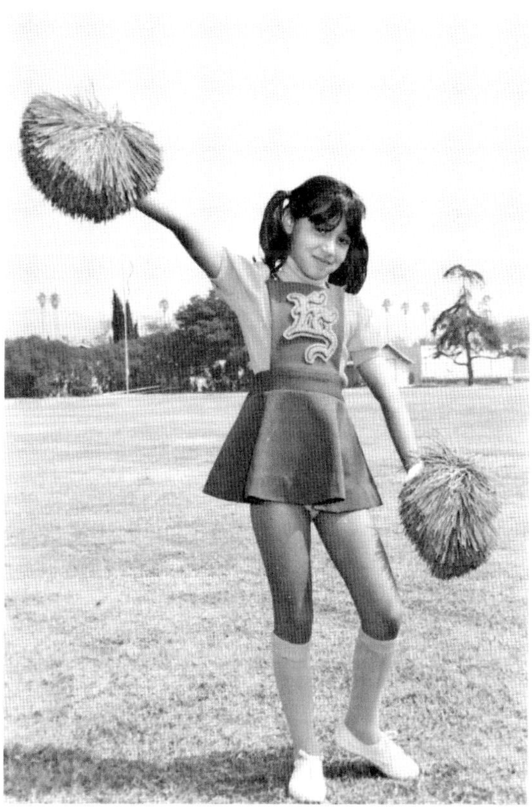

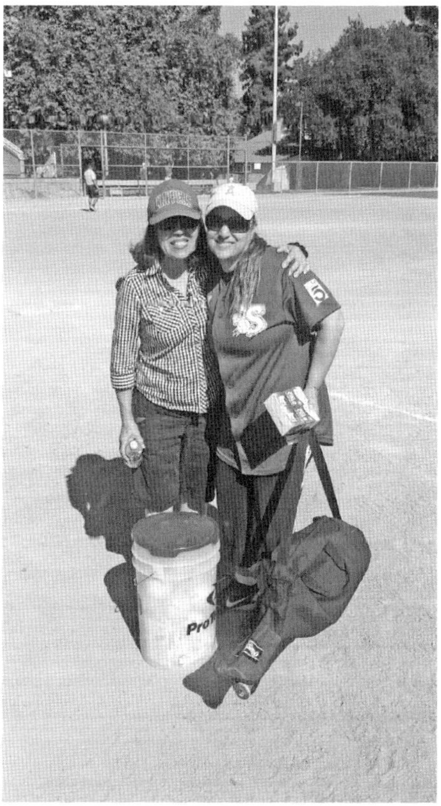

Dianne Sánchez (right) is the daughter of Teresa M. Santillán (left). Sánchez played for the KTLA Channel 5 news department softball team, the Sunset Sluggers—the station is on the famous Sunset Boulevard in Hollywood—and in the 2015 season she became the team manager and played first base. She is the mother of Román and Rhiannon Mejía, who played various sports in Alhambra. Teresa graduated from Belmont High School and attended East Los Angeles Community College and graduated from California State University at Los Angeles in 1999. She retired in 2008 after 25 years as an elementary school teacher with the Los Angeles Catholic Archdiocese, mainly with Assumption School in East Los Angeles. Since 2011, she has traveled to over 25 countries, plays golf and bowls, and is one of the coauthors of *Mexican American Baseball in East Los Angeles*. (Courtesy of Teresa M. Santillán.)

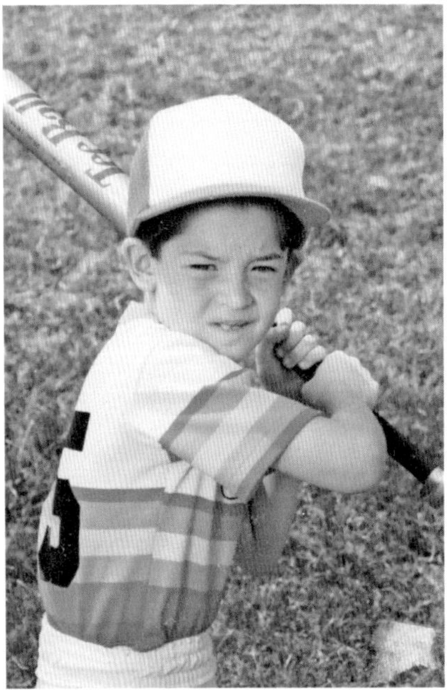

Mel Sánchez V was born at Valley Vista Hospital in San Gabriel in 1984 and graduated from Rancho High School in Arcadia. He played youth tackle football for the Junior All-American League for both Temple City and Arcadia and played for the Arcadia Apaches for one season and for the Temple City Rams for two years. He played middle linebacker and wore the number 57 like his football hero, Ricky Jackson of the New Orleans Saints. Mel IV was the defensive coach for his son's Rams team. He and his father, Mel III, were huge Saints fans because of their hard-hitting style. (Courtesy of Mel Sánchez IV.)

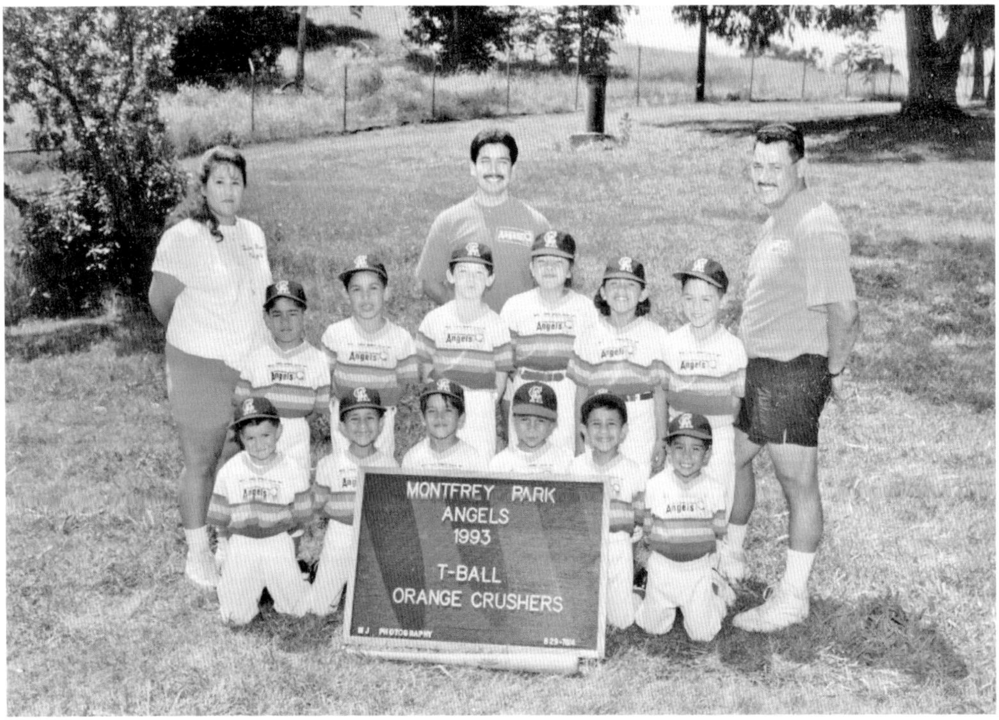

Mel Sánchez V (second row, third from left) played for the Monterey Park Angels in 1992 and 1993. There were several teams called the Angels, but each had a specific color to tell them apart, like the Orange Angels and the Red Angels. Mel V's father, Mel IV, is a musician who played in two popular thrash metal bands, Abattoir and Evildead, performing throughout Europe. Mel IV resides in Alhambra as of 2018. (Courtesy of Mel Sánchez IV.)

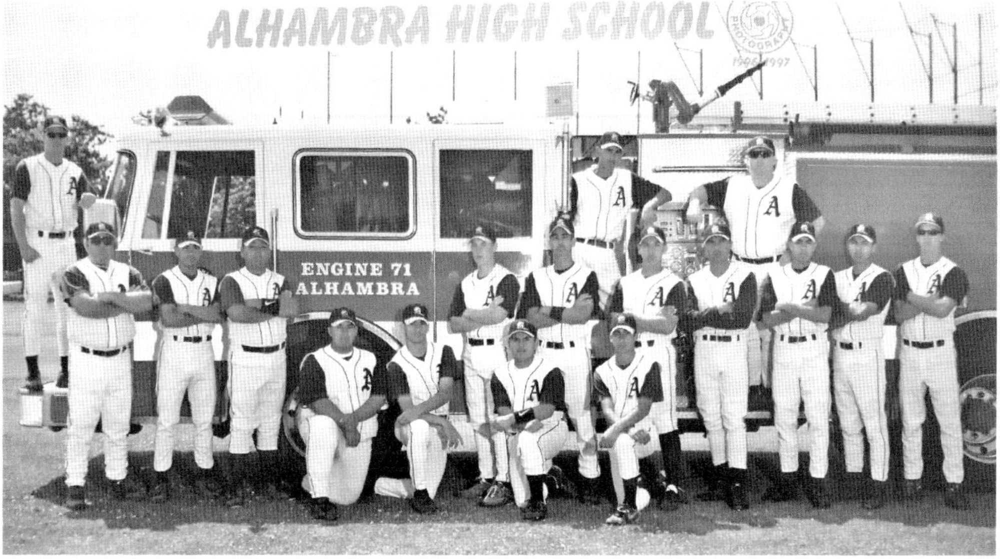

The 1997 Alhambra High School Moors are, from left to right, (first row) Sal Pérez, John Hoyos, Joel Valles, and David López; (second row) coach Kevin Heaton, Fred Uribe, James García, Bryan McIntire, Sergio Ramírez, Marin Chávez, Ryan Tan, Jovan Ramírez, Martín Díaz, and coach Ryan Hart; (third row) head coach Steve Gewecke, Nathan García, and coach Robbie Greep. Sergio Ramírez and Jovann Ramírez earned first-team honors. Fred Uribe later played at East Los Angeles College. Joel Valles played at Pasadena City College and the University of Missouri. (Courtesy of Steve Gewecke.)

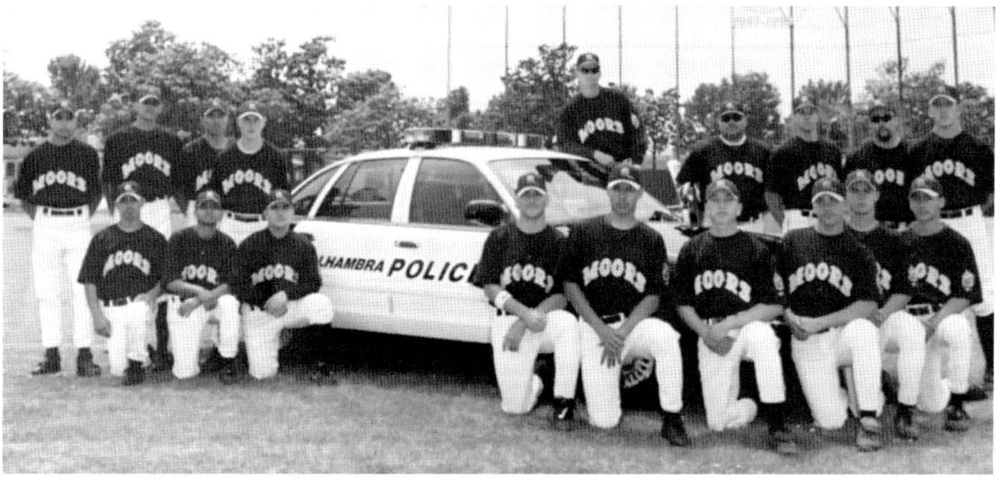

The 1998 Alhambra High School Moors had a good team. From left to right are (first row) Steve Zúñiga, Misael Artaega, Joel Valles, John Hoyos, Martín Díaz, Jorge Gómez, Fred Uribe, Michael Tade, and David López; (second row) Jovan Ramírez, Nathan García, Ryan Tan, Bryan McIntire, head coach Steve Gewecke, coach Kevin Heaton, coach Pat Hart, coach Shawn Clingan, and Pat Fitzgerald. They won nine out of their last 10 games to make the playoffs, where they defeated league champions Bell Gardens on back-to-back days. Joel Valles, Fred Uribe, Michael Tade, and David López earned first-team honors. (Courtesy of Steve Gewecke.)

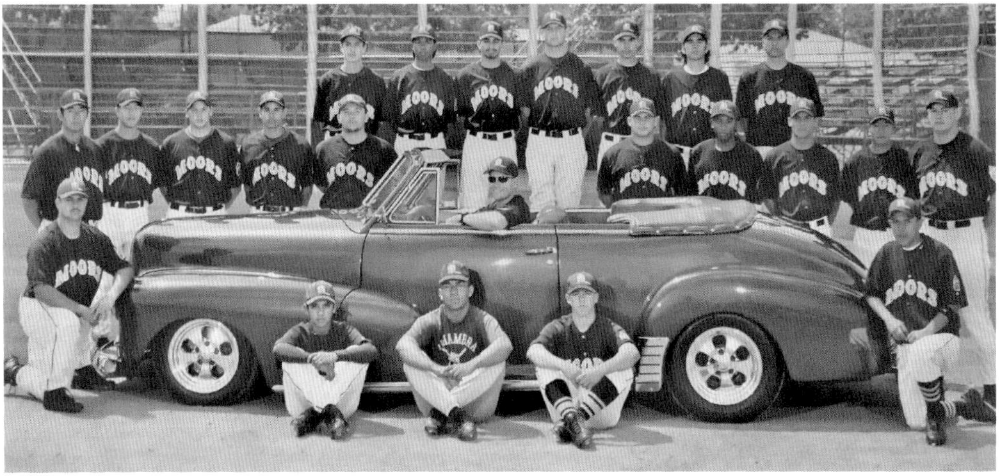

The 2003 Alhambra High School Moors finished in second place in their league. From left to right are (first row) Tony Nieto, César Martínez, Eric Aguirre, Joey Blanco, and Alex Maciel; (second row) coach Wataru Tomita, Darren Hasegawa, Jerrod Carr, John Kirby, Shaun Cerecedes, head coach Steve Gewecke, Robert Vargas, Deric Allen, Ralph Carmona, Daniel Hasegawa, and coach Fred Werner; (third row) Steven Díaz, Jeremy DeVore, Adan Encinas, Wes Frias, Pablo Cortés, Mark Freeborn, and Jacob Proctor. Jeremy DeVore, Shaun Cerecedes, Alex Maciel, and Wes Frias earned first-team honors. Frias played at Benton Community College in Oregon. (Courtesy of Steve Gewecke.)

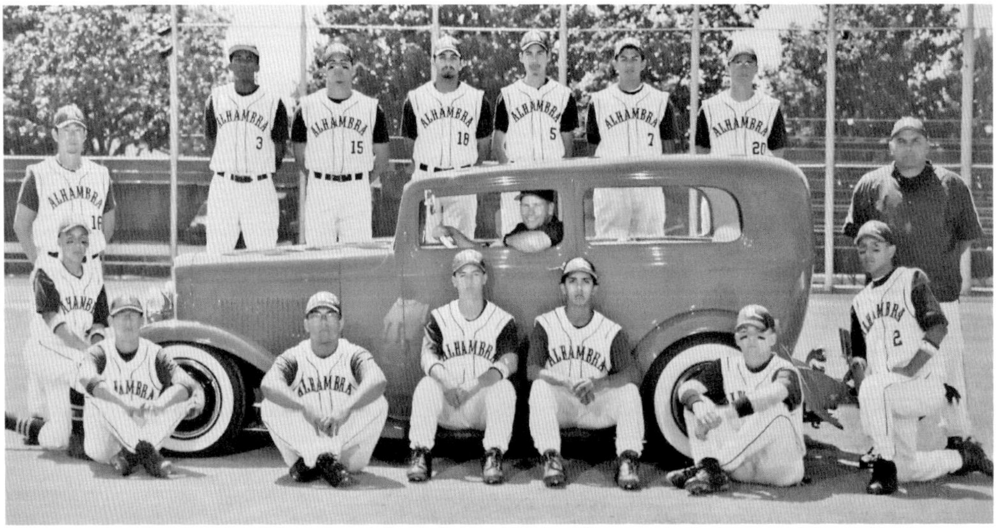

The 2004 Alhambra High School Moors had outstanding players. From left to right are (first row) Dennis Zapata, Ronnie Kurihara, Eric Aguirre, Joey Blanco, César Martínez, Javier Estrada, and Alex Maciel; (second row) coach Wataru Tomita, head coach Steve Gewecke, and coach Bobby Gonzáles; (third row) Deric Allen, Robert Vargas, Adan Encinas, Pablo Cortés, Gabriel Illingworth, and Adam Varnes. Robert Vargas and Deric Allan earned first-team honors and went on to play ball at Chicago State University. César Martínez played at East Los Angeles College. Ronnie Kurihara played at Upper Iowa University. Major-leaguers Max West and Ralph Kiner played for Alhambra. (Courtesy of Steve Gewecke.)

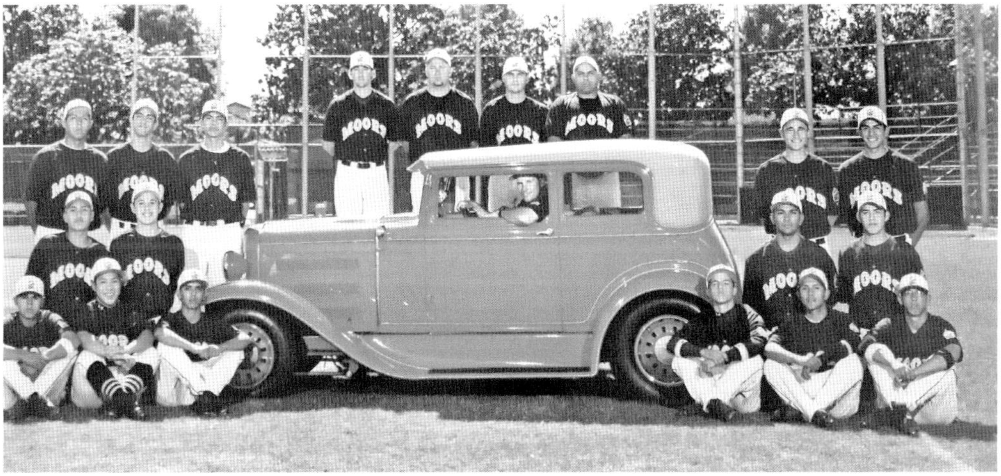

The 2005 Alhambra High School Moors finished first in their league, the first league championship for coach Steve Gewecke. From left to right are (first row) Jesús Ventura, Jon Chong, César Martínez, Joey Blanco, Alex Marciel, and Ronnie Kurihara; (second row) Aaron Soto, Alex Ponce, head coach Steve Gewecke, Eric Aguirre, and Gilbert Reynoso; (third row) J.R. García, Casey Martin, Noe Ramírez, coach Chris Cosbey, coach Shawn Clingan, coach Dave Gálvez, coach Bobby Gonzáles, Adam Varnes, and Gabriel Illingworth. Noe Ramírez was named California State Freshman by Cal High Sports. He is pitching for the Anaheim Angels in 2018. (Courtesy of Steve Gewecke.)

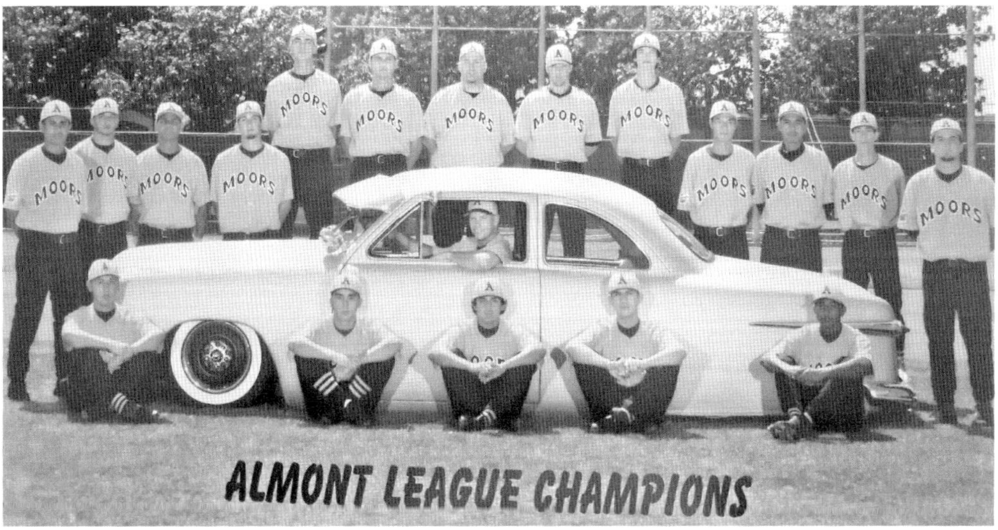

The 2008 Alhambra High School Moors won the Almont League for the fourth year in a row. The team set two school records, winning 17 consecutive games and 23 games overall. From left to right are (first row) Richard García, Ryan Águilar, Jonathan Beltrán, Greg Saldate, and Eric Allen; (second row) Christian Alas, Chris Rosario, Joshua DeVore, Rob Olivarez, Noe Ramírez, coach Dave Gálvez, coach Shawn Clingan, coach Chris Cosbey, Tim Lewis, Stanley Yu, Irvin Reyes, Quinn López, and Cody Heaton. Head coach Steve Gewecke is in the car. (Courtesy of Steve Gewecke.)

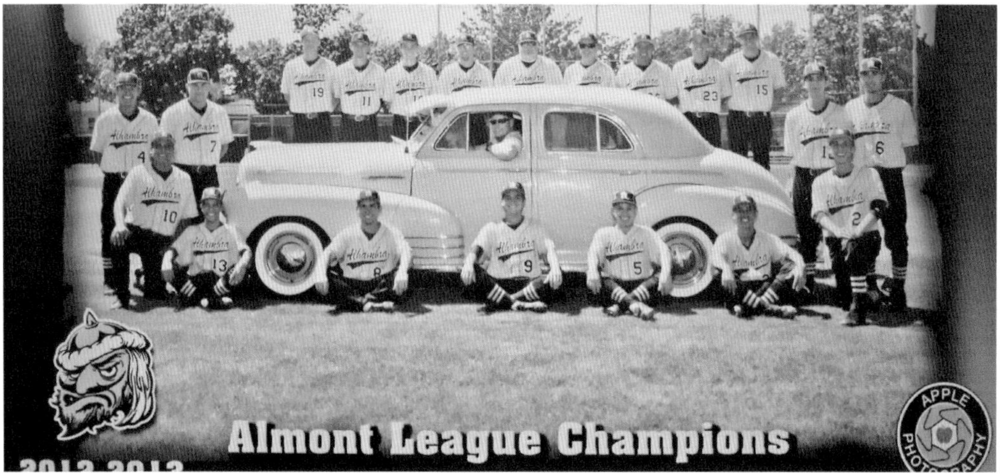

The 2012 Alhambra High School Moors won the Almont League, setting a team record with 24 wins and finishing in second place in CIF Division 3. The last time the Moors were in the CIF championship game was 1926. From left to right are (first row) Brandon Morales, Juan Crespo, Andrew Arroyo, Andrés García, Marco Briones, and Cory Yip; (second row) Christian Marcel, coach Chris Cosbey, coach Colin Danielsen, Nathan Quiñónes, Blake Kuehnie, Jeremy Durán, Jonah Lybarger, Jesús López, Enrique Landero, Gilbert Quesada, Chance Beal, coach Rich Cosbey, and Charles Gibson. Head coach Steve Gewecke is in the car. (Courtesy of Steve Gewecke.)

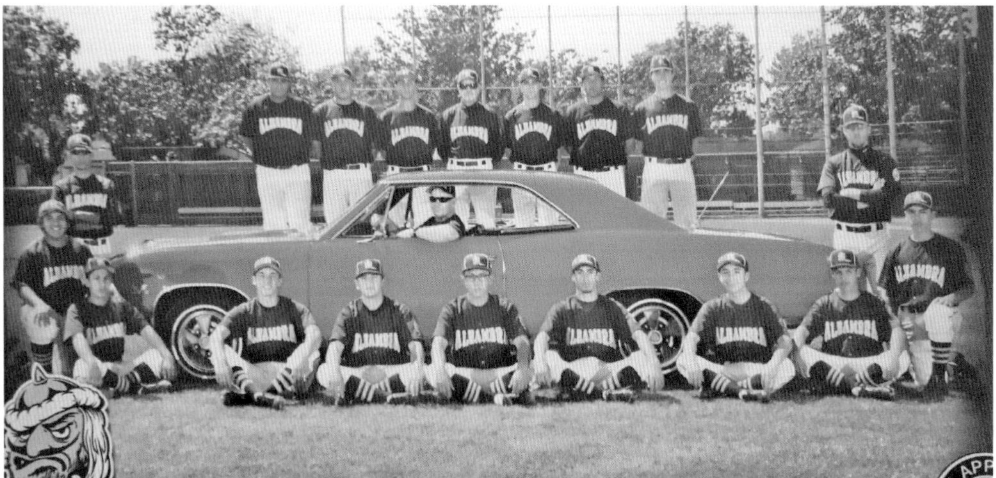

The 2014 Alhambra High School Moors won the league title and were the first Moors team to go undefeated in league play. Pitcher Marco Briones's career record at Alhambra was 30 wins and one loss. He is pitching at Utah Valley University in 2018. From left to right are (first row) Adrián Cerón, Marco Briones, Joseph Barajas, José Loera, James Giambalvo, Óscar Peralta, and Michael Corral; (second row) Andrew Prieto and Gabriel Figueroa; (third row) coach Andrew Águilar, Vance Tovalin, Adam Rodríguez, Julian Zermeño, coach Rick Cosbey, David Saldate, Christian Maciel, Nick Giambalvo, and coach Chris Cosbey. Head coach Steve Gewecke is seated in the car. (Courtesy of Steve Gewecke.)

Noe Ramírez was one of the best players at Alhambra High School. He plays for the Los Angeles Angels in 2018, having previously played for the Boston Red Sox. He pitched for the USA Baseball Collegiate National Team in 2010 and earned a silver medal at the International University Sports Federation World University Baseball Championship in Tokyo, Japan. He made his major-league debut with the Red Sox on July 3, 2015, at Fenway Park. On August 8, 2017, he joined the Angels. (Courtesy of Steve Gewecke.)

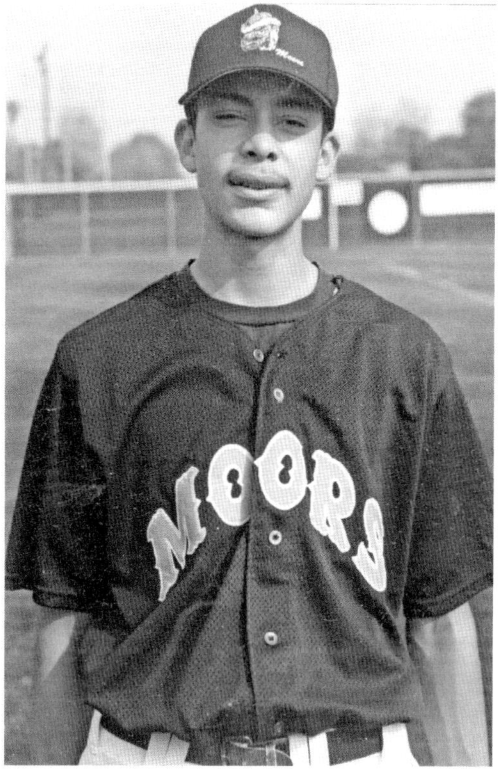

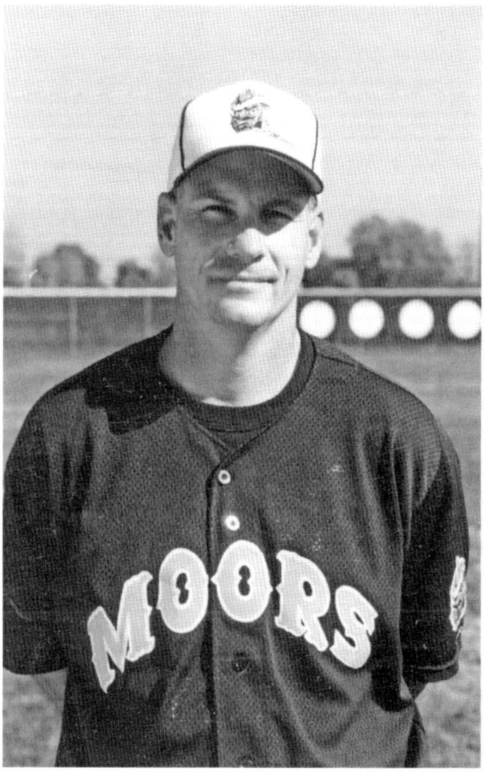

Steve Gewecke is the head coach at Alhambra High School in 2018. His father, Roger, and grandfather Clifford Sr. played ball and coached. Steve played ball at Arcadia High School, Glendale Community College, the University of Nebraska, and the University of Southern California. He played for the St. Louis Cardinals A-Ball affiliate Springfield Cardinals in Illinois. He has coached at several San Gabriel Valley high schools, including Arcadia, San Gabriel, Mountain View, and Alhambra. Steve was named the *Star-News* Coach of the Year in 2005, 2008, and 2012. His record at Alhambra is quite impressive, with 11 league championship titles. (Courtesy of Steve Gewecke.)

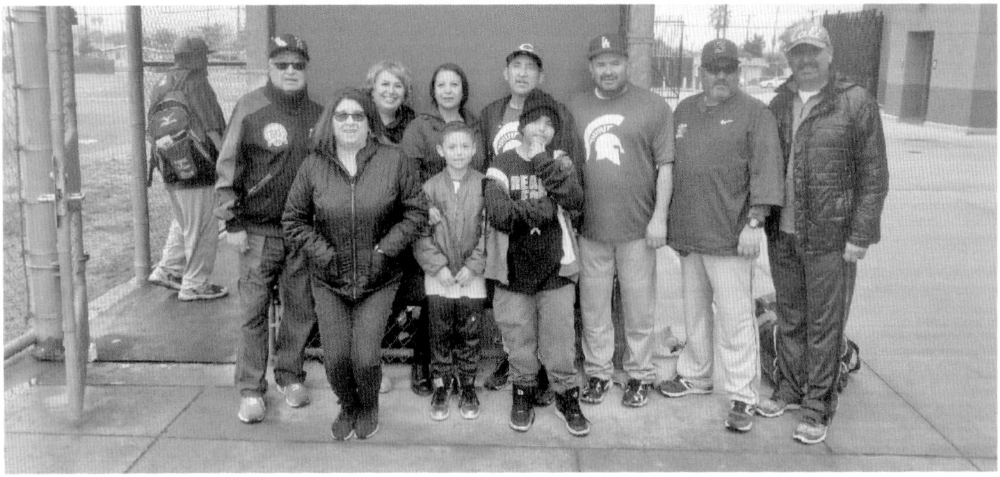

This 2018 photograph representing five generations of Pérez ballplayers was taken at Pioneer High School in Whittier, where the Pérez boys played ball and graduated. Tommy Pérez Sr. was an outstanding player during the 1930s and 1940s. Tom Pérez Jr. was a very good player and remarkable coach. His sons and their children have carried on the family tradition of baseball and softball. From left to right are (first row) Michelle Tamayo, Ian Loza, and Noah Pérez; (second row) Tom Pérez Jr., Rebecca Pérez, Heather Loza, Nick Pérez, Michael Pérez, Tommy Pérez III, and Robert Pérez. (Courtesy of Nick Pérez.)

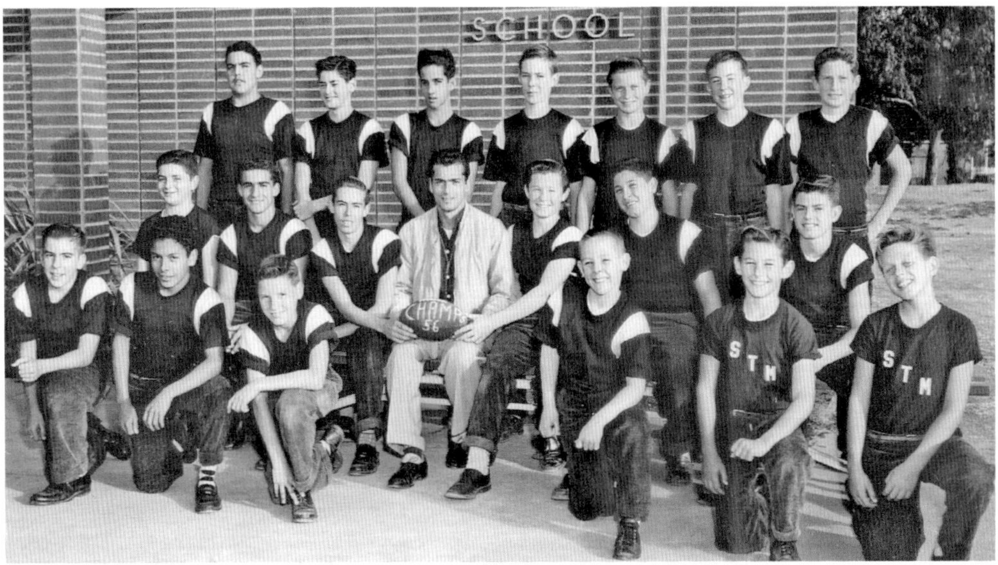

Fred Padilla (first row, second from left) was born in El Paso in 1943. His parents had come to the United States from Mexico as children due to revolution and hardship in 1920. Fred attended St. Thomas More in Alhambra, where he played Catholic Youth Organization basketball, football, and softball. At Bosco Tech, he ran track and played football until he suffered a knee injury. After receiving his bachelor's and master's degrees in materials science and engineering from UC Berkeley, he worked at Alcoa, Aerospace Corp., and the Jet Propulsion Laboratory, but also enjoyed a 50-year teaching career at Bosco Tech and Los Angeles Trade-Tech College. (Courtesy of Fred Padilla.)

S.Sgt. Brian Henninger Aguirre served on the Iraq-Kuwait border in 2008. He was born in San Gabriel in 1969, joining the Army at the age of 18 and serving more than 25 years as a military police officer. He has been deployed throughout the world including combat training. His three daughters, Monique, Victoria, and Emily, are very proud of his dedication, sacrifice, duty, and honor to his country. His family heritage includes Native American, Spanish, Mexican, German, and Irish. He was an outstanding baseball player in little league, high school, and in the military. (Courtesy of James Henninger Aguirre.)

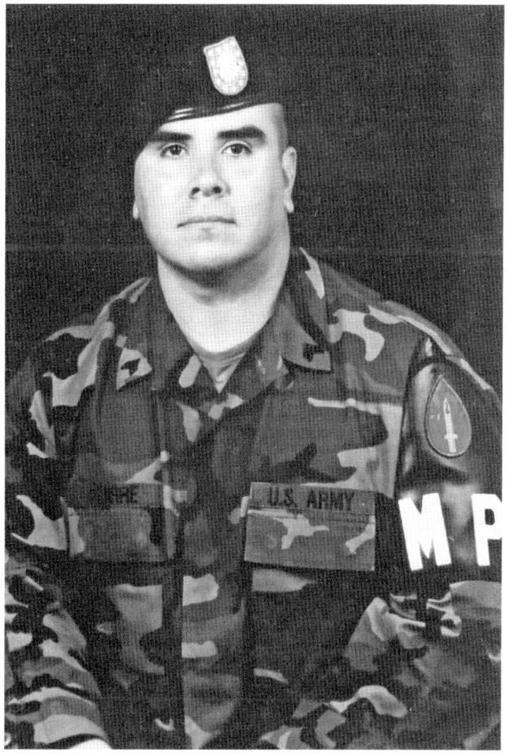

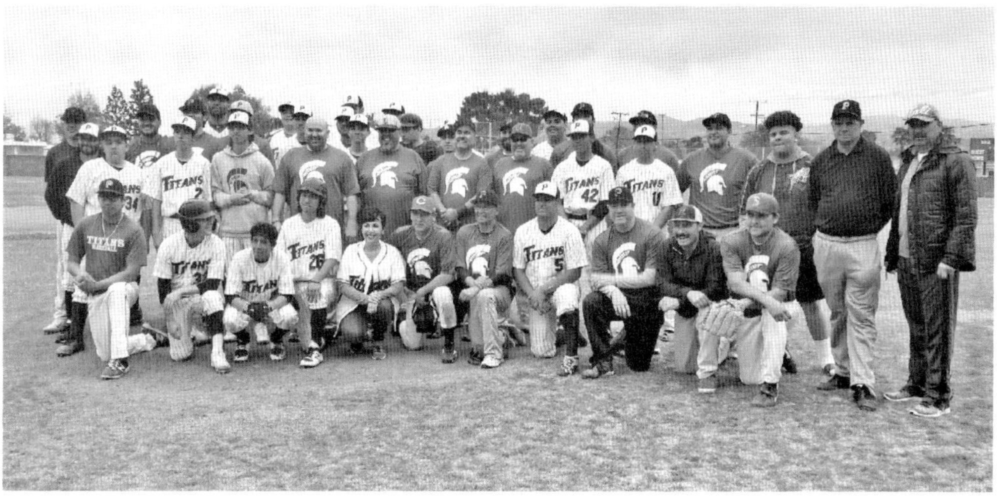

On Saturday March 10, 2018, a friendly yet competitive game was played at Pioneer High School in Whittier between alumni and the current varsity team. Despite the threat of rain, there was a nice turnout to cheer both teams on. Throughout the San Gabriel Valley, more and more high schools are hosting these contests, bringing back the "old-timers" to compete against the current team. It is a nice tradition that expresses to the former players that they are not forgotten and that they still are greatly appreciated. Needless to say, there is always ribbing, joking, and teasing, but it is done in a respectful manner. Nick Pérez (first row, sixth from left) was the winning pitcher in 2017 and 2018. (Courtesy of Nick Pérez.)

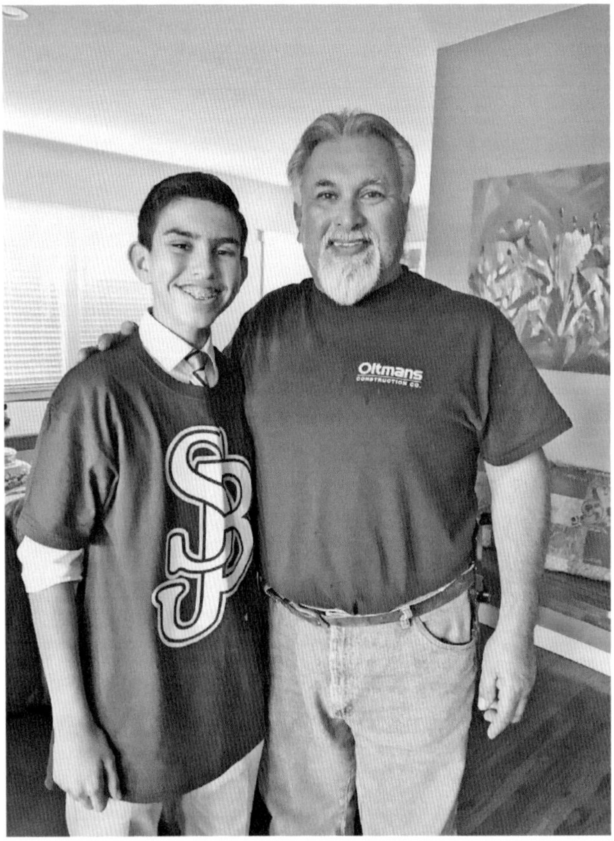

Joe Santillán (right) was born at Lincoln Hospital in East Los Angeles in 1957. He was raised in Norwalk, where he attended Norwalk High School. He and his wife, Eva, have two grown children, Melissa and Carlitos, who played several sports, including baseball, softball, football, and soccer in the Norwalk-Artesia-Cerritos area. Melissa has three children who also play several sports in both the community and school. Joe is seen with his grandson Nicolas, who attends St. John Bosco in Bellflower, where he runs track and plays on the soccer team. (Courtesy of Joe Santillán.)

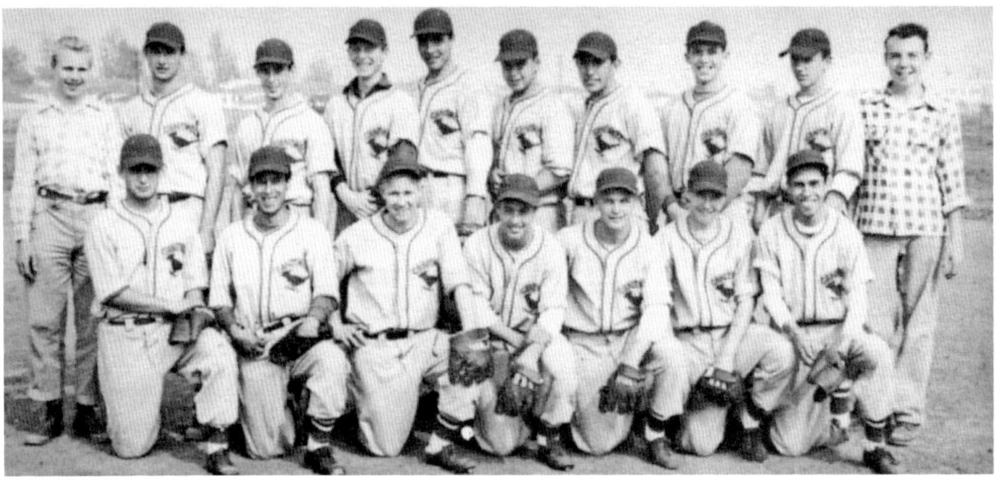

Edward Rodríguez (first row, far right) played on the 1951 Cantwell High School baseball team in Montebello. Other players included R. Rodríguez, J. Villa, and A. Salazar. He attended our Lady of Lourdes Elementary School in East Los Angeles in 1947. At Cantwell, he was on the C football team, played varsity baseball for four years, was a member of the Glee Club, and majored in business. He played ball during his military service. He currently lives in Carlsbad, California. (Courtesy of Edward Rodríguez.)

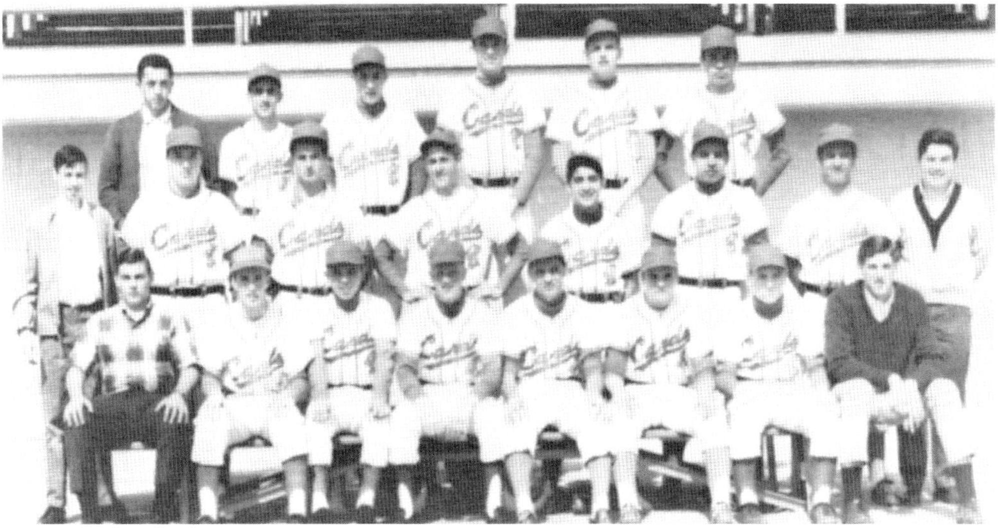

Steve Pedroza Gilles (third row, third from left), class of 1966, is still regarded by many as Cantwell's best hitting and most feared first baseman. He was a pure line-drive left-handed hitter, possessing a near-perfect swing. He was a three-year starting varsity letter-winner in baseball and the starting quarterback for the varsity football squad. He started on the 1964 CIF semifinalist team and the 1966 Angelus League Championship team. He was the league's batting champion in 1966, when he hit for a remarkable batting average of .512. (Courtesy of Lauro Montes.)

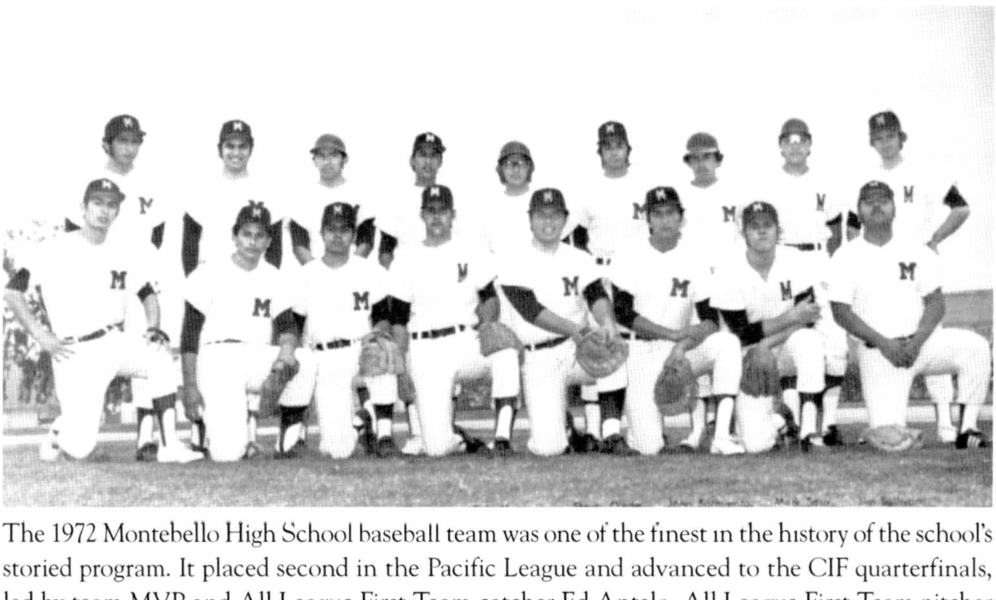

The 1972 Montebello High School baseball team was one of the finest in the history of the school's storied program. It placed second in the Pacific League and advanced to the CIF quarterfinals, led by team MVP and All-League First Team catcher Ed Antelo, All-League First Team pitcher Billy Daniels, pitcher and Most Inspirational Player Eddie Herron, All-League Second Team right fielder Rene Beltran, and Defensive Player of the Year at Montebello High School and All-League Second Team second baseman Jimmy Montez (second row, fourth from left). Head coach Jim Douglas's squad had great pitching and defense and a very potent offense. (Courtesy of Helen Fuentes Gonzáles.)

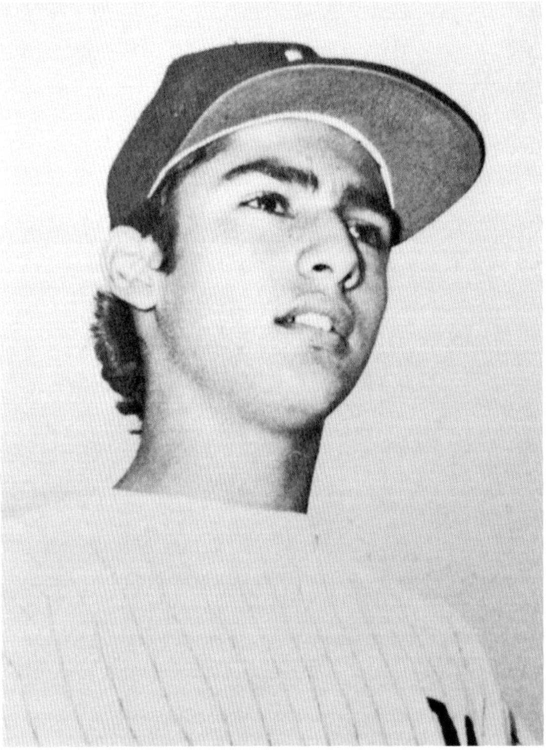

Jimmy Montez, Montebello High School class of 1973, discovered early on that he was a natural at second base. He began honing his fielding and hitting skills in the Montebello little leagues. Montez continued his baseball success, earning the Montebello Stars' prestigious Perpetual Trophy Award, and was a two-time All-League player and the 1972 Defensive Player of the Year. He played at East Los Angeles Community College and earned an athletic scholarship to Whittier College, where he finished his baseball career. His success was due to his talent, work ethic, team-first attitude, and endless passion for the game. (Courtesy of Helen Fuentes Gonzáles.)

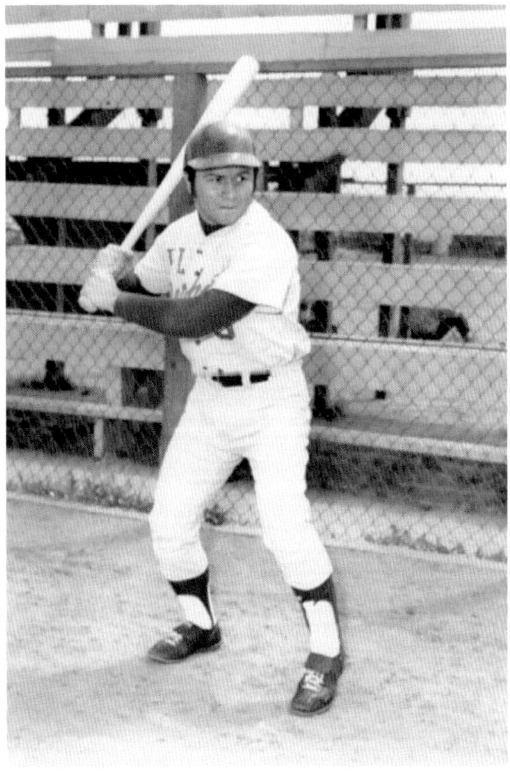

Jack Arenas is the youngest of 12 siblings and son of Joaquín and Maria Paz Arenas who migrated from Mexico in 1928. Jack started playing T-ball at Rose Hill Recreation Center in Los Angeles. He played all sports, but baseball was his favorite. At 11, he pitched on a travel team, the Baldwin Park Blue Jays, playing in different cities including Mexicali, Mexico. Two years later, he pitched for the East Los Angeles Cardinals. At Lincoln High School, he played on the junior and varsity teams and was voted first team all-league on the JV team. After years as a pitcher, his varsity coach, Dave Chávez, converted Jack to shortstop. He was voted first team all-league twice, and first team all-city at shortstop. He later played two years at East Los Angeles College and two years at Whittier College. (Courtesy of Jack Arenas.)

Growing up in Boyle Heights, Gene Aguilera idolized the great Dodger teams from the late 1950s and 1960s. As a young man, he walked to Evergreen Park to play baseball with his neighborhood friends from East Fourth Street while emulating his favorite Dodger, Duke Snider. He is seen in his front yard with his "Black Beauty" bat, wearing his much loved Dodger T-shirt, as David Acosta plays catcher. After graduating from Lakewood High School and the University of Southern California, Aguilera returned to his East LA roots to work and serve the community. (Courtesy of Gene Aguilera.)

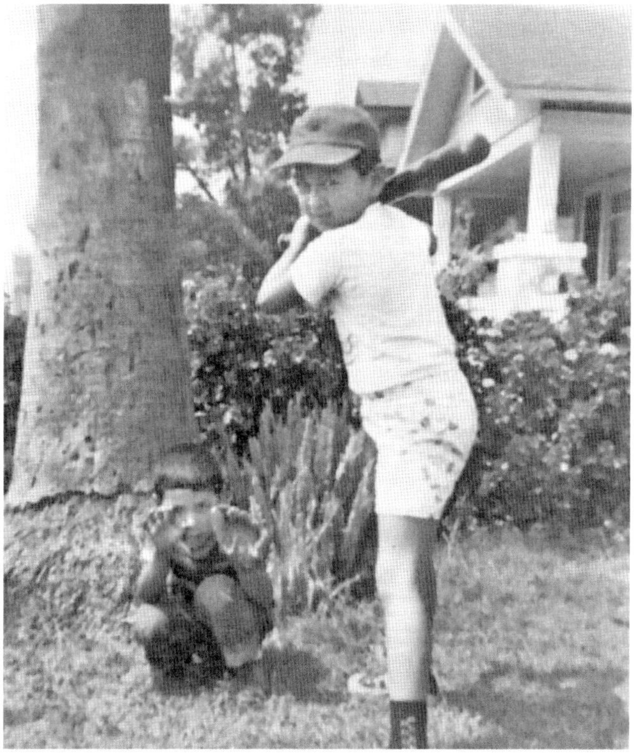

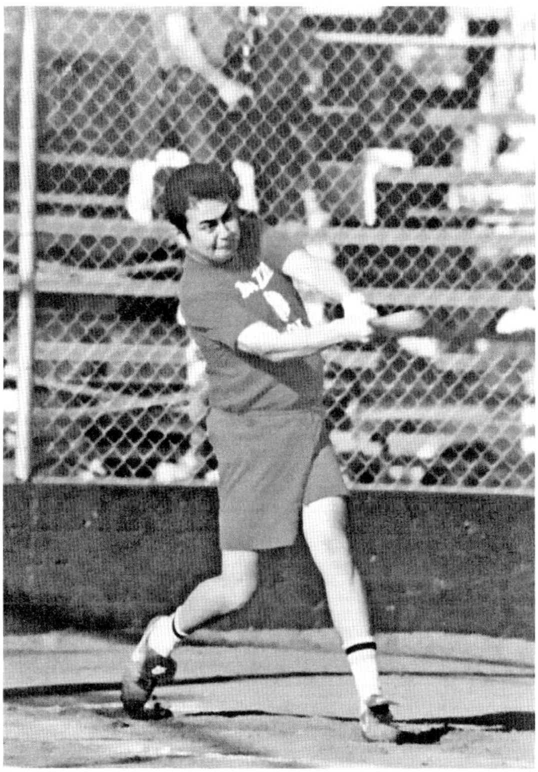

Gene Aguilera, president of the East Los Angeles Lions Club, gets a key hit in his team's thrilling, extra-inning, 10-9 victory over the Montebello Lions Club at Montebello City Park on August 14, 1988. Jack Duran and Dan Rosas also contributed key hits for the win. The East Los Angeles Lions Club was declared Champs of the Eastside after defeating the Montebello Lions in softball. Gene is one of the nation's foremost experts on the history of Mexican American and Mexican boxing history. He has published two books on the subject with Arcadia Publishing. (Courtesy of Gene Aguilera.)

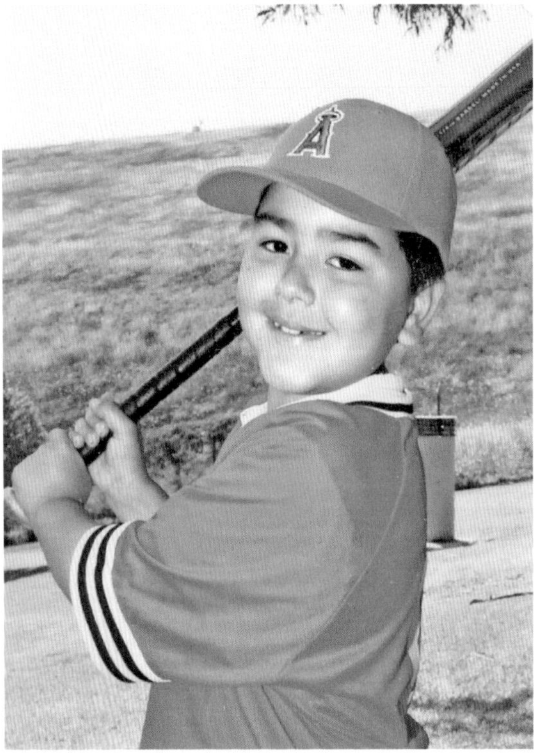

Vincent Pimentel was born at Garfield Hospital in Monterey Park and played for the Monterey Park Angels in 1995 under coach Andrés Nieto. He attended Brightwood Elementary School and graduated from Mark Keppel High School in 2012. Pimentel is currently attending East Los Angeles Community College and is a manager with McDonald's. His great uncle William played ball with the Belvedere Pee Wees, Ford Market, and Ramírez Mortuary. (Courtesy of Victor Pimentel.)

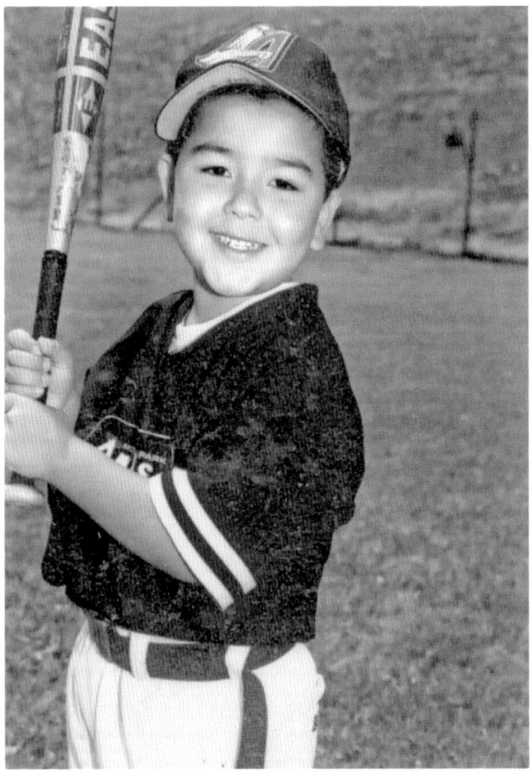

Vincent Pimentel comes from a long line of sports figures. His parents are Victor and Linda Pimentel. His paternal grandparents were Carlos and Emma Pimentel. His great uncle Jesús Pimentel played ball in the 1950s at Laguna Park (now Ruben Salazar Park) in East Los Angeles. Jesús later became a world-class boxer known as "Little Poison." Jesús married María Elena Torres, and they have four children. Jesús's brother, José Luís, also played ball around East LA and was an outstanding boxer known as "Big Poison." Both brothers were inducted into the Boxing Hall of Fame. (Courtesy of Victor Pimentel.)

Fidel Elizarrez played six years of little league ball, including two with the Pirates. The Pirates teams included Mario Valadez, Tony Pérez, Frank Rodríguez, and Ray Arce and coaches Ray Arce Sr. and Tony Pérez Sr. Elizarrez played second base for the Montebello High School Oilers. In his senior year, the team won the Pacific League Championship, beating Arcadia at Blair Field in Long Beach in 1966. His teammates included Mike Torres, Ben Negrete, and Jerry Rodríguez. After graduation, Elizarrez played Connie Mack Baseball, the American Legion, and for the Montebello Stars, managed by Armando Pérez. He is named after an uncle killed in World War II. (Courtesy of Fidel Elizarrez.)

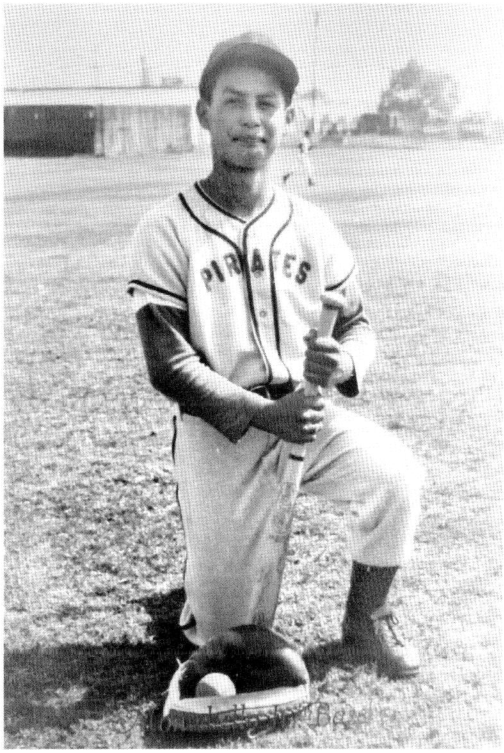

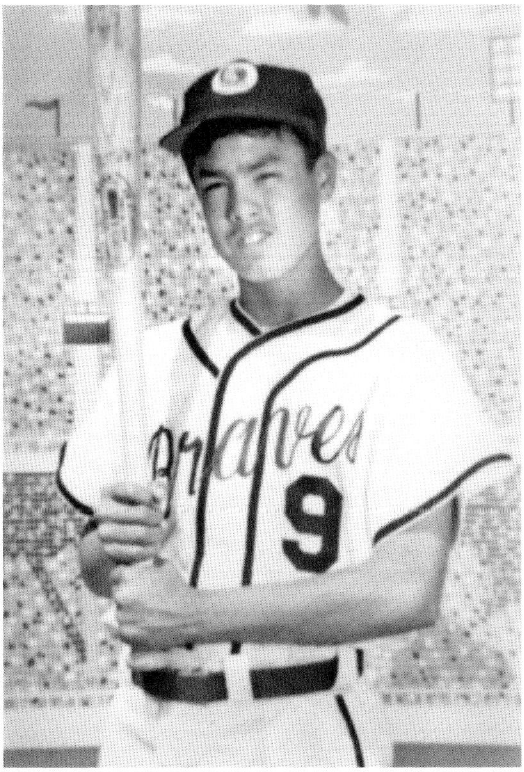

Gilbert Elizarrez is the brother of Fidel. He attended St. Benedict Catholic School in Montebello and played little league at Grant Rae Park in 1968 and 1969, and at Montebello Park. The league games were sponsored by the Montebello Baseball Association. Gilbert played several sports at Montebello High School, including baseball and football. He and his wife, Marina, have a son, Nickolaus, and a daughter, Jenaya. Gilbert is now retired and lives in Montebello, where he volunteers for the Sons of the American Legion. (Courtesy of Fidel Elizarrez.)

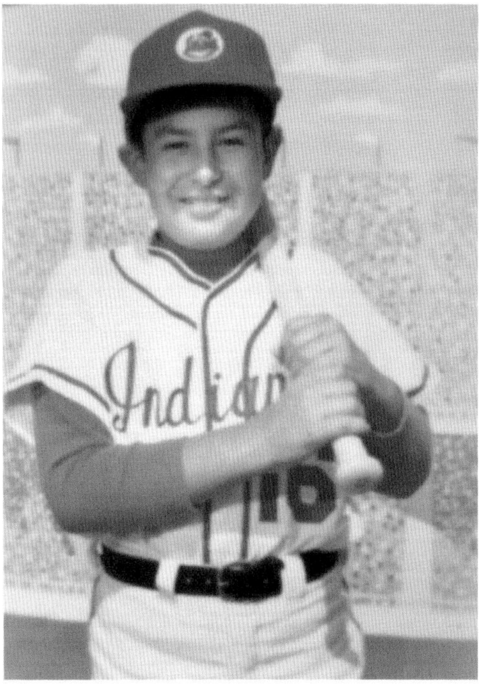

Michael Elizarrez, born in 1958 at Beverly Hospital in Montebello, is the brother of Gilbert and Fidel Elizarrez. He attended St. Benedict and Cantwell Catholic Schools. He played little league at Grant Rae Park, and baseball and basketball at Cantwell as a first baseman and shooting guard. He later played for the semipro Montebello Stars, managed by the legendary Mando Pérez. Elizarrez played on a Babe Ruth World Series team in 1971 that traveled to Texas, leading his Yankees team in hitting. He and his wife, Martha, have three children, Adela, Elijah, and Gabriel. He currently lives in El Sereno and enjoys golfing at Whittier Narrows, Montebello, and Luminaries. (Courtesy of Fidel Elizarrez.)

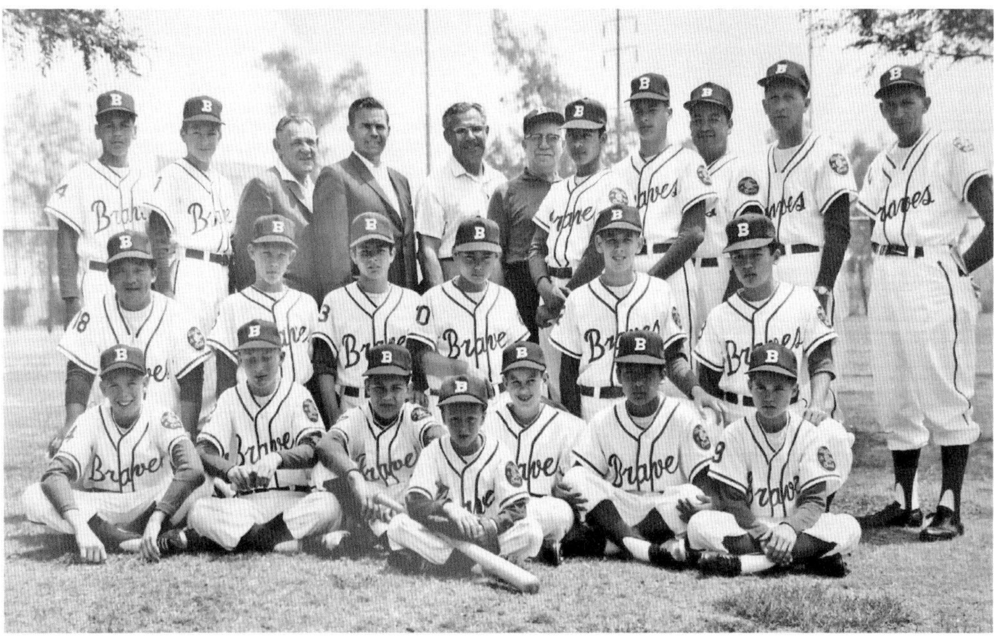

The 1958 Montebello Braves were composed of boys from Montebello, San Gabriel, Whittier, Pico Rivera, Monterey Park, and East Los Angeles. The Braves were an affiliate of the California State Association. Some of the players were Chris Jaramillo Jr., Mike Sepulveda, Ralph Arzate, Eddie Garza, and Jim Kreutzer, and the team was coached by Armando Garza and Chris Jaramillo Sr. The team was sponsored by Local 11 of the International Brotherhood of Electrical Workers. (Courtesy of Jim Kreutzer.)

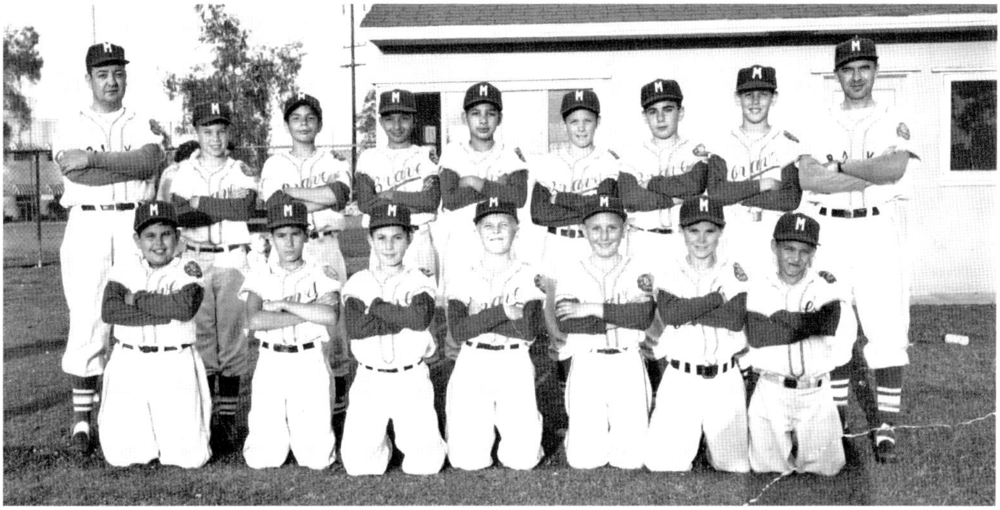

The So-Cal Pee Wee League Golden State Braves are seen in 1960 in Monterey Park. The year before, the Braves won the San Gabriel Valley championship, sponsored by the popular company Formula 42 Shampoo. Unbeknownst to the players, the owner of Formula 42 was comedian and actor Jerry Lewis. They were invited to his large secluded house in the Beverly Glen area of West Los Angeles. There was a barbecue, swimming, and all the burgers, hot dogs, and desserts they could devour. The pool house was even equipped with a piano. (Courtesy of Jim Kreutzer.)

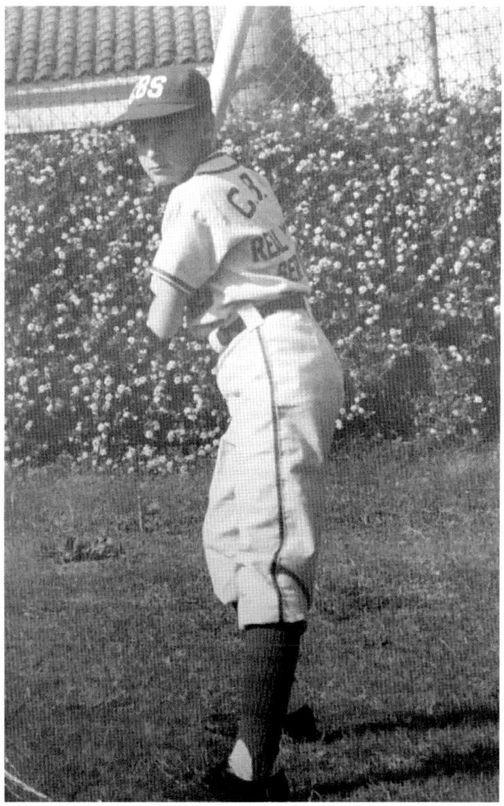

Edmund James Nájera was born in 1950 to Edmund and Cecilia Nájera in Maywood, California. He went to school in Montebello at St. Benedict's. During the 1960s, he played little league baseball with the Cubs and Angels' teams. He graduated from Cantwell High School in 1968 and from East Los Angeles Community College in 1973. Nájera was drafted into the Army Security Agency from 1970 through 1972 and was sent to Okinawa. During that time, he played baseball for the headquarters team. He eventually graduated from California State University at Los Angeles in 1976 with a bachelor's degree in science and accounting. He worked for several large companies including Sunkist, Northrop, Rockwell, Dole, and Northrop. He currently lives in Thousand Oaks with his wife, Norma. They have twin boys, Edmund and James, and four grandchildren. (Courtesy of Edmund James Nájera.)

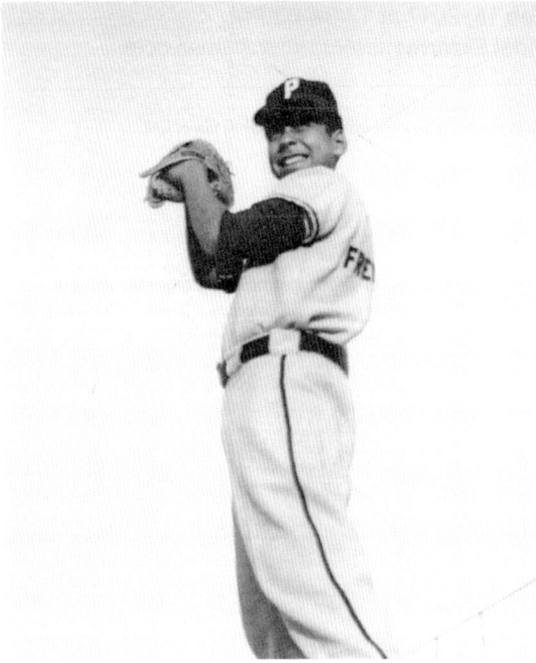

Tony Pérez played and coached for nearly 50 years in the San Gabriel Valley. His father, Maxie Pérez Jr., played ball in the Belvedere area and coached Tony's teams. Tony served in the US Navy in the Mekong Delta in Vietnam and was discharged in 1974. In 1977, he joined the US Marine Corps Reserves and was activated during Operations Desert Storm and Enduring Freedom. After 30 years, he retired as a chief warrant officer four. He taught at Montebello High School for 25 years and Bell Gardens High School for 10 years. He and his wife, Barbara, have three grown children, Yolanda, Kara, and Paul, and one grandson, Ronan. (Courtesy of Tony Pérez.)

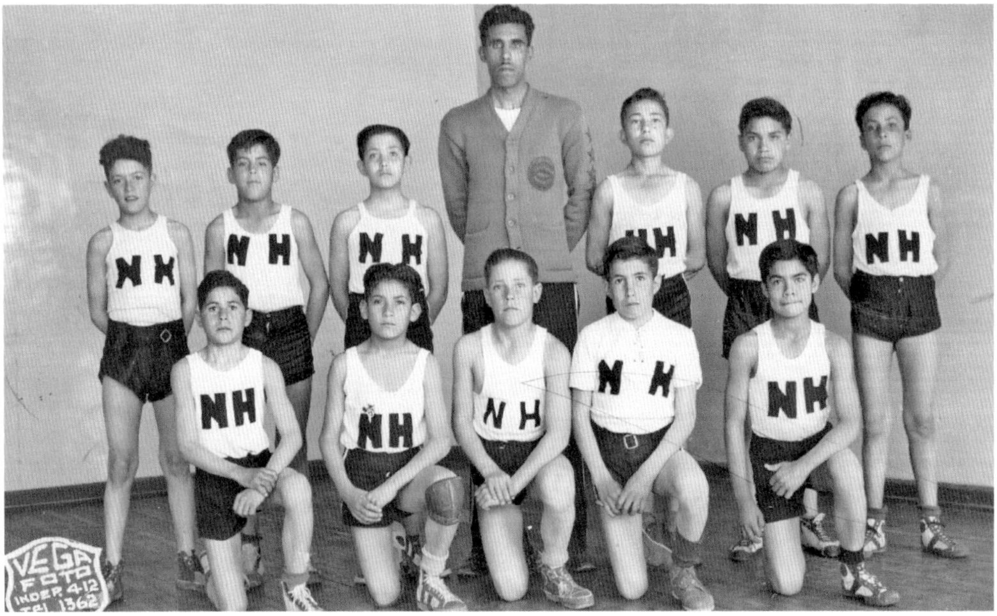

Andrés Nieto (first row, second from right) is a legend in Mexico and the United States. He played for La Escuela Niños Heroes ("the school of the boy heroes") in Chihuahua in 1942. Coach Nezi Santos (second row, center) played on Mexico's Olympic basketball team in 1956. In Mexico, Andrés was a member of the Boy Scouts, joined the Mexican Army in 1948, received his certificate in physical education in 1955, and was a union member. Nieto has been acknowledged by the California Assembly, the US Congress, Boys Town, and Monterey Park for his generous dedication to youth sports. (Courtesy of Andrés Nieto.)

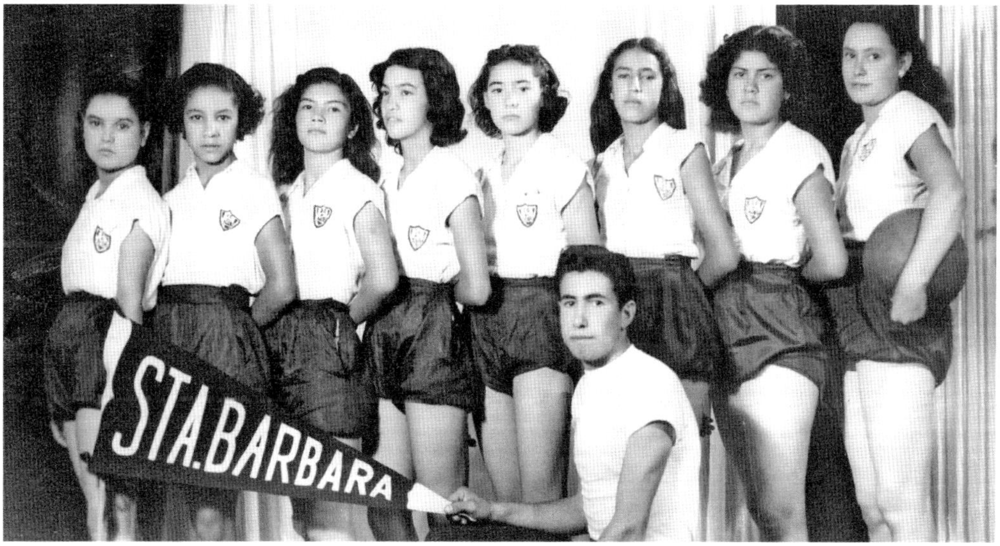

Andrés Nieto coached this young women's basketball team in Santa Barbara, Chihuahua, Mexico, in 1948. His was a professor of physical education in the Chihuahua schools. Nieto was born in the city of Chihuahua, earning a degree in business administration and physical education. He migrated to El Paso in 1955 and moved to Los Angeles in 1959. He and his wife, Ana, had four children, Andy, Angie, Tony, and Adrian. Andrés became a US citizen in 1970. In 2009, the Continental Amateur Baseball Association (CABA) bestowed its most prestigious award, membership in its hall of fame, upon Andrés. (Courtesy of Andrés Nieto.)

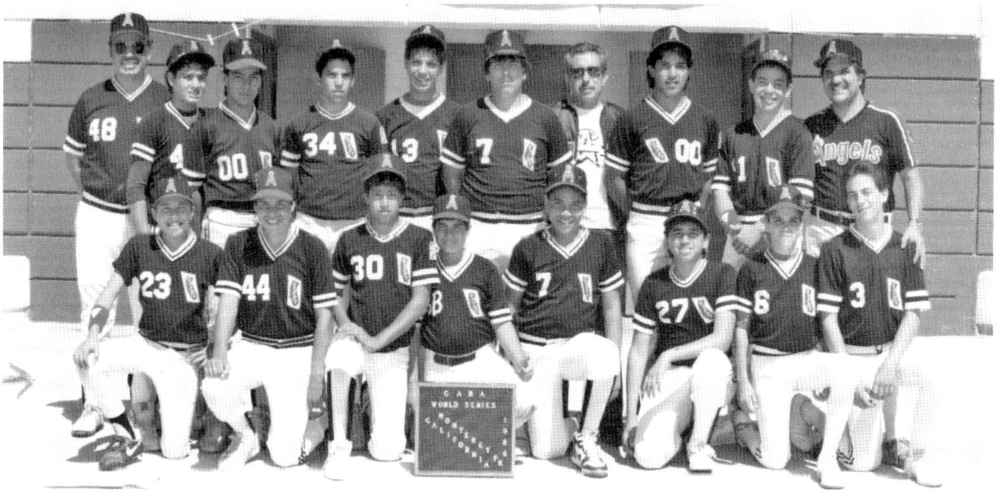

Andrés Nieto (second row, fourth from right) has devoted nearly 30 years to youth sports activities in the Monterey Park area and has coached and managed teams with the Monterey Park Sports Club for more than 10 years, including basketball, baseball, and soccer. He is the cofounder of Pee Wee Basketball, the founder of the Monterey Park Angels traveling team, and the CABA Director of the Year. He earned a city proclamation for 25 years of service, and in 1995, he served as CABA's southwest regional director. His son, Tony, is at far left in the first row. (Courtesy of Andrés Nieto.)

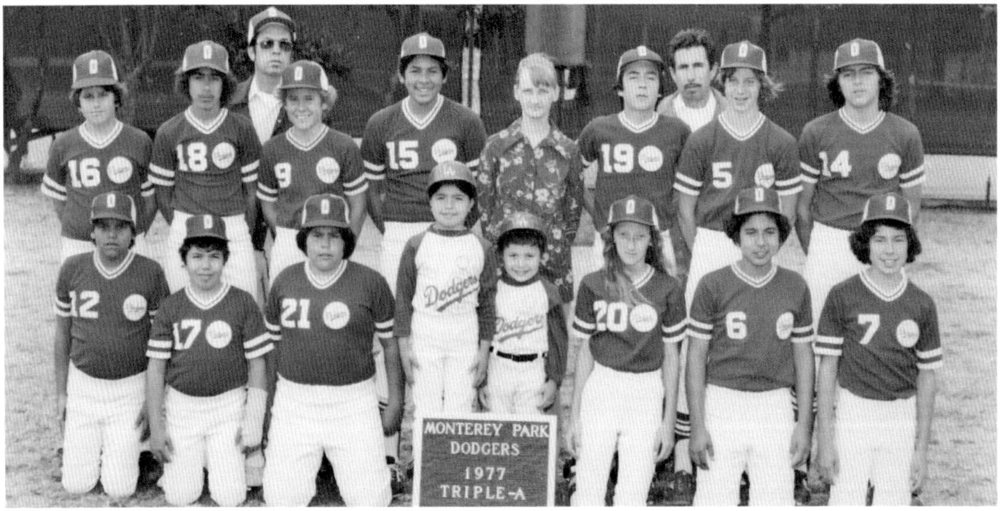

Andy Nieto (first row, second from left) played youth baseball for several years in Monterey Park. His sister Angie and brother Tony are the batgirl and batboy in the middle of the first row, and his father and coach, Andrés, is third from right in the second row. The Nieto children played football, baseball, basketball, softball, and soccer in the Monterey Park area. Andy graduated from Schurr High School in Montebello, where he was a three-year infielder who earned 1982 CIF honors. Andy and his wife, Judy, have two children, Samantha and Andrew-Cody. (Courtesy of Andy Nieto.)

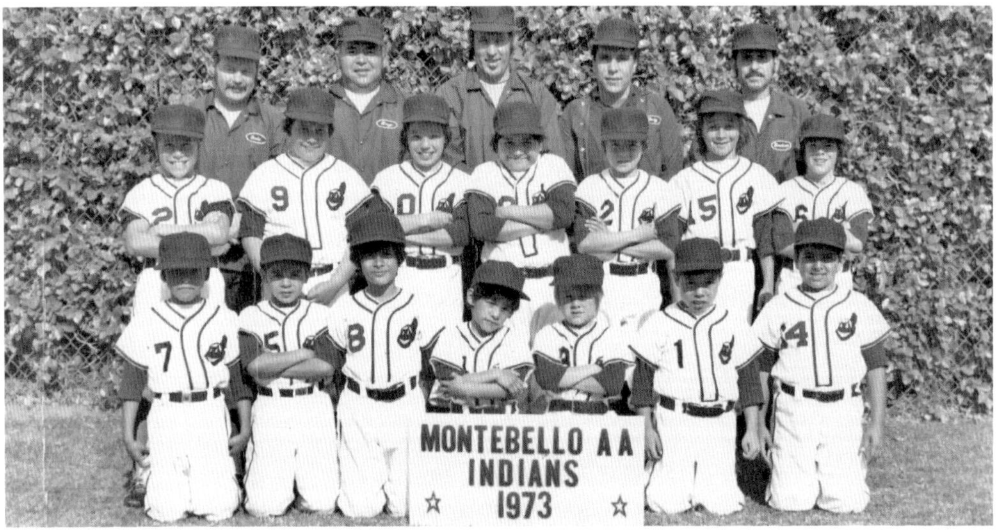

Andy Nieto (first row, second from right) played for the Montebello Indians in 1973. Nieto was a designated hitter–infielder for two seasons (1985–1986) at Cal State–Fullerton after starting at second base at Mount San Antonio Community College in Walnut, California, in 1984. He played in the Chicago White Sox and Detroit Tigers organizations from 1986 to 1989. Nieto served as the head baseball coach at Glendale Community College in 1996 and was the head assistant coach and recruiting coordinator for East Los Angeles Community College. He was the hitting coach for the USC baseball program for several seasons. (Courtesy of Andy Nieto.)

Andy Nieto (center) is seen with fellow coaches Mark Olsen (left) and Angel Sandin on a Monterey Park traveling team in 1989. Following his professional baseball career, Nieto earned his bachelor's degree in physical education from USC in 1991 and a master's degree from Azusa Pacific in 1996. He worked as an associate scout for the California Angels (1993–1996) and regularly serves as an instructor at several Southern California baseball camps. He was coach for the 714 Angels team in the high school Area Code Games in 1993 and 1994. Sandin eventually married Andy's sister Angie. (Courtesy of Andy Nieto.)

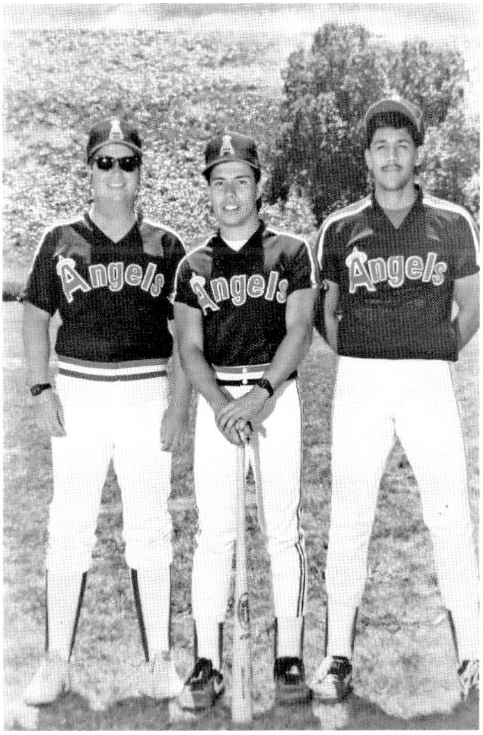

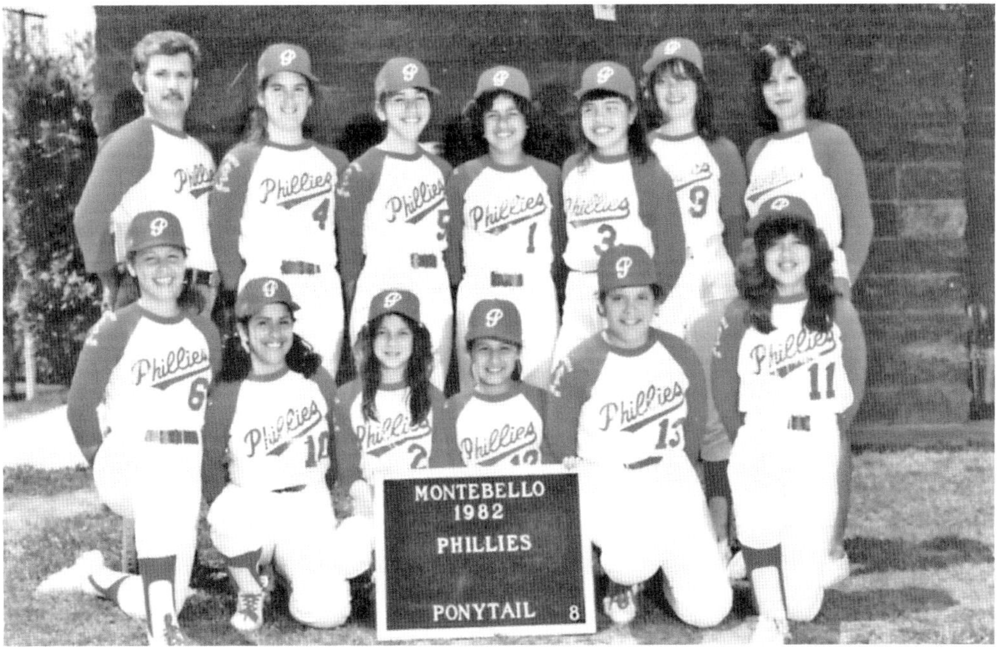

Angie Nieto (No. 10) continued the long family tradition of sports, especially in softball. She played for the Montebello Ponytail Association Clovers in 1981. She also played for the Montebello Honey Bees in 1981 and the Montebello Phillies in 1982. She played travel ball with the Monterey Park Angels and was on the Schurr High School softball team in 1986. (Courtesy of Angie Nieto.)

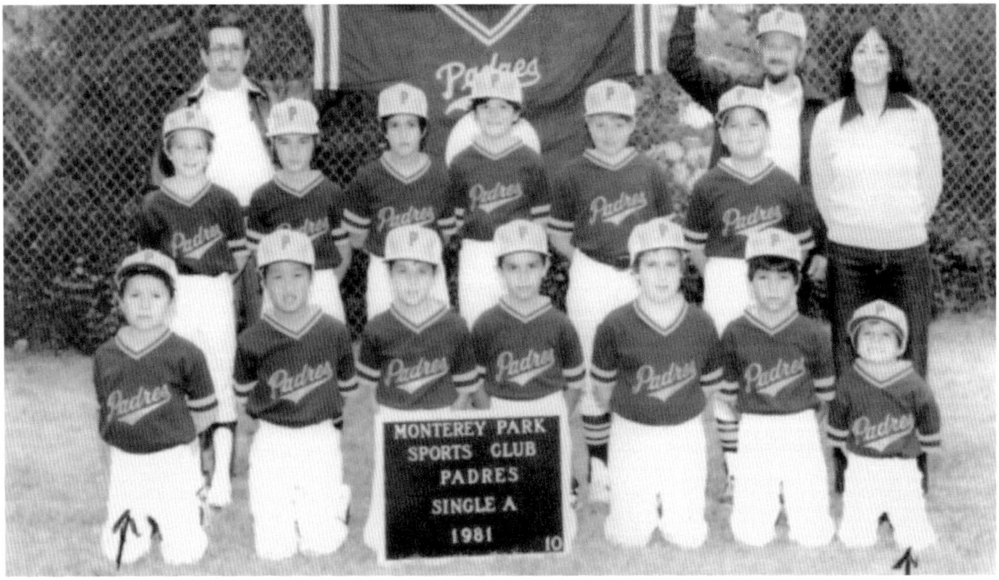

Adrian Nieto (first row, far left) has followed in the sports footsteps of his father (third row, far left), two brothers, and sister. He played for several youth teams, including the Monterey Park Angels of the Willie Mays Division in 1986. Adrian played for the Monterey Park Angels in 1990 and went on to play for Cantwell–Sacred Heart of Mary High School in the early 1990s. (Courtesy of Adrian Nieto.)

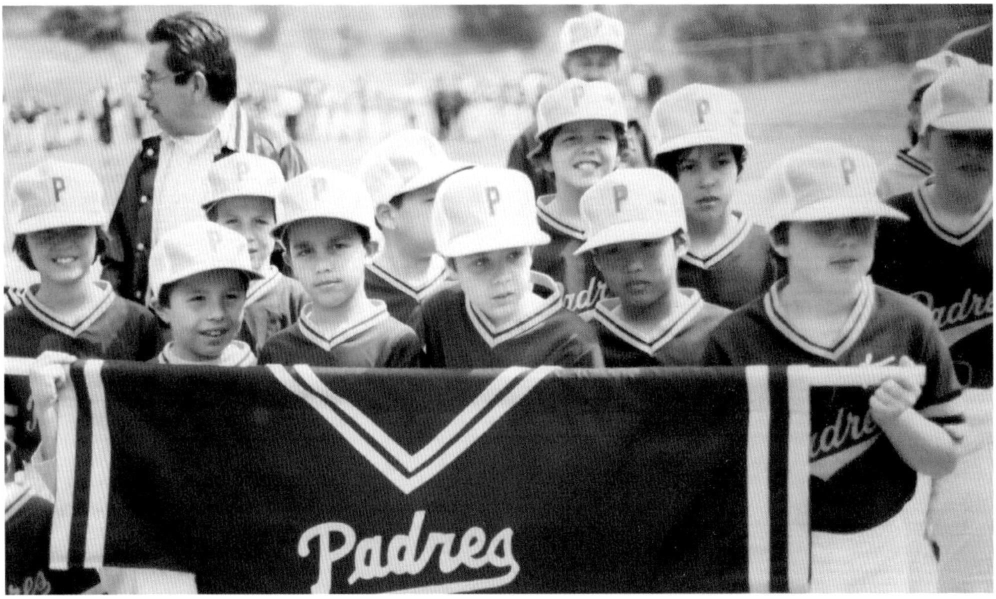

Tony Nieto (first row, far left) played several years in the Monterey Park area. In 1981, he was coached by his father, Andrés. Tony learned his skills and passion for baseball from his father, his brother Andy, and a host of dedicated coaches. He played ball at Schurr High School and was named to the All–Football League Team and All-Area Team in his senior year. He played four years of baseball at USC and was named captain of the 100th team in USC history. (Courtesy of Tony Nieto.)

Tony Nieto was an outstanding baseball star at Schurr High School in Montebello. In his four years at the University of Southern California, Nieto started every position except second base and centerfield, and pitched during his senior year. In 1994, he was drafted by the Cincinnati Reds, playing two seasons in the Reds organization before playing one year in the Baltimore Orioles system. Nieto was the coach, pitching coach, and recruitment coordinator at Loyola Marymount University in 2000-2001, guiding the Lions to a third consecutive West Conference championship in 2000. (Courtesy of Tony Nieto.)

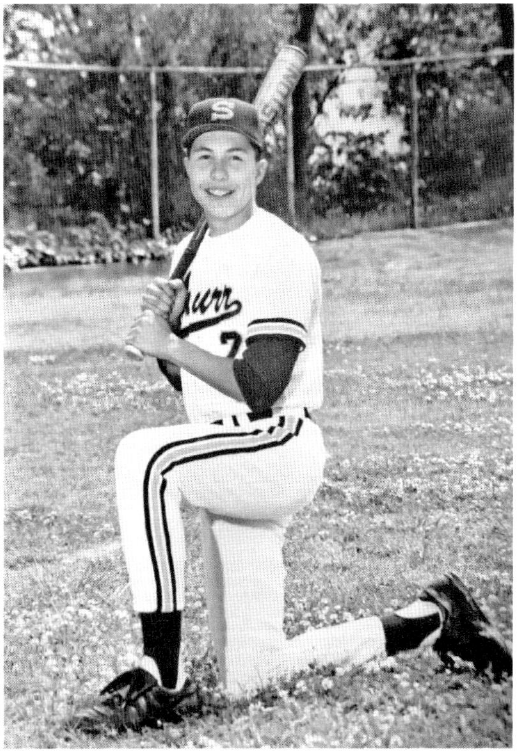

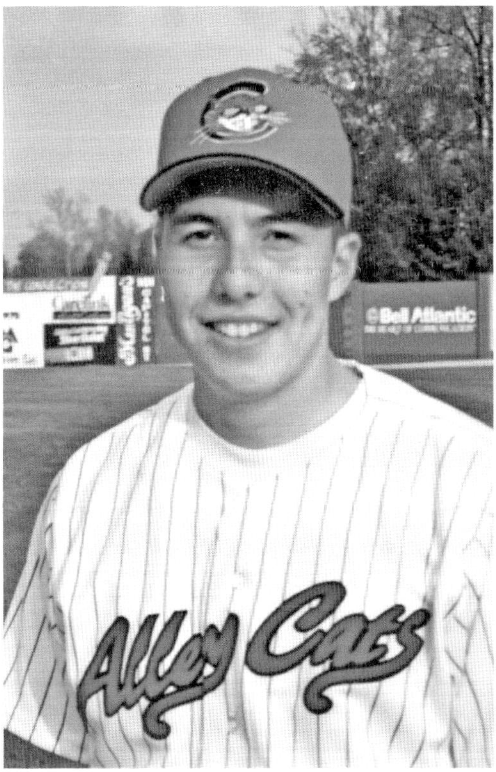

Tony Nieto played a handful of seasons with the Reds and Orioles organizations, including the Single-A Charleston, West Virginia, Alley Cats. He graduated from the University of Southern California in 1995 with a bachelor's degree in communication, and in 2005, earned his master's degree in special education. Nieto became the head coach at California High School in Whittier in 2003 and has led the Condors to seven league titles, a school record of five consecutive titles from 2012 to 2016. His teams have appeared in four consecutive California Scholastic Federation quarterfinals, and two semifinals. In 2012 and 2015, Nieto was named the Daily News Coach of the Year. He and his wife, Veronica, reside in Whittier with their three children, Noah, Dylan, and Aidan. (Courtesy of Tony Nieto.)

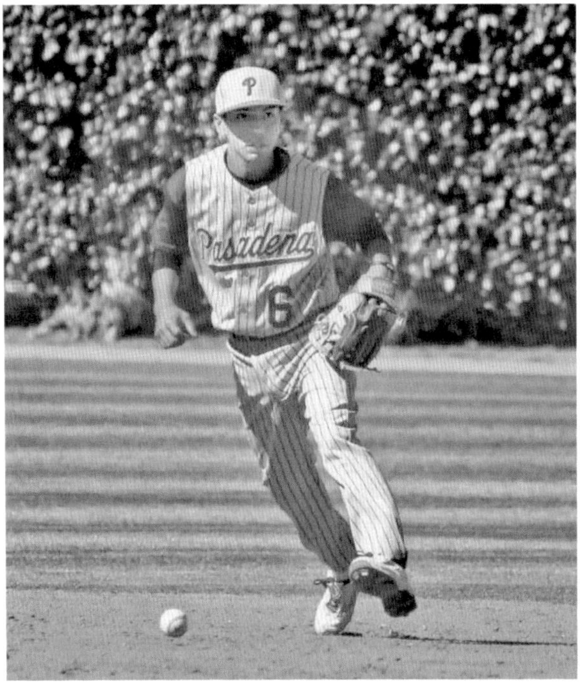

Tyler Blue Domínguez grew up in El Monte, where he played travel ball and four years of varsity baseball at Arcadia High School. He went on to play two years of college baseball at Pasadena City College. He sought a career in law enforcement, and in 2014, became a police officer in the San Gabriel Valley. In 2015, he went back to Arcadia High School and volunteered as a junior varsity baseball coach. (Courtesy of Tyler Blue Domínguez.)

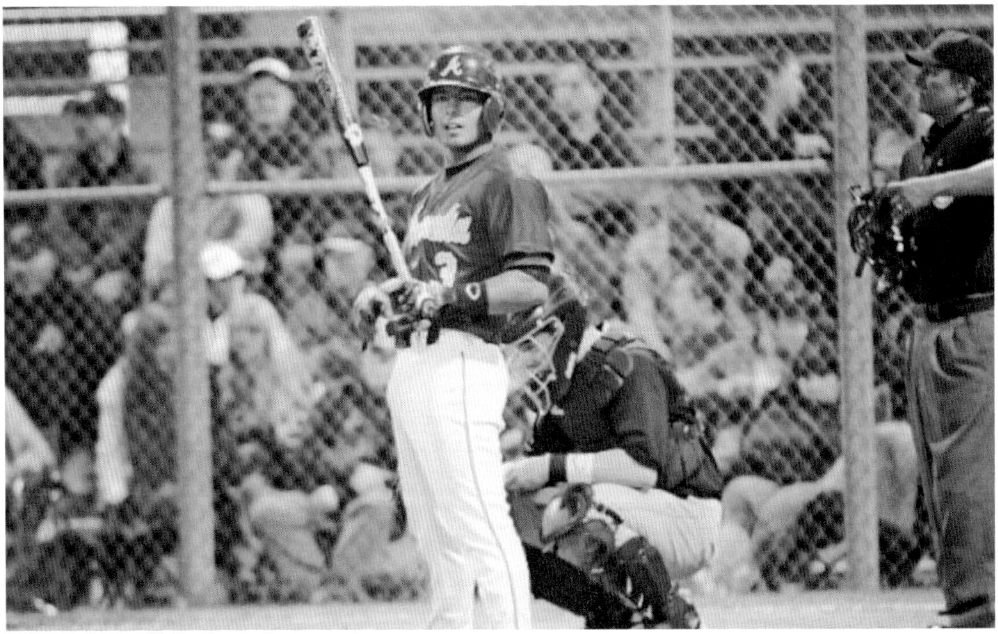

David Domínguez played four years of varsity baseball at Arcadia High School, playing two years with his brother Tyler in the middle infield (2010 and 2011). After high school, he played ball at Rio Hondo College, helping the team win the Foothill Conference. He transferred to Pasadena City College and joined new coach Patrick McGee in the South Coast Conference. Domínguez is a student at California State University at Northridge and is ready to graduate with a degree in kinesiology. He is pursuing a career in firefighting. (Courtesy of David Domínguez.)

Monica Laird Fox was born in 1970 and raised in Buena Park, California. She attended Raymond Temple Elementary School, La Palma Junior High School, and John F. Kennedy High School. She played softball for three years. In junior high school, she played basketball, and later played on a company softball team. Her older sister, Lisa, was a cheerleader in school, and Monica was the mascot. Monica's mom, Martha Holguín Laird, briefly attended Mark Keppel High School in Alhambra and later served as team mother and scorekeeper at Monica's games. Monica has several relatives who played baseball and softball in the San Gabriel Valley. (Courtesy of Martha Holguín Laird.)

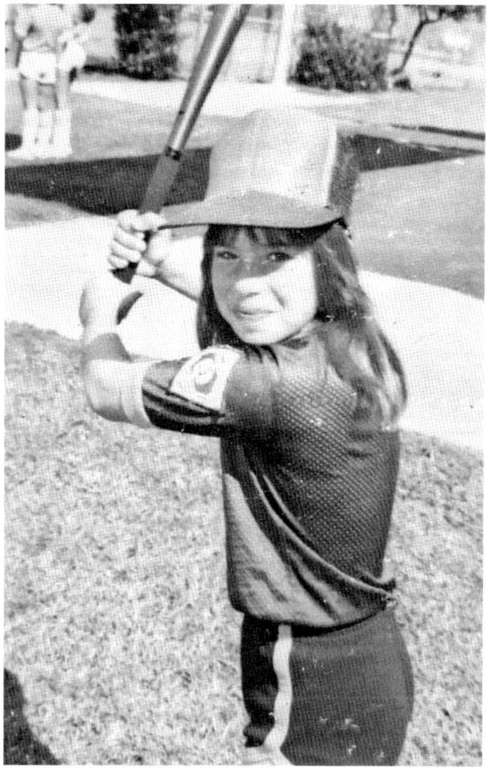

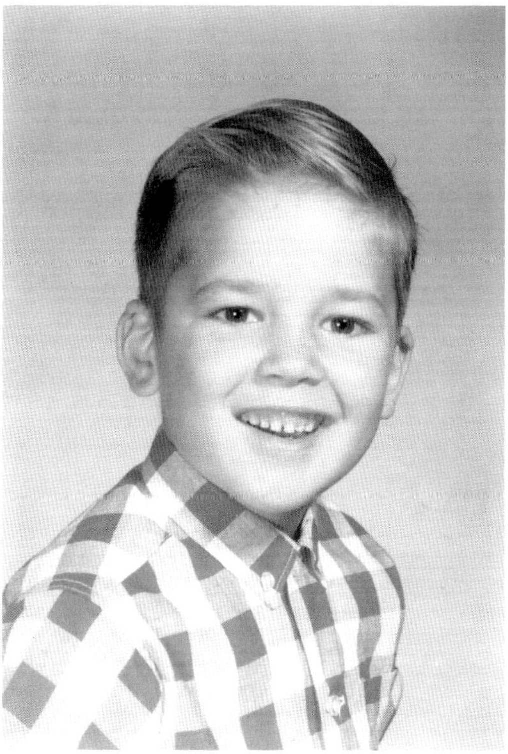

Lorenzo "Larry" J. Laird was born in 1960 at Garden Park Hospital in Buena Park, California, to Jack and Martha Laird. His sisters are Monica Laird Fox and Lisa Durkovic. Martha named him after her father Cresencio's brother, Lorenzo. Laird attended Raymond Temple Elementary, La Palma Junior High, and Kennedy High School in Buena Park. He played T-ball, softball, and later football in high school. His true love, however, was outdoor sports—he hunted, fished, swam, and rode boats, motorcycles, and snowmobiles. Like his outdoor activities, Laird enjoyed several occupations including truck driving, landscaping, roofing, taking flying lessons and working at an airport, Sadly, he died in a car accident in 1986 in Idaho, leaving sons Jordan and Teddy, a wife, Allison, and four grandchildren born after his death. (Courtesy of Martha Holguín Laird.)

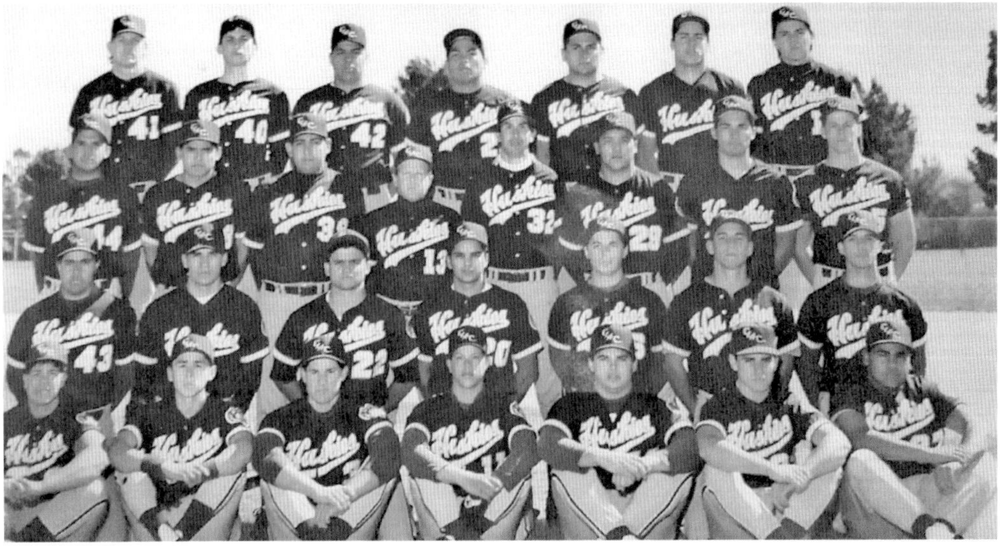

Rafael Gutiérrez (fourth row, far right) played baseball under coaches Anthony Pérez, Bill Drulias, and Rich Montez at Montebello between 1984 and 1988 in the Whitmont League against Bell Gardens, El Rancho, Whittier, Pioneer, Santa Fe, La Serna, and California High Schools. He played at East Los Angeles Community College under coaches Roger Lawson and Al Cone. Gutiérrez was scouted by Steve Flores and signed with the Kansas City Royals. He played minor-league ball in Eugene, Oregon, and rookie ball in Florida. (Courtesy of Rafael Gutiérrez.)

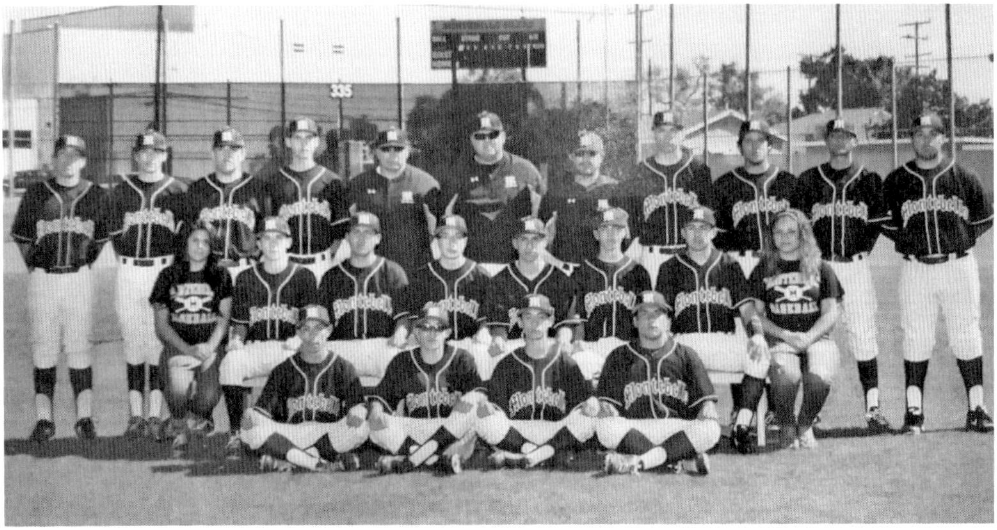

Rafael Gutiérrez (third row, center) was released by the Royals, but with the pitching help of knuckleballer Charlie Hough, he signed with the Los Angeles Dodgers and played in Vero Beach and in the Northwest League in Yakima, Washington. He had pitching mentors such as Claude Osteen, and Luis Tiant. He tried Mexican ball with Mike Brito but decided to attend Cal State–Long Beach, where he earned his degree in education and teaching credentials. He was the pitching coach for the Montebello High School Oilers in 1994, head coach between 1997 and 2013, and is now is the athletic director. (Courtesy of Rafael Gutiérrez.)

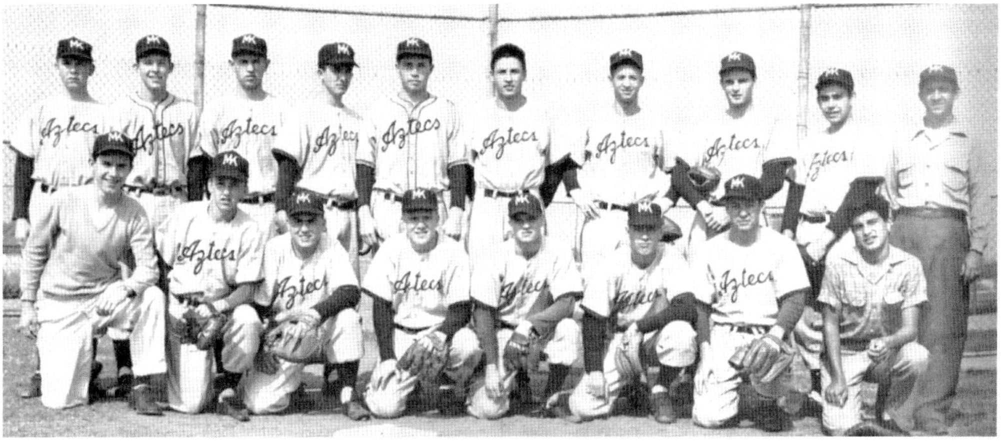

The 1954 Alhambra Mark Keppel High School Aztecas had several outstanding players and coaches, including Larry Burright (first row, sixth from left), Mike McCormick (second row, fourth from left), Frank Nieto (first row, far right), and coach Maynard Horst (second row, far right). Mike McCormick played 16 years in the major leagues for the New York and San Francisco Giants, Orioles, Senators, Yankees, and Royals. Larry Burright played for both the Mets and the Los Angeles Dodgers. Frank Nieto played football and served as the manager for the baseball team. (Courtesy of Maynard and Pauli Horst.)

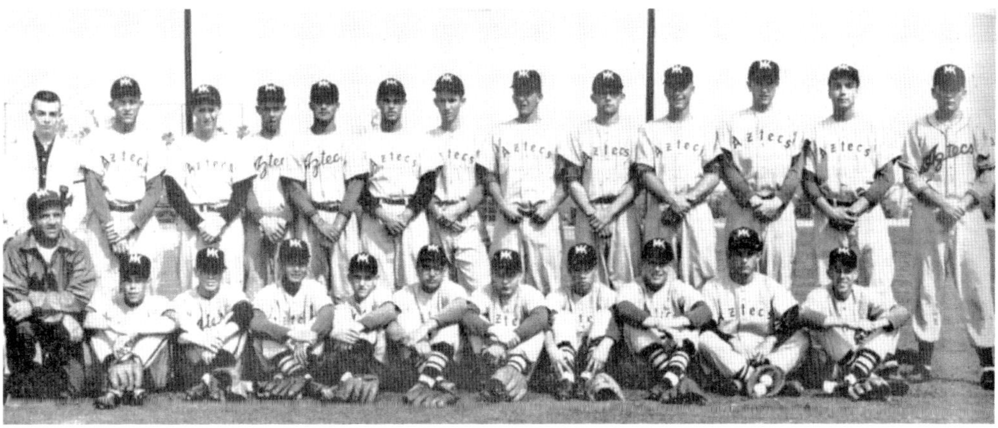

The 1956 Aztecas were another powerful Keppel team. Keppel won the Pacific League championship in 1955, 1956, and 1957. They played their home games at Almansor Park because they did not have a school field. Ralph Martínez (first row, fifth from left) and Frank Nieto (first row, fifth from left) played with future major-leaguers Mike McCormick (second row, fifth from left) and Pete Mikkelsen (second row, fourth from right). Mikkelsen played eight years in the majors, including with the Dodgers. Martínez later played for the freshman team at USC. (Courtesy of Maynard and Pauli Horst.)

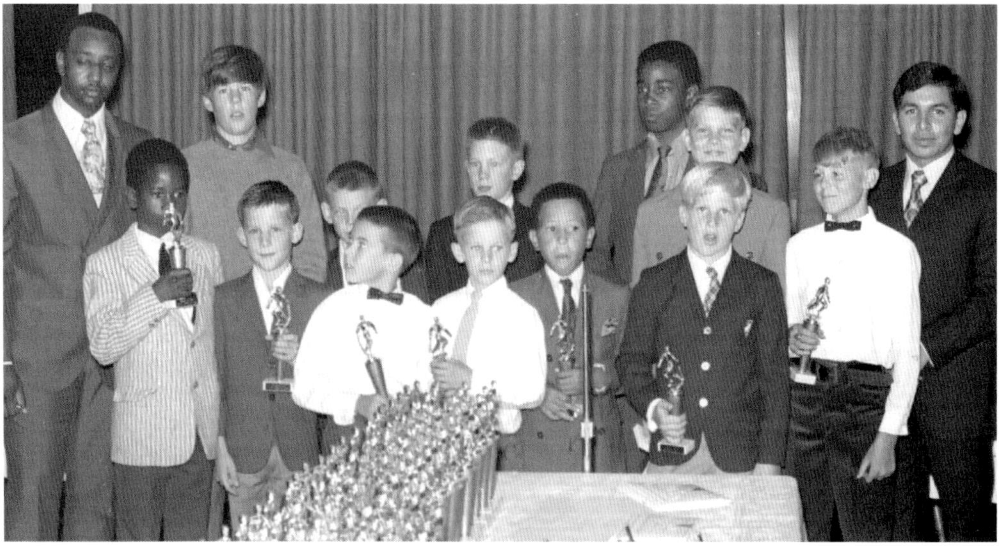

Sgt. Charles Santillán (far right) was born in East Los Angeles in 1949. In 1954, his family moved to Norwalk, where he played little league as a catcher. He graduated from Norwalk High School in 1967. Santillán enlisted in the Army as a paratrooper in 1968, following in the footsteps of his father, Carlos, who was a paratrooper during World War II. Charles coached little league for the children of servicemen. When he and manager Ted Brown (far left) were on training exercises, Charles's wife, Sandy, and Brown's wife coached the team. (Courtesy of Charles Santillán.)

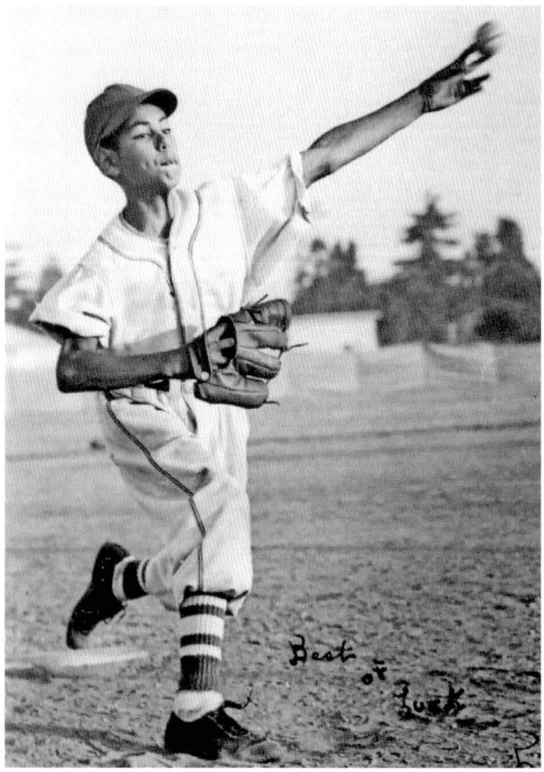

Carlos Salazar played in two leagues in 1952, the Pasadena Baseball School and Pasadena's first little league season. The Baseball School games were played at Brookside Park, the spring training facility for the Chicago White Sox. The school was divided into three divisions and played teams from Fullerton, Anaheim, Chino, and Whittier on regulation diamonds. The little league comprised eight teams sponsored by Pasadena merchants. Salazar is pictured in his Midget A's uniform at Brookside Park. That same day, he played a little league game at Victory Park in Pasadena. He later became an all-star for the West Pasadena little league. (Courtesy of Carlos Salazar.)

4

Whittier, Pico Rivera, and Norwalk

Pico Rivera, Whittier, and Norwalk are on the southeast end of the San Gabriel Valley and have produced outstanding players, teams, coaches, and umpires. Pico Rivera traces its beginnings to the 1870s, when the Atchison, Topeka & Santa Fe and the Union Pacific Railroads completed rail lines through the area. The city is about 11 miles from Los Angeles and was incorporated in 1958, merging the two unincorporated communities of Pico, named after Pio Pico, the last Mexican governor of California, and Rivera.

A Spanish land grant was given to retired soldier José Manuel Nieto (Rancho Los Nietos) in 1784 that included parts of Whittier, Fullerton, and Brea. After Mexico's independence from Spain, another land grant was issued to Juan Crispín Pérez that included parts of present-day Whittier. At the time of the Mexican-American War in 1846, Pio Pico owned much of the land that is today Whittier. He built a *hacienda* near the San Gabriel River, known today as the Pio Pico State Historic Park. After the defeat of Mexico in 1848, the property changed hands several times until Quakers purchased the land with the intent of founding a community. As the city grew, the citizens named it after John Greenleaf Whittier, a respected Quaker poet, and deeded a lot to him. Whittier College was founded by the Quakers during the late 1890s. The school mascot is the Poet.

Norwalk was incorporated as a city in 1957. Norwalk's sister cities are Morelia, Michoacan, and Hermosillo, Sonora, in Mexico. The famous El Camino Real traversed the area. Rancho Los Nietos included Norwalk. For years, Norwalk was home to nearly 50 families associated with farming and the dairy industry. It was home to some of the largest sugar beet farms in all of Southern California. Most of the farmers were Dutch.

The southeast region of the San Gabriel Valley included Mexicans who worked for the railroads, in agriculture, and in construction, especially during the housing boom after World War II. Most Mexican Americans lived in distinct neighborhoods. Due to the GI Bill and employment and educational opportunities, the Mexican American population is significant. Generations have played baseball and softball in Pico Rivera, Whittier, and Norwalk. This is their story.

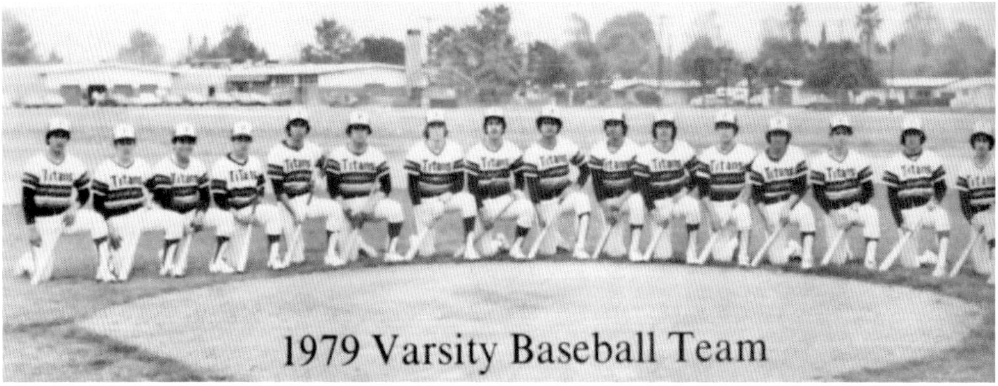

Nick Pérez played for the 1979 Titans varsity team at Pioneer High School in Whittier. Nick's grandfather Tommy Pérez Sr. and father, Tom Jr., were both outstanding players and remarkable coaches. The 1979 Titans included David Gonzáles, Tom Padilla, Ben Jocobo, Mel Cázarez, Duke Límon, Art Alva, Gilbert Fragozo, Ernie Magaña, John Pasillas, Perry Ullo, Mark Tamayo, head coach Anthony Gonzáles, and assistant coach Ron García. (Courtesy of Nick Pérez.)

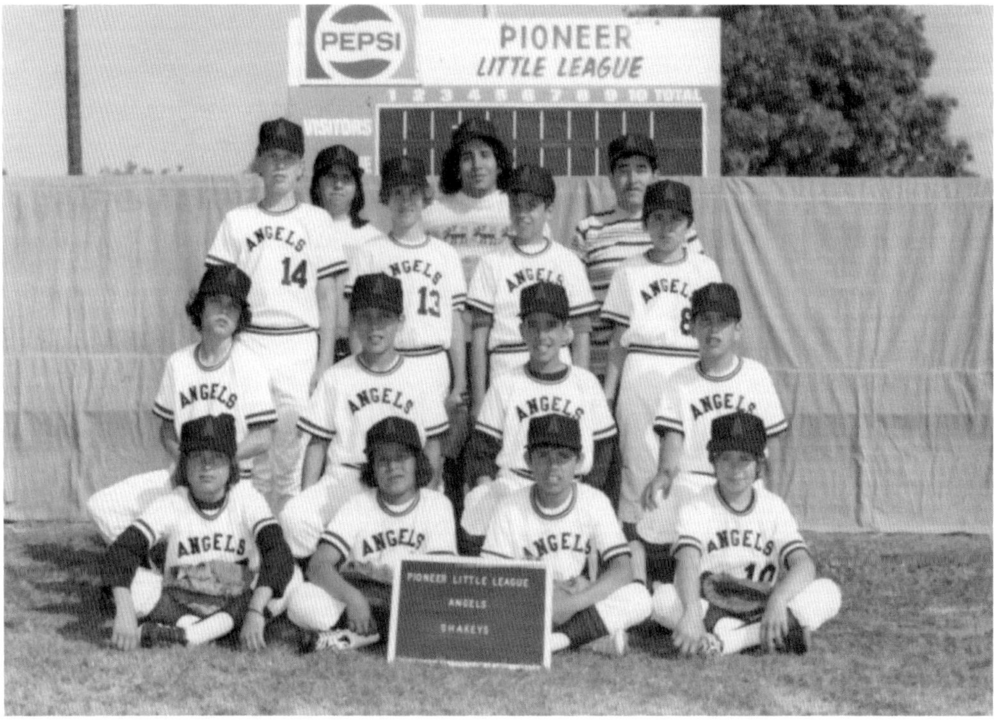

Nick Peréz (first row, far left) played all positions. He enjoyed playing pitcher, catcher, and outfielder. Coach Dennis Chávez (fourth row, center) and his father and manager, Danny Chávez (fourth row, far right) were active in the Pioneer little league. The Angels, who played in the major division, surprised everyone by tying the Dodgers for first place in 1972. Peréz hit a home run against the Dodgers, chipping off the top of the fence. This was his last season in the majors before moving on to the senior league. Other players included Danny Chávez and Chris Cardoza. (Courtesy of Nick Pérez.)

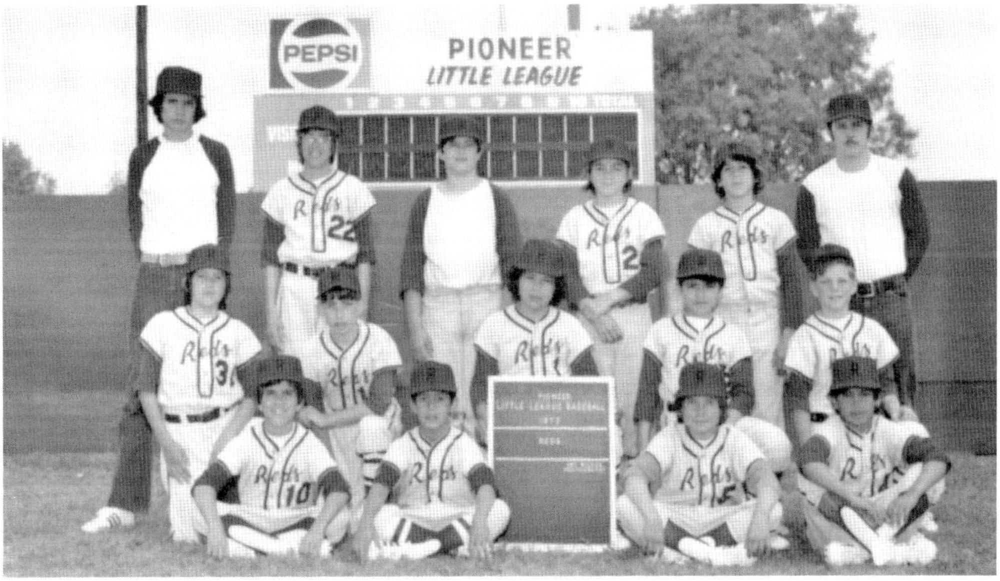

The 1973 Reds played in the Pioneer little league at Coffman Field in Whittier. There were two fields, one for the minor league and one for the major league. They were coached by Anthony Gonzáles (third row, far left), who later became head baseball coach at Pioneer High School. Four of his players on this team also played for him at Pioneer. Gonzáles later became the head baseball coach and athletic director at California High School. After winning a championship in the early 1990s, he retired and hired Andy Nieto to coach the baseball team. Other players included Mark Tamayo and Ernie Magaña. (Courtesy of Nick Pérez.)

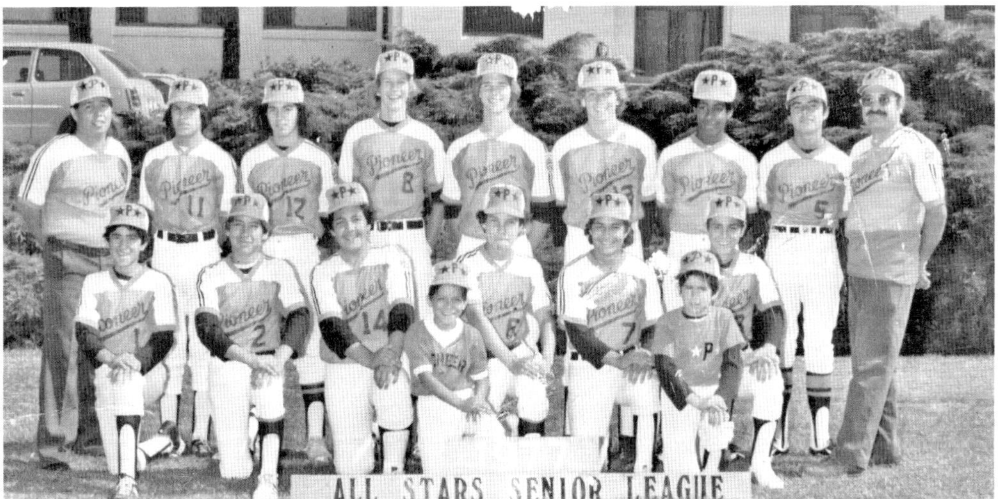

Nick Pérez (first row, second from left) and his brother Tommy (first row, far left) were coached by their father, Tom Jr. (second row, far right), on the 1977 All-Stars for the senior league. This photograph was taken in front of Pioneer High School. Most all-star teams comprise players wearing the jersey of the team they are representing, but this team had matching uniforms so that they played as one team. (Courtesy of Nick Pérez.)

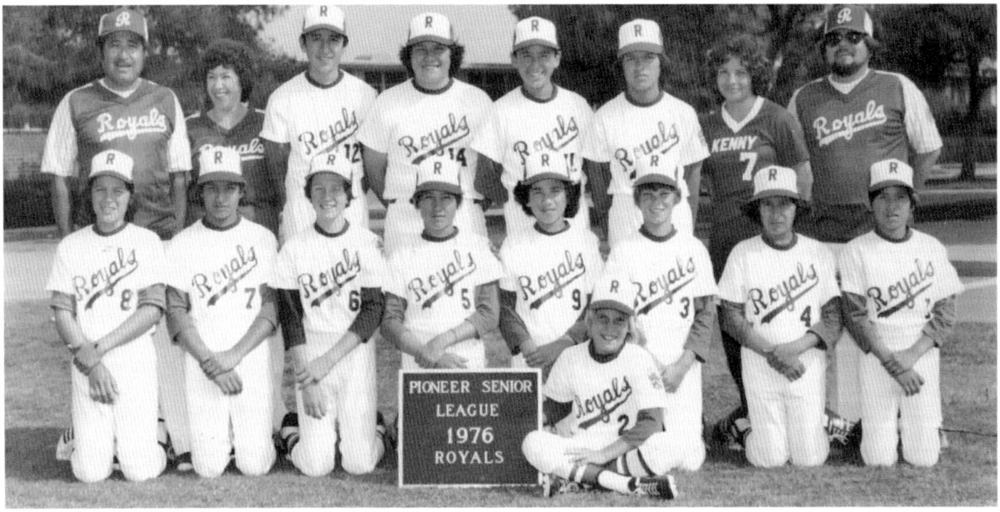

The 1976 Pioneer Senior League Royals were champions. The Pioneer little league played at Coffman Field in Whittier, but the senior league played at Pioneer High School. Nick Pérez (No. 5) and his brother Tommy III (first row, far right) were coached by their father, Tom Pérez Jr. (second row, far left), while their mother, Alice (second row, second from left) served as team mom. Both Nick and Tommy played catcher and pitcher. Other players included Pete Martínez (No. 4), Anthony Pacillas (second row, third from right), Danny Luna (No. 14), and Tommy Mays (No. 12). (Courtesy of Nick Pérez.)

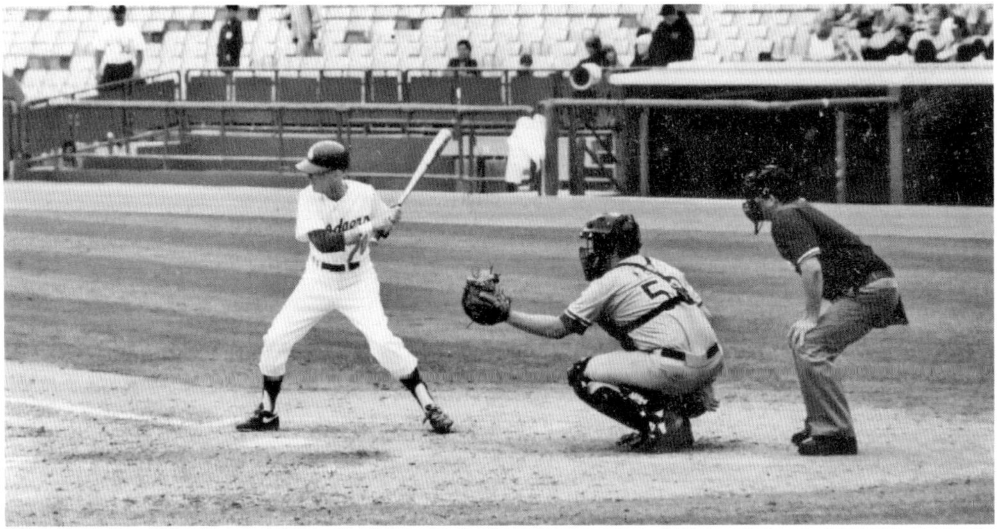

Nick Pérez is seen in 1989 umpiring a Dodgerstown Men's League game. Nick became an umpire in 1983, umpiring several levels including little league, high school, community college (Orange Coast and South Coast Districts), Triple-A, Double-A, and Division III baseball. He umpired two high school championship games at Dodger Stadium. Nick has officiated high school basketball and football games. His father, Tom Jr., started umpiring in the 1970s, and he and Nick have umpired the same game. Nick has umpired on fields where he played little league and high school. (Courtesy of Nick Pérez.)

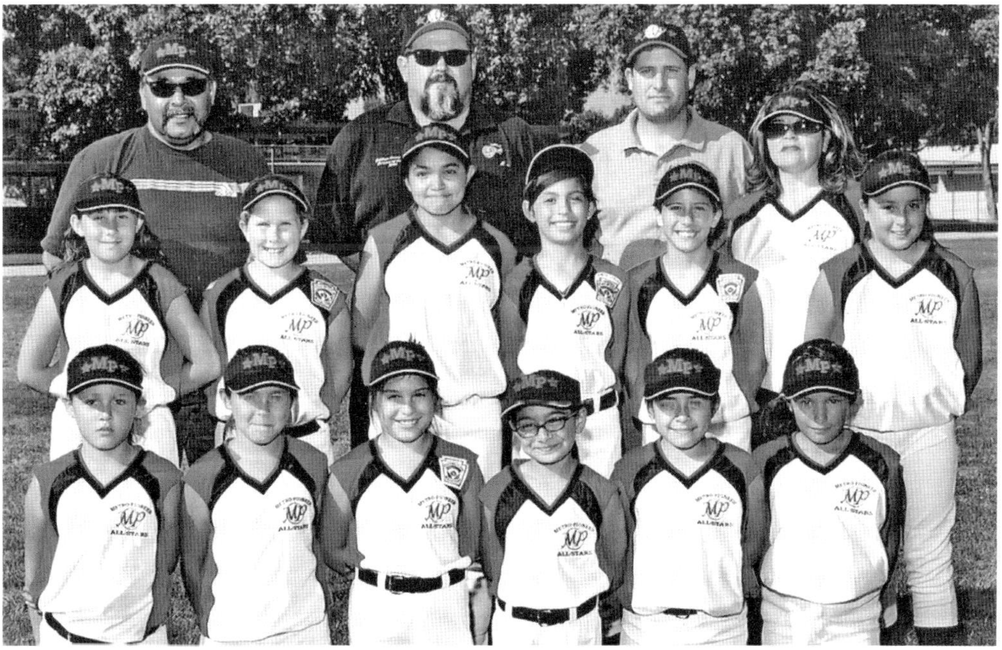

Sophía Espinoza was born in 1995 and raised in Norwalk. Sports were a major part of her life growing up. She cannot remember a time when she was not playing sports or cheerleading all year. She started playing girls' softball when she was only four years old and continued playing at Metro Park in Santa Fe Springs. She started cheerleading at four years old and continued through high school, winning two national championships in 2012 and 2013. Her father, Tomás, and two brothers played for many years in Norwalk and other surrounding communities. (Courtesy of Sophía Espinoza.)

This photograph of Tommy Pérez III (center), his dad, Tom Jr., and Kelsey Grammer was taken in early 2004, when Tommy returned home from deployment in Kuwait. Tom decided to take Tommy, his wife, April Lynn Molina-Pérez, and two other guests to watch a live recording of *Frasier*. Afterwards, Tommy and his party were introduced to the cast members. The original plan was that Grammer would sit in the chair, but he refused, saying that Tommy was really the biggest star on the set and deserved to sit. (Courtesy of Tommy Pérez III.)

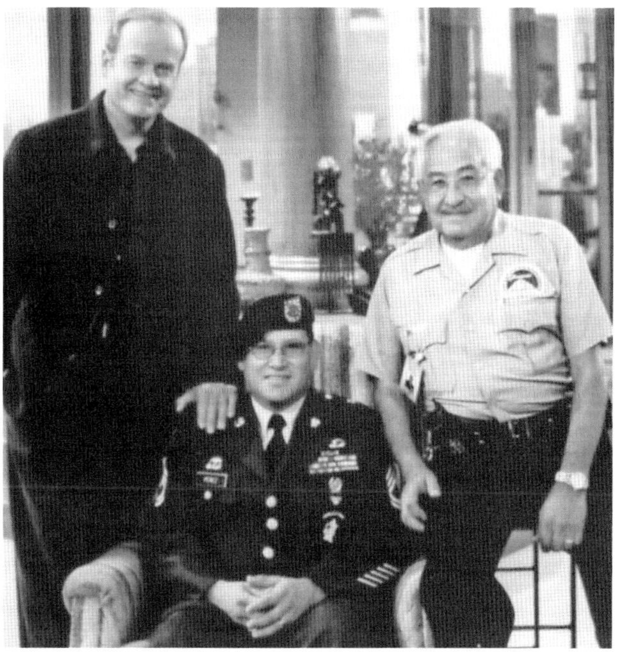

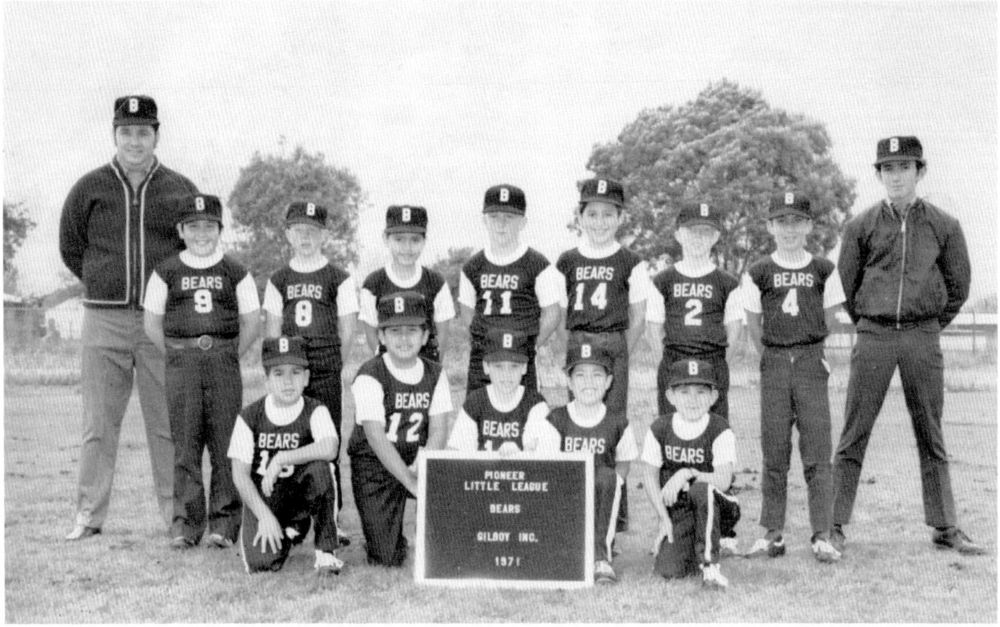

Tommy Pérez III (first row, far right) comes from a long, rich family tradition of baseball and softball. His paternal grandfather, Tommy Pérez Sr., was an outstanding player and coach in the late 1920s, especially in East Los Angeles, where he coached for Mario López's teams, Mario Service Station, and Carmelita Provisions Company. Tommy III's father, Tom Jr., played ball as well throughout Southern California and Baja California. Tommy III started in 1971 at the age of seven as a batboy for the Pioneer little league Giants, who played their games at Coffman Field in Whittier. (Courtesy of Tommy Pérez III.)

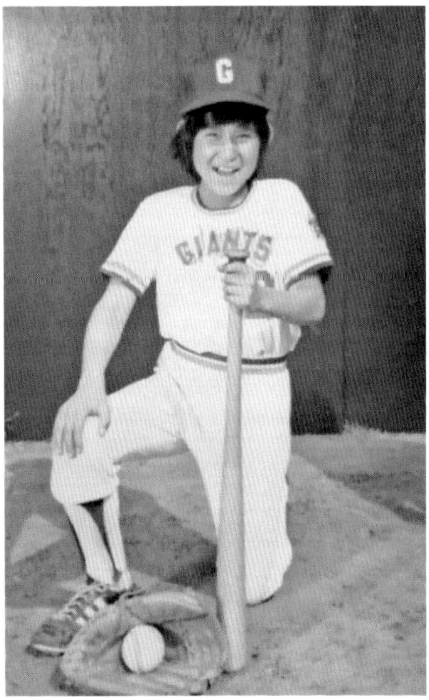

In 1972, Tommy Pérez III played right field for the Pioneer little league Minor-B Bears. The following year, he played shortstop and batted lead-off for the Minor-B Athletics. He was selected to the All-Star Team and lost in the All-Star Tournament, held in Pico Rivera. His 1974 Minor-A Cardinals won the league championship with a 19-1 record but lost in the regional championship game. Pérez had a distinguished career at Coffman Field, playing for the Giants and the Senior Royals. In 1976 and 1977, his brother Nick played with him on the Royals while their dad, Tom Jr., managed. (Courtesy of Tommy Pérez III.)

Tommy Pérez III recalls one 1975 game when he and his brother Nick were on opposing teams. Tommy, playing third base, threw Nick out at home plate. Nick was so angry he went after Tommy but was restrained by the umpire. Nick had the last laugh—his team won the championship that season. Tommy played at Pioneer High School in Whittier. Besides baseball, he played football both ways. Tommy's father, Tom Jr., and Anthony "Tony" González organized a team for a youth countywide baseball tournament of champions at Whittier Narrows Park. The team, Los Nietos ("the grandchildren"), won the Junior Division against a team from Helen Keller Park. The guest speaker at the banquet was the legendary Brooklyn Dodger Roy Campanella. (Courtesy of Tommy Pérez III.)

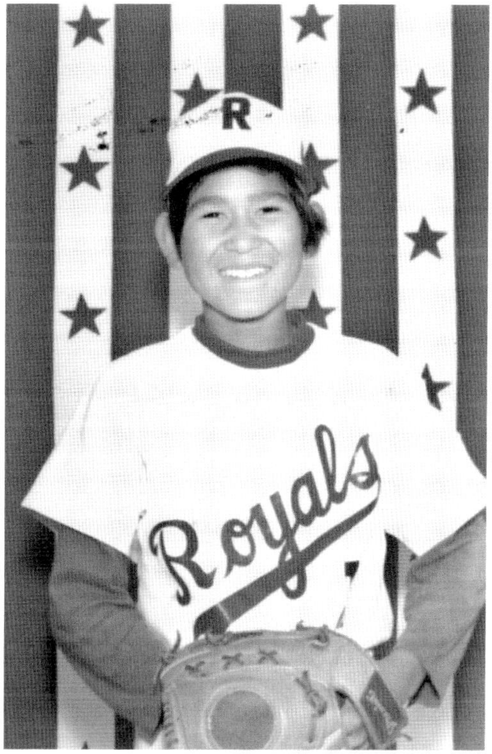

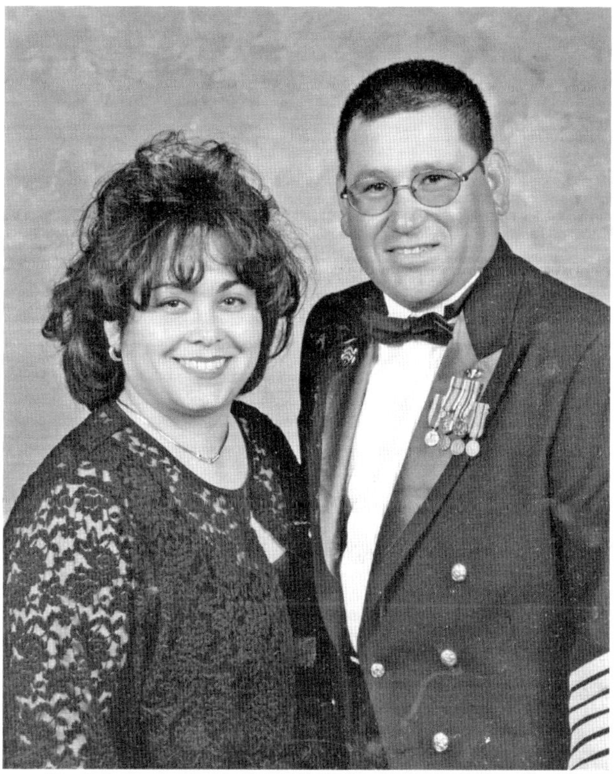

Tommy Pérez III and his wife, April L. Molina-Pérez, currently reside in Victorville, California. They have two daughters, Lauren Nicole and Sarah Jessica Molina-Pérez. Lauren, with Troy Livingston, has three children, while Sarah Jessica and Robert Camacho have Phoenix. April was an all-star in youth softball between the ages of 8 and 15 in Montebello, California. Lauren played two years of softball, and Sarah took six years of Tae Kwon Do. Tommy's father, Tom Jr., grew up in East Los Angeles and played and coached for several teams. Tommy's mother, Alice, devoted countless hours over 20 years serving as team mom. (Courtesy of Tommy Pérez III.)

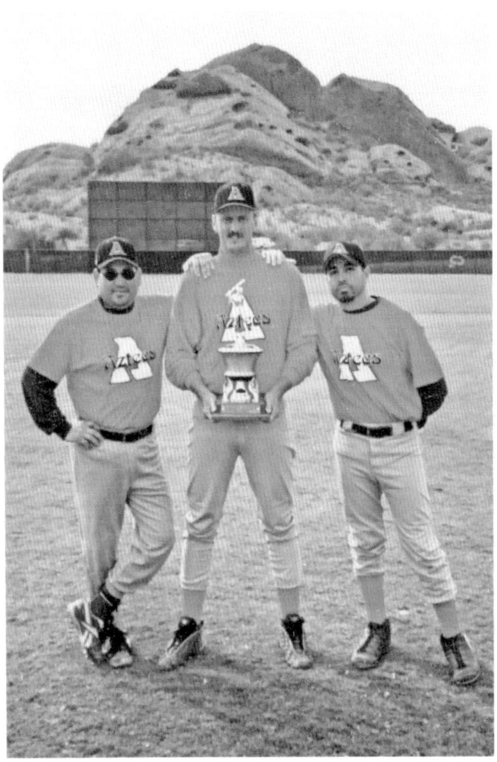

Tommy Pérez III (left) is seen here with Randy Kassinger (center) and Pete Sanchez as they celebrate their championship in Arizona in the 28-and-over Wood Bat Men's Senior Baseball League (MSBL) World Series tournament. Teams from all over the United States and other countries compete in the MSBL and Men's Adult Baseball League. Pérez has played on several teams that traveled to Las Vegas, Arizona, San Diego, and Tijuana, Mexico. His father, Tom Jr., and grandfather Tommy Sr. both played and coached in East Los Angeles, and traveled to Mexicali and Tijuana to compete against Mexican teams. Three generations of Pérez illustrate the long tradition of Mexican and Mexican American teams crossing the border to showcase their talents, and to speak the common languages of baseball and Spanish. (Courtesy of Tommy Perez III.)

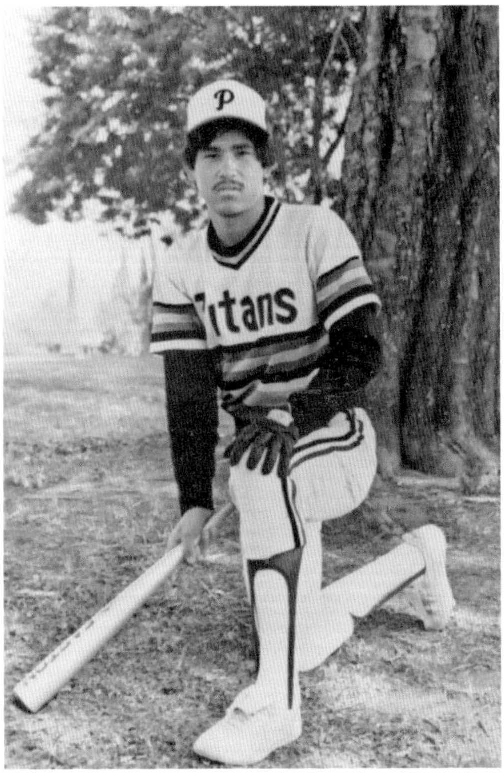

Tommy Pérez III played both football and baseball at Pioneer High School in Whittier. He excelled in both sports, was voted to the first team All Whitmont League as a football defensive back, second team All Whitmont League in baseball as a second baseman, and first team All Southern California All-Area, also at second base. Gil Gamez, a scout for the Kansas City Royals, had shown some interest in Pérez during high school. Pérez's brothers, Robert, Marc, Nicholas, and Michael, played little league and all attended Pioneer High School. Robert did not play in high school, while Marc and Michael played junior varsity baseball and varsity football. Nicholas (Nick) was an outstanding player in both sports. At a recent alumni game at Pioneer, brothers Tommy, Nicolas, Michael, and their father reminisced about the old days of glory. (Courtesy of Tommy Pérez III.)

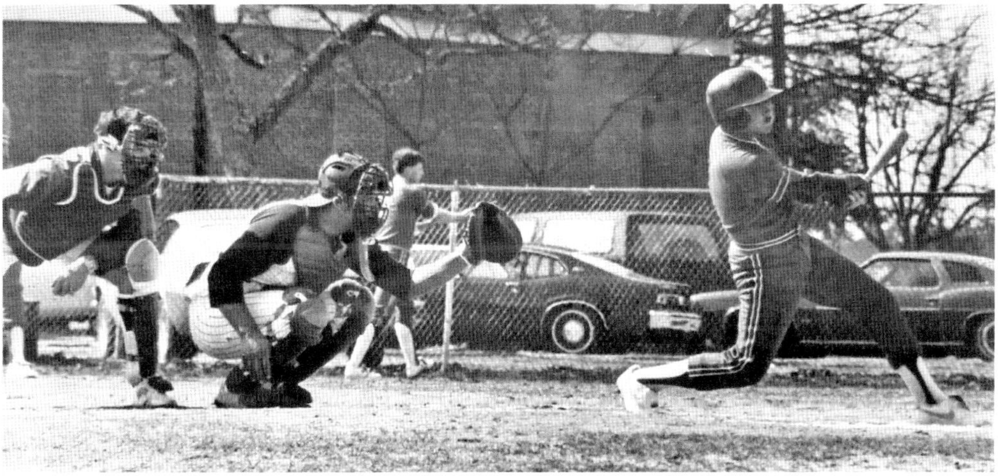

Tommy Pérez III joined the US Army in 1982, becoming a paratrooper with the 82nd Airborne Division, Delta Company, 782nd Maintenance Battalion. He played football and baseball for the Fort Bragg Dragons against local community colleges, including Spring Valley and Littlefield. He is seen in 1985 taking a swing during a preseason game against Littlefield at the 18th Airborne Corps Stadium at Fort Bragg. He was later stationed at Fort Benning, Georgia. Pérez was deployed to Grenada to rescue American hostages in 1983 and served in Kuwait, Iraq, and Afghanistan. (Courtesy of Tommy Pérez III.)

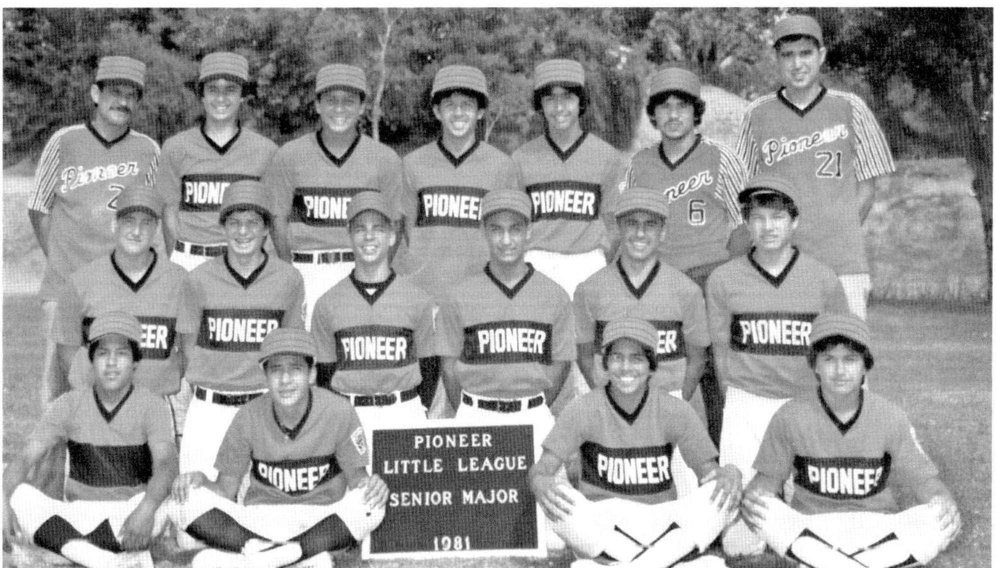

Tommy Pérez III (third row, second from right) started coaching and playing baseball in 1981 after he graduated from Pioneer High School in Whittier. He was an all-star coach in the Whittier Pioneer little league Senior Division. He played for a team in the City of Commerce, made the All-Star Team, and went on to play against a team from Aguascalientes, Mexico. Since his military service, Pérez continues to coach and play ball, including with the MSBL. In 2000, his team won the MSBL World Series. Pérez proudly wears his championship ring. (Courtesy of Tommy Pérez III.)

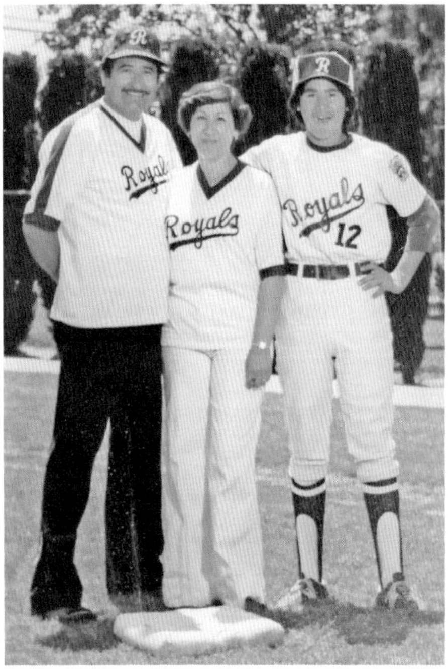

Tommy Pérez III (right) is pictured with parents Tom Jr. and Alice. Tommy is a highly decorated veteran with several medals and citations from his 34 years of military service, including deployment to Grenada, Kuwait, Iraq, and Afghanistan. His mother, Alice, was born in East Los Angeles to Mariano and Nellie Carranco Roldan from Zacatecas and Leon, Mexico. She had two brothers, Joe and Tommy, and a sister, Dolores. Her father played ball in East Los Angeles and later worked for Capitol Records. Sadly, he died at the young age of 38. Alice attended Marianna Elementary, Belvedere Junior High School, and Garfield High School. She tried playing ball at a young age but was hit with the ball and never played again. (Courtesy of Tommy Pérez III.)

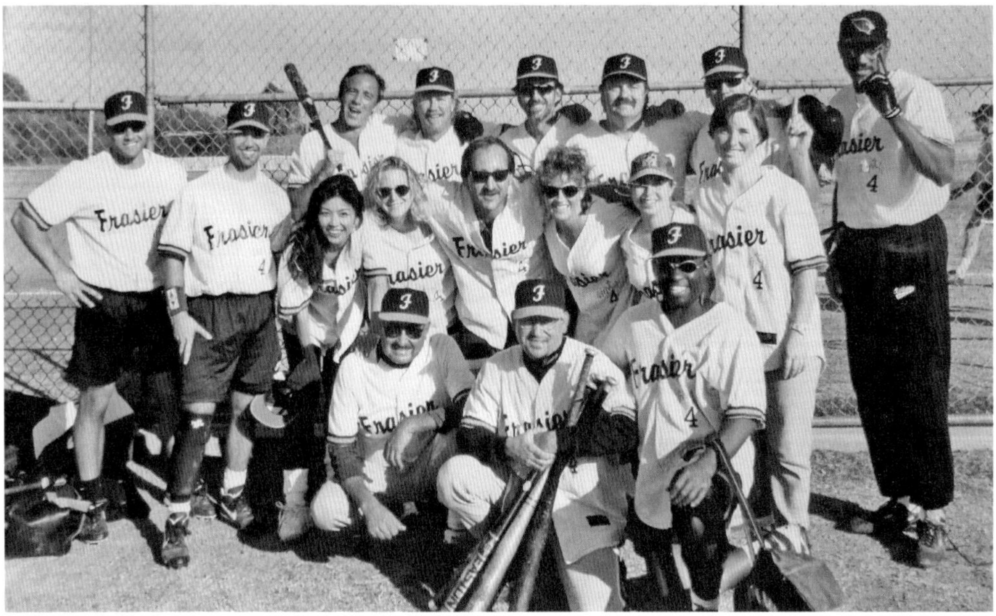

Tom Pérez Jr. (first row, far left), the father of Tommy III (center, kneeling), was a security guard for *Cheers* and *Frasier*, becoming a close friend of the cast and crew. When the *Frasier* team joined the Primetime Softball League, Tom served as manager, while his sons Tommy (first row, center), Mark, and Mike played. The team played in two championship games, in 1997 and 1999. They played against *Hill Street Blues*, *Third Rock from the Sun*, *Beverly Hills 90210*, *ER*, *The Golden Girls*, *Home Improvement*, *LA Law*, *Married with Children*, *Roseanne*, *Wings*, and *Charmed*. Tommy III played on the *Frasier* team for six years. (Courtesy of Tommy Pérez III.)

Dave Salazar was born in 1895 near Griffith Park in Los Angeles. He and his brother Mike, who was raised in San Gabriel, were outstanding baseball players from the 1920s through the 1950s throughout California, the Southwest, and Mexico. Dave is seen here leaving for spring training in 1924 with the San Francisco Seals. On that team were Paul and Lloyd Waner, known as "Big Poison" and "Little Poison." The catcher for the Seals was Andy Vargas. In the 1930s and 1940s, Dave Salazar, and later, his two sons Carlos and David Jr., played overhand softball at Brookside Park (now Jackie Robinson Park) near the Rose Bowl using a 10 inch ball and playing regular baseball rules. Carlos and David played for the UniVets, a Mexican American team comprised of veterans. David had served in the Korean War. (Courtesy of Carlos Salazar.)

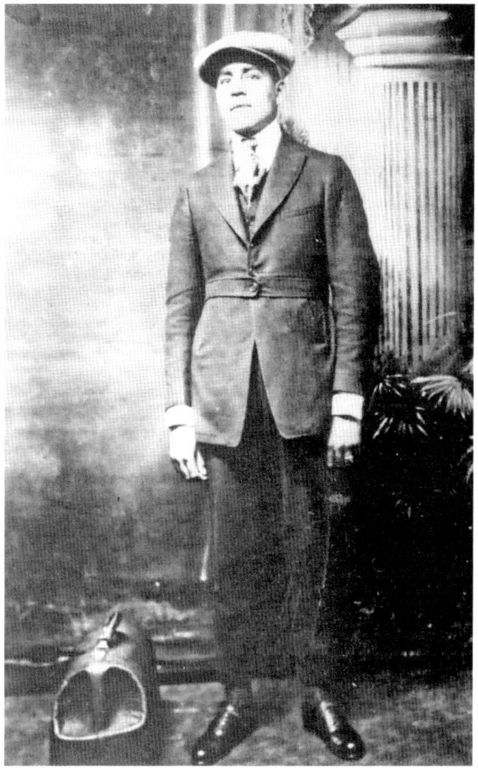

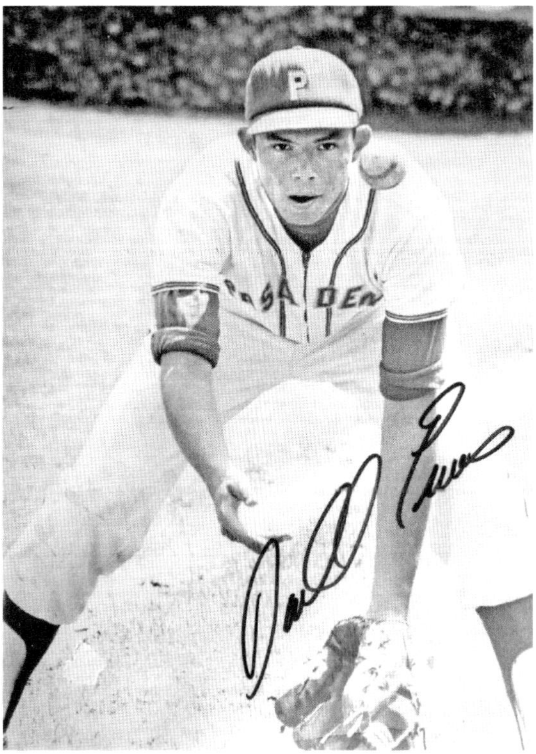

Darrell Wayne Evans is the grandson of Dave Salazar, whose daughter Eleanor gave birth to Darrell in 1947 in Pasadena, California. Evans is a former third baseman and first baseman who played in the major leagues from 1969 to 1989 with the Atlanta Braves, San Francisco Giants, and Detroit Tigers. In his career, he had over 2,223 hits, 414 home runs, and 1,354 runs batted in. He appeared in the 1973 and 1983 All-Star games and won the World Series with the Detroit Tigers in 1984. He is one of the few players to have hit over 400 home runs without being seriously considered for induction into the Baseball Hall of Fame. Baseball expert and author Bill James has said that Evans is the most underrated player in baseball history, absolutely number one on the list. (Courtesy of Carlos Salazar.)

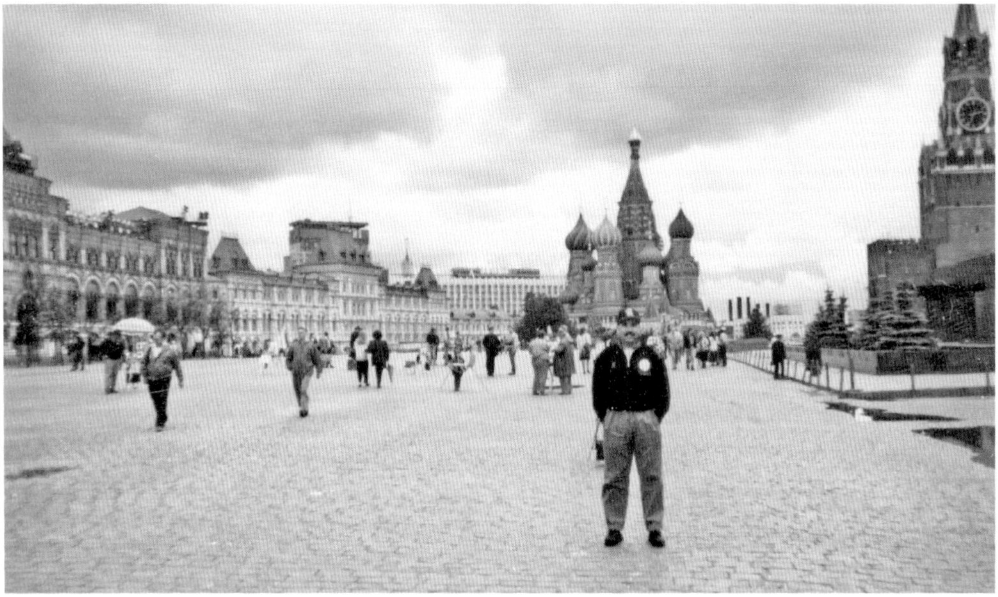

In 1994, Mark R. García from Arcadia in the San Gabriel Valley was the administrative assistant for international baseball operations for the California Angels. He and Bob Protexter were sent to Moscow and St. Petersburg to scout and hold tryouts on a Russian army base, at the home of the Moscow Red Army Baseball Club, and at Moscow State University. García is seen here in Red Square. (Courtesy of Mark R. García.)

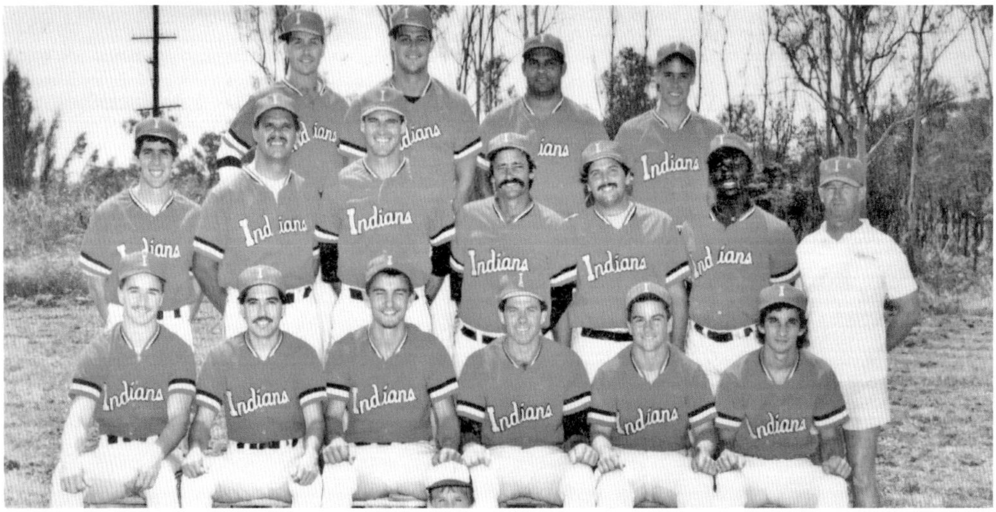

Mark R. García (first row, second from left) attended Bishop Amat High School and Pasadena City College in the San Gabriel Valley. He is seen here with the Brisbane Southside Indians in Australia, during the 1985–1986 season. García's teammate, Tony Palaygi (second row, fifth from left) played ball with García in high school and also played at California State University at Pomona. García has been a baseball scout for nearly 25 years and gives thanks to his scouting mentors Frank Amaya, Rueben and Ernie Rodríguez, David Garcia, George Zabala, Jesse Flores Sr. and Jr., Steve Flores, Angel Figuroa, and Fred Mazuca. (Courtesy of Mark R. Garcia.)

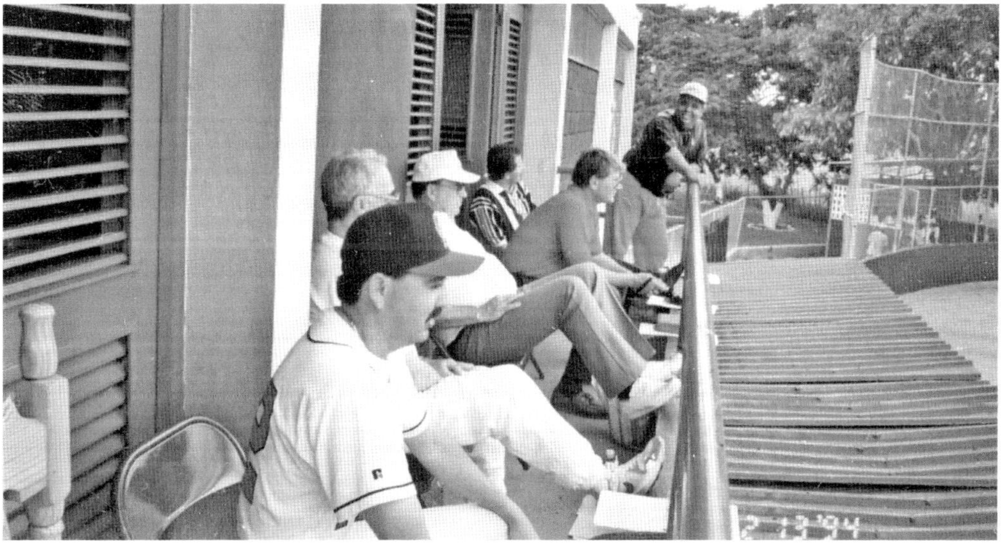

Mark R. García (foreground) is seen here scouting for the California Angeles in San Pedro de Macoris in the Dominican Republic. García played ball at all levels including youth, high school, college, professional, and international. He decided that the baseball scouting life was the way to go and has been a scout for several major league teams for 25 years, especially active in international scouting in Russia, Latin America, and Asia. (Courtesy of Mark R. García.)

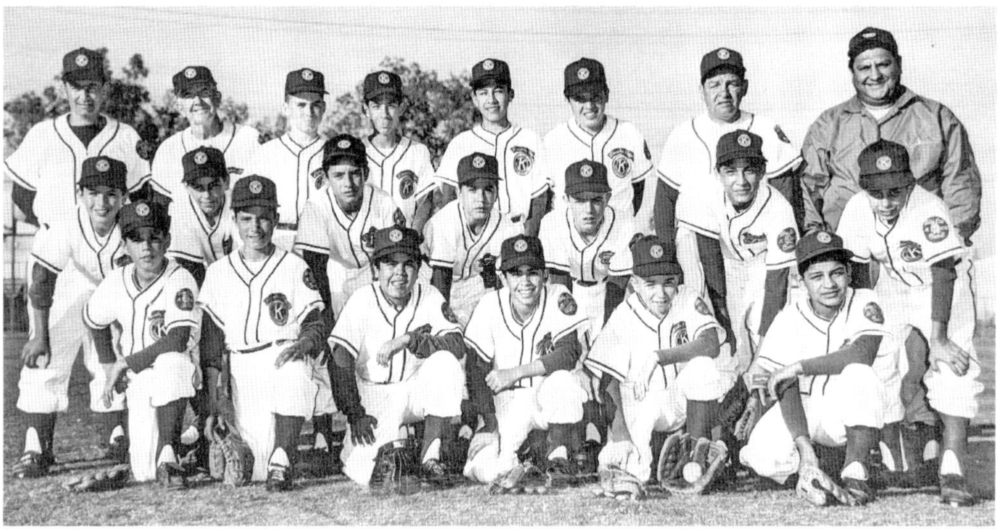

Tony Ortega (second row, center) played for the 1960 Kiwanis Lincoln Heights team. Players who later played for the Cathedral High School Phantoms included Ortega, Richie Castro (first row, far left), David Contreras (first row, fourth from left), Rick Auerbach (first row, second from right), Ray Mellado (second row, far right), Dan Guerrero (second row, far left), and Larry Morán (third row, third from left). Contreras later taught and coached at Santa Barbara High School, Auerbach became the Los Angeles County tax assessor, Guerrero played ball at Cal Poly–Pomona, Mellado was the founder of the Great Minds in STEM program, and Morán played for LA Wilson. (Courtesy of Tony Ortega.)

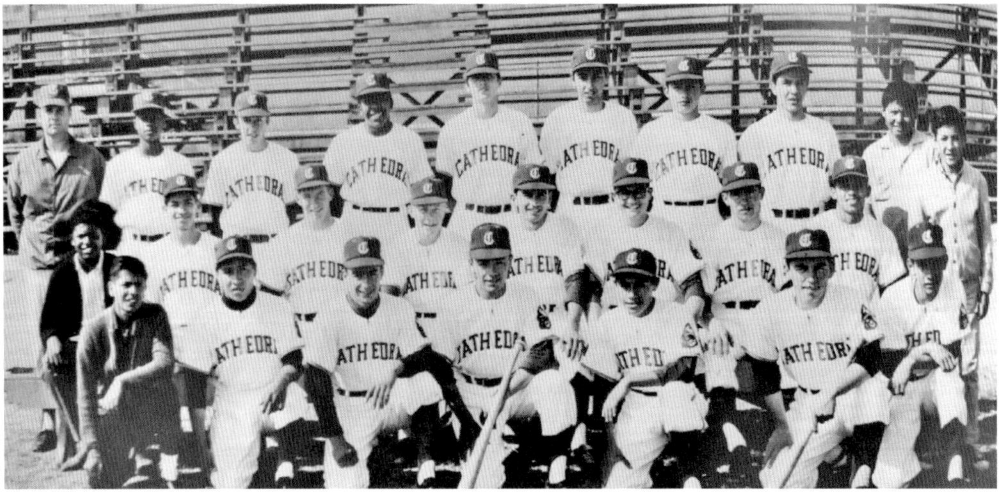

The Cathedral High School Phantoms had outstanding players in 1963, 1964, and 1965. Tony Ortega (standing, far right) played second and third base. The team practiced at Elysian Park, driving through the Dodger Stadium parking lots in vans. Their coach was Dick Salter, who also coached football and was the athletic director. He was also the academic counselor who encouraged Tony to pursue careers in teaching and coaching. Teammate Ken Rudolph (second row, second from left) played nearly a dozen years in the major leagues, while Matt Machetti (second row, third from right) played third base at East Los Angeles College and Cal State–Fullerton and was drafted by the Angels. (Courtesy of Tony Ortega.)

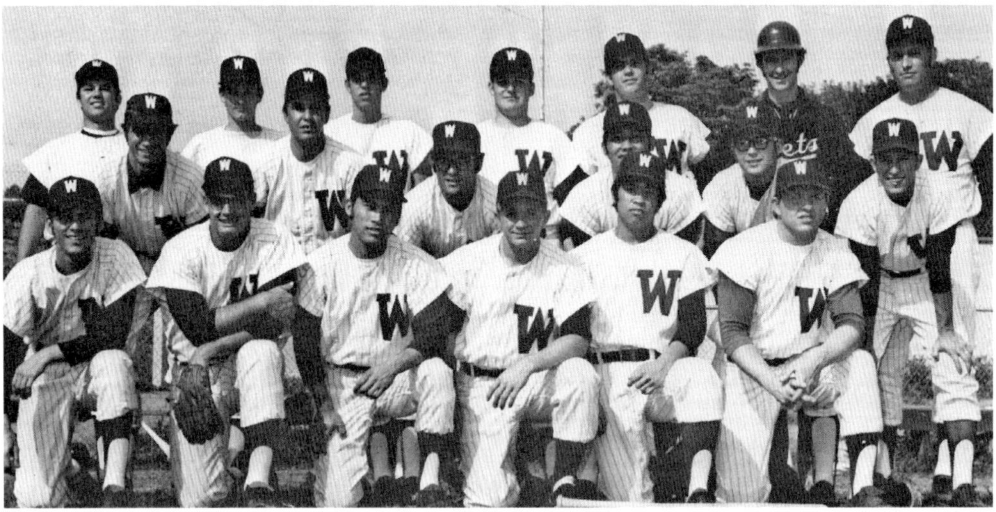

Tony Ortega (second row, second from left) played ball at Whittier College in the late 1960s, graduating in 1970 with a bachelor's degree in kinesiology and social sciences. Another Mexican American on the team, Joe Román, had played at Cerritos College in Norwalk and later became an attorney. Ortega earned a master's in school administration from Cal State–Fullerton and received his administrative credentials in 1980. His first teaching job was in Pomona at Palomares Middle School, where he coached freshman football. He later taught at Duarte High School, where he coached football and baseball. (Courtesy of Tony Ortega.)

David Trujillo (right) was born in Albuquerque, New Mexico, in 1945. His uncle Benny was a left-handed pitcher, while David's father, Eugene, coached during the 1950s. David played ball in little league, grammar school, and at Valley High School. He eventually moved to Norwalk, California, where he coached for 25 years. He took the Norwalk All-Stars to Hermosillo, Mexico, for seven years, winning the championship each time. He is seen here receiving a trophy from a Mexican official. Trujillo also coached in San Bernardino, California, for two years. He and his wife, Tina, currently live in Newton, Kansas. (Courtesy of David Trujillo.)

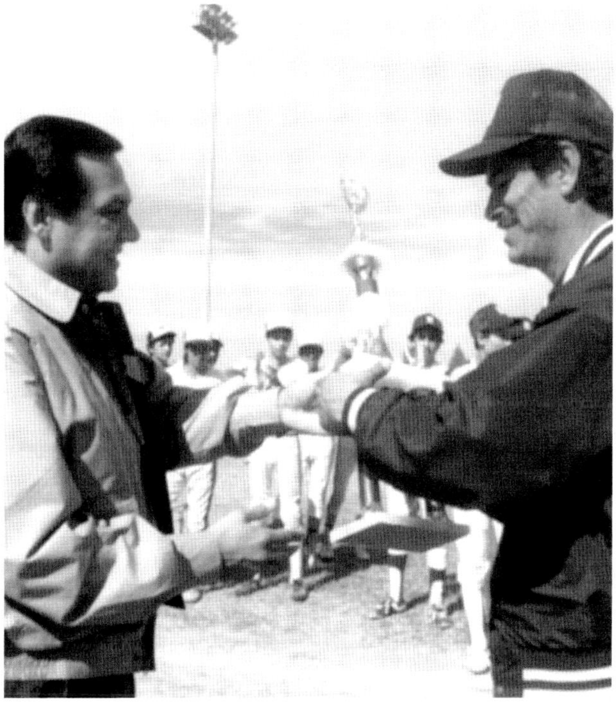

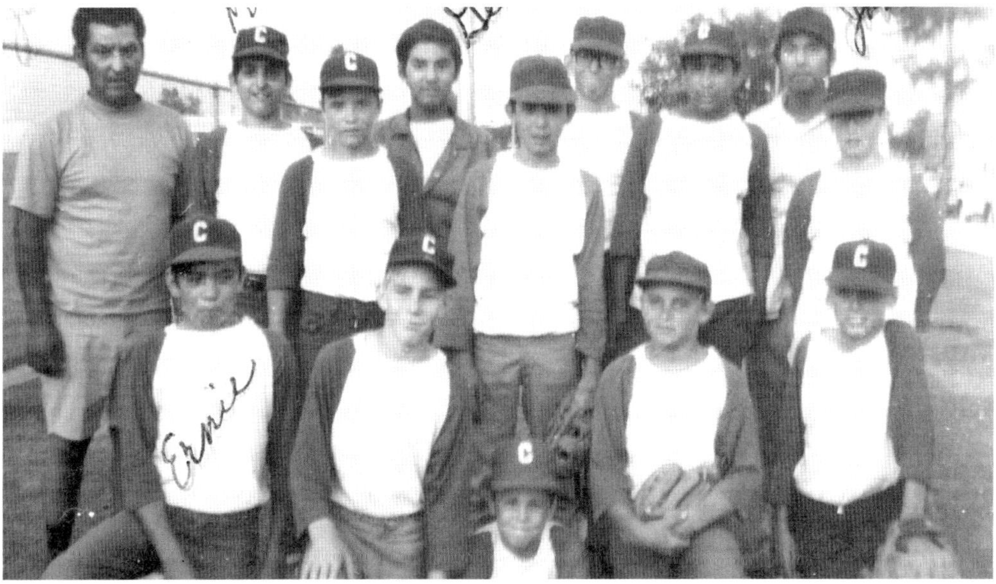

Johnny R. Ramírez (standing, far left) coached for many years in Norwalk, Artesia, and other surrounding communities. He coached his sons John Jr. (third row, far right) and Geno (third row, third from left) for years. Ramírez was active with youth ball organizations and served a term as president of his local little league. His daughter, Eva, played right field in the Artesia Parks and Recreation Department in the 1960s. Her sister Linda played ball, too, while another sister, Laura, was a cheerleader. Tragically, Ramírez was killed in a construction accident in 1972, leaving his young widow, Mabel, to take care of their nine children. (Courtesy of Eva Santillán.)

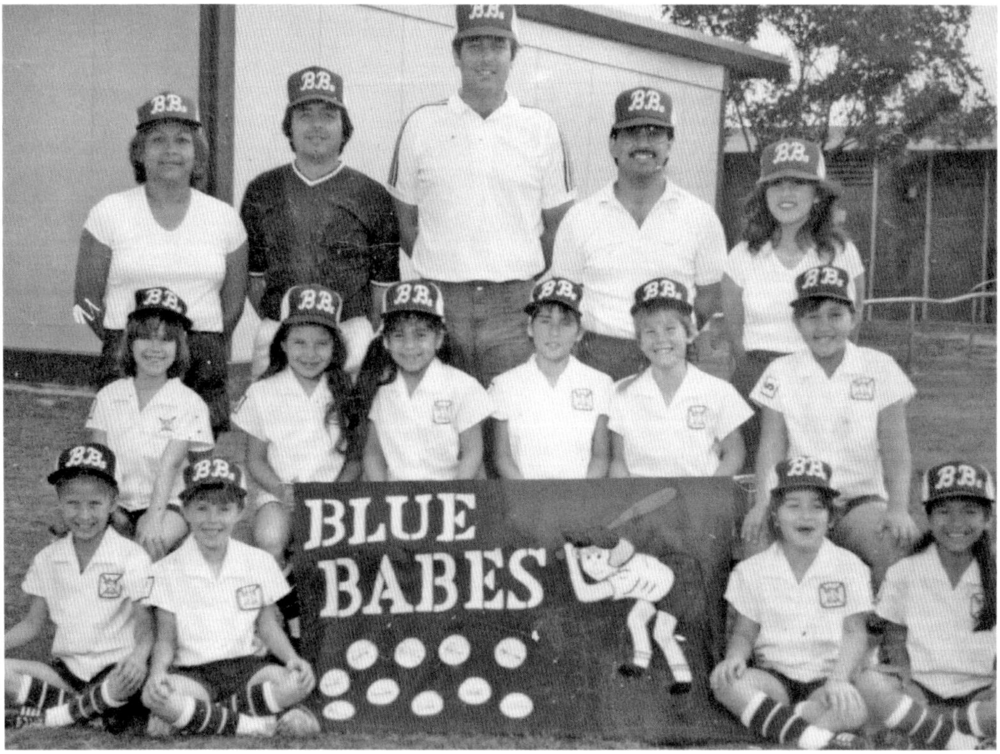

Melissa Santillán Toney (first row, far right) played one year of T-ball with the undefeated Blue Babes in Cerritos in 1980. Mother Eva (standing right) was the team mom, and father Joe (standing second from right) was a coach and made the banner. Melissa graduated from Artesia High School in 1992. She played soccer and was a cheerleader. She was one of two girls on the boys' soccer team at Artesia High School and played soccer at Long Beach City College. She still plays recreational league soccer. She and her husband, Aaron, have three children, Nicolas, Sophia, and Bella. (Courtesy of Melissa Santillán Toney.)

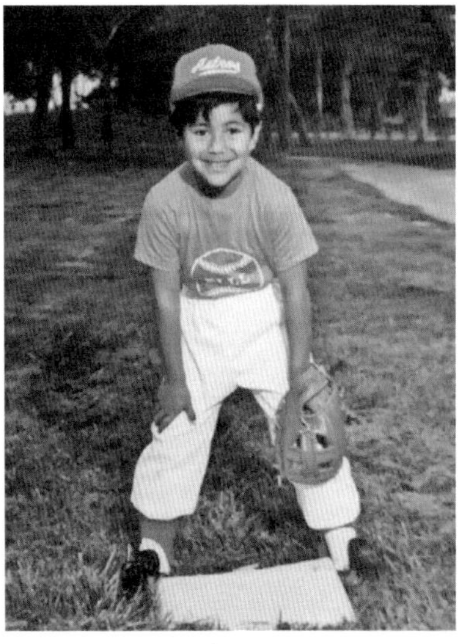

Carlitos Santillán was born in 1979 at Cerritos Gardens General Hospital in Hawaiian Gardens. He attended Melbourne Elementary School, Bancroft Middle School, and Lakewood High School. Sister Melissa attended Melbourne Elementary School in East Lakewood and Tetzlaff Middle School. Carlitos played little league at Heartwell Park in Long Beach and Pop Warner football. In high school, he continued playing both sports, wearing No. 33 as a running back and striking out 18 consecutive batters. He has served as a soccer coach to his nephew Nicolas. (Courtesy of Carlitos Santillán.)

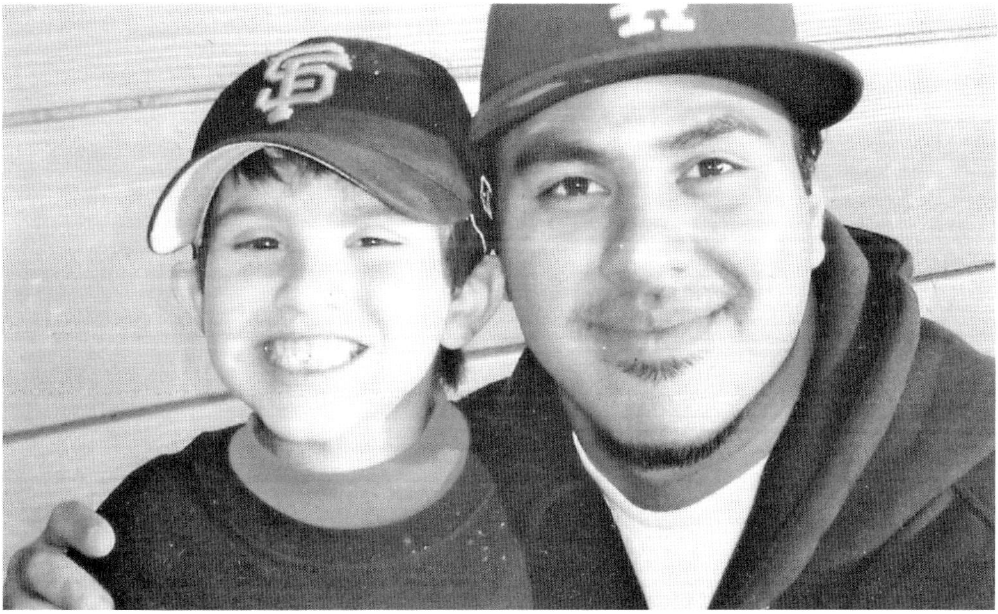

Nicolas Toney (left), seen here with his uncle Carlitos Santillán, started playing sports as a four-year-old in Cerritos and Norwalk. Aaron, his father, played soccer at Iowa State. Nicolas participated in wrestling and T-ball and played on several baseball, soccer, basketball, and cross-country teams in school and the community. In 2018, he is the only freshman on his varsity soccer team. He has visited England, France, Germany, Belgium, the Netherlands, Austria, Germany, the Bahamas, several eastern states, and Washington, DC. (Courtesy of Melissa Santillán Toney.)

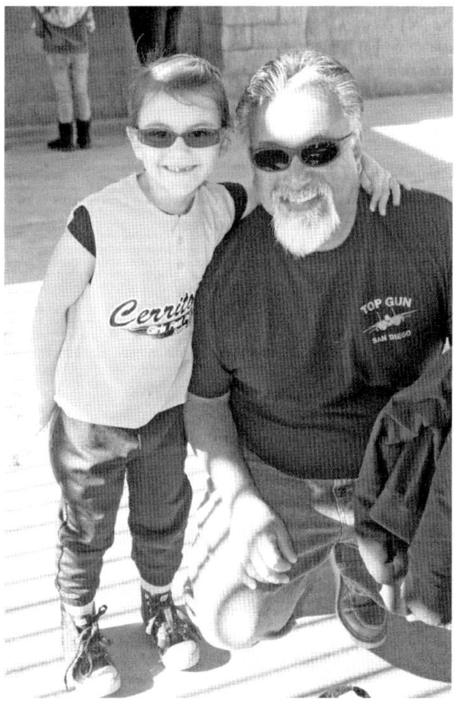

Bella Toney, Nicolas's sister, seen here with her grandfather Joe Santillán, started playing soccer at four years old and later played T-ball and softball in Cerritos. At 10, she joined her school's track team and placed first in her division in a district meet. Even though she played baseball, soccer was her true love. Her 2017 team won the national championship of US youth soccer, the National President Cup. Bella is an honors student, a member of the Green Engineering Club, and a Distinguished Scholar in Science. She hopes to become a college professor like her great-uncle Richard A. Santillan. (Courtesy of Melissa Santillán Toney.)

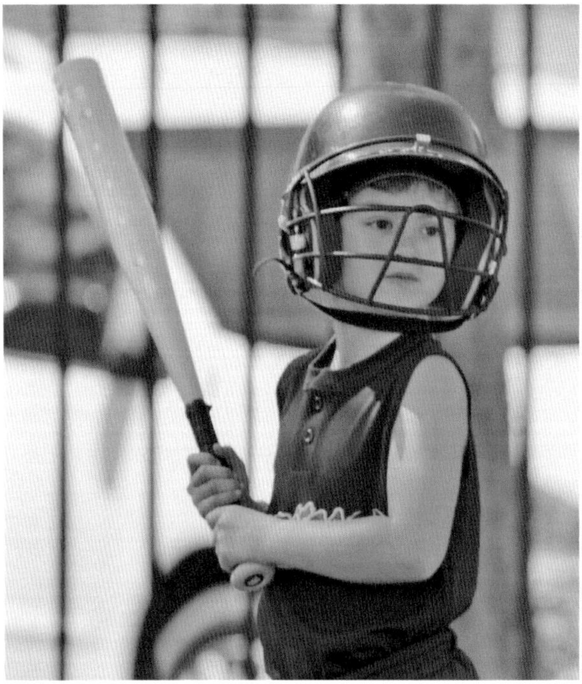

Sophia is the youngest of the Toney family. Like her brother Nicolas and sister Bella, Sophia played multiple sports at a young age, including softball, basketball, track, volleyball, and soccer in Cerritos and Cypress. Besides sports, Sophia enjoys participating in school plays and talent shows and is active with volunteer groups and student government. She is a member of the Reading Olympics team and the Good News Club, is a class representative for the student council, is on the yearbook committee, and mentors younger students in the library and computer lab. (Courtesy of Melissa Santillán Toney.)

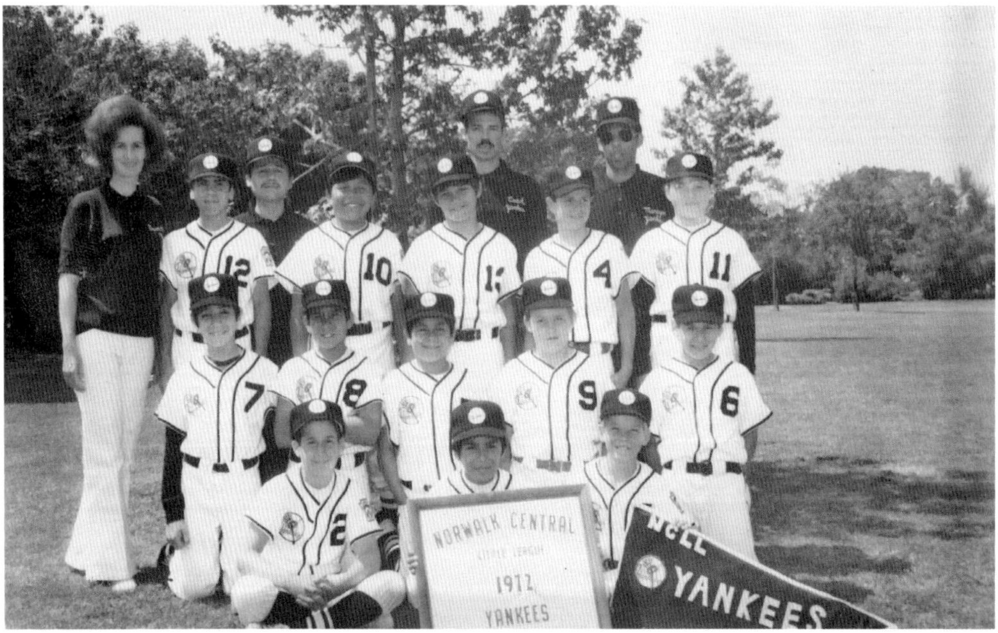

Mike Álvarez grew up in Norwalk and played for the 1972 Norwalk Central little league Yankees. The team included, from left to right, (first row) Mickey Stevens, Art Moreno, and Ricky Baker; (second row) Mike Álvarez, Pat Padilla, Reyes Orozco, unidentified, and Louis González; (third row) team mom ? Scroggins, Richard Vásquez, coach ? Vásquez, Patrick Rico, Mike Fernándes, coach ? Scroggins, Chuck Scroggins, Ron Mora, and head coach Mike Hernández. Nearly half of the team went on to have successful baseball and softball careers. (Courtesy of Mike Álvarez.)

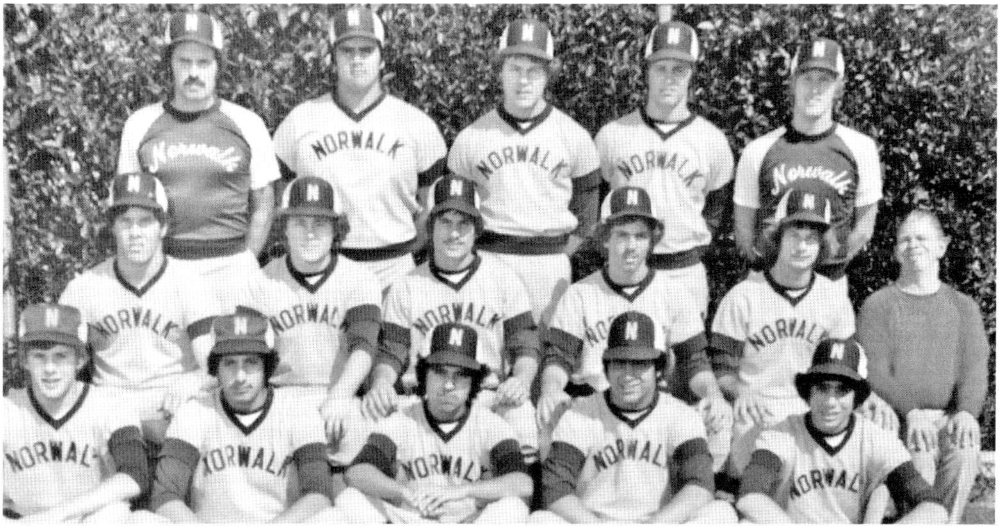

Mike Álvarez (first row, far right) was a centerfielder at Norwalk High School known for his outstanding batting, his passionate play, and his awesome throwing arm, and was a Suburban League All-League selection in 1977 and 1978. The 1978 team won the CIF championship. His father, John Sr., was an outstanding fastpitch softball pitcher. Mike also played American Legion and Connie Mack ball and was selected to play in Mexico as part of the sister city program between Norwalk and Hermosillo in 1976. He also had a remarkable softball career, winning two state championships in 1983 and 1984 with the Amigos team from Norwalk. (Courtesy of Mike Álvarez.)

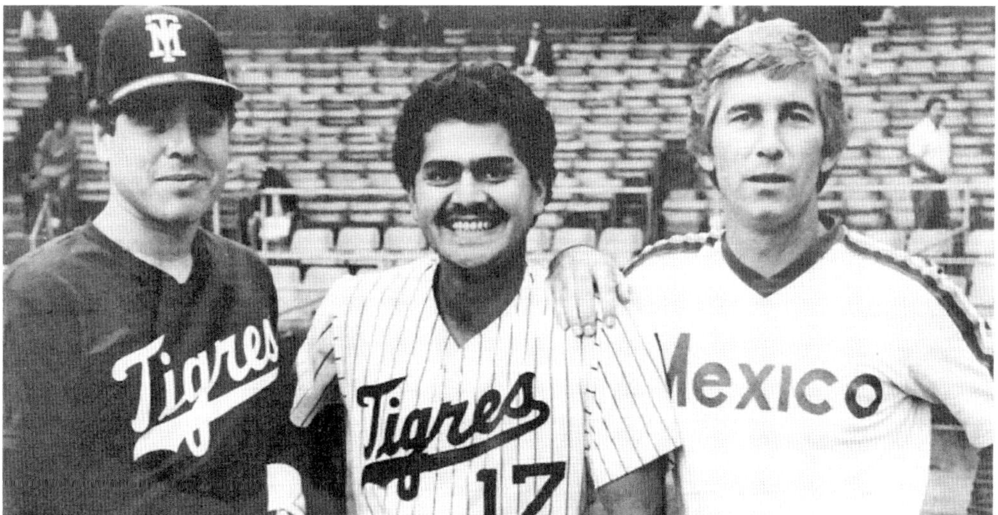

John Álvarez (left), Andy Pasillas (center), and Mike Paul (right) played baseball for Cerritos Community College in Norwalk. Álvarez played at Norwalk High School and with the San Diego Padres organization, Pasillas grew up in Hawaiian Gardens and played for Artesia High School and the Chicago White Sox, and Paul grew up in Detroit and played for the Texas Rangers. Álvarez was a third baseman, batting and throwing right-handed. He was drafted by the Padres in the 13th round of the 1977 amateur draft from California State University Fullerton. (Courtesy of John Álvarez.)

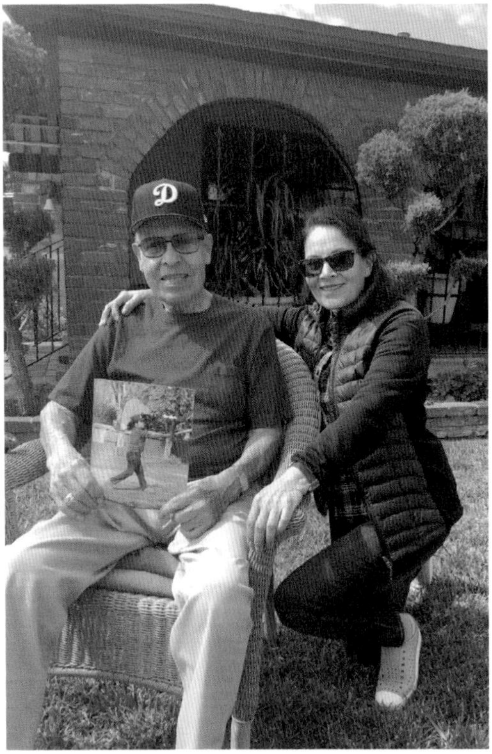

Seen here are Leo Herrera and his daughter Sandy Santillán. Herrera was born in Montebello in 1928 and married Alta Contreras in 1947. She was born in Downey, California, and grew up in the company town of Simons Brickyard, now Montebello. They had three children, Sandy, Yolanda, and Ron, three grandchildren, and three great-grandchildren. Leo worked for the ONC Freight Company and retired in 1997 after 41 years. He joined the company team in 1963, playing shortstop for five years. His team played at Lou Costello Park in Los Angeles. Sandy was born at Beverly Hospital in Montebello, grew up in Whittier, and graduated from California High School. Her family and relatives grew up on land that Sandy's paternal grandfather, Gabriel, had allocated to them. As children, Sandy and her siblings and cousins cleared fields to play baseball. (Courtesy of Sandy Santillán.)

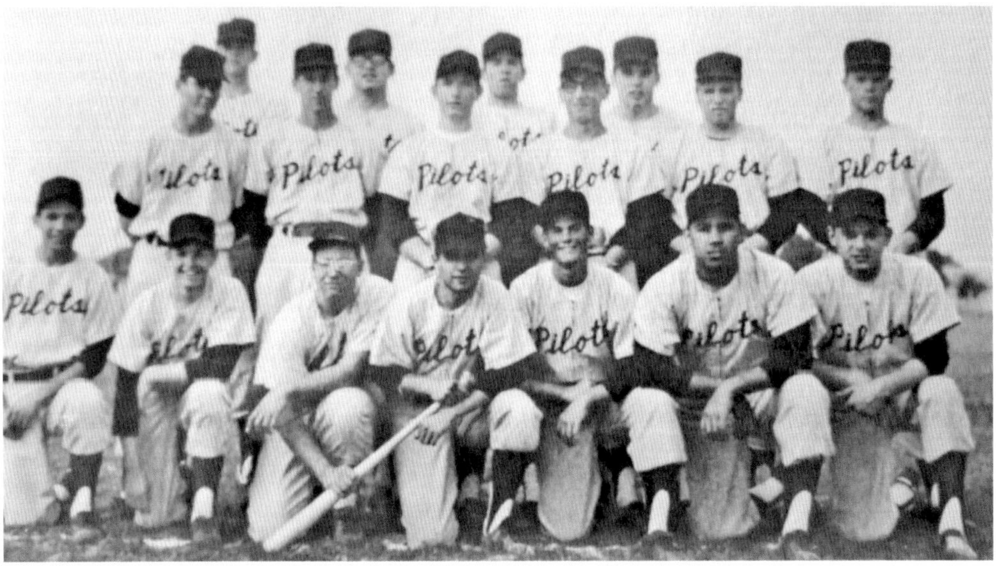

The 1965 Excelsior High School Pilots from Norwalk are, from left to right, (first row) R. Álvarez, D. Hansburger, J. Kammel, O. Salcido, L. La Place, G. Zabala, and B. Manzo; (second row) D. Hopkins, T. Swoinek, R. Ings, R. Cox, R. Stokey, and L. Larson; (third row) G. Rowen, S. Stewart, T. Tanner, and E. Tweit. The school was founded in 1903 and suffered massive damage during the 1933 Long Beach earthquake. At one time, it enrolled students from Cerritos, Artesia, and Bellflower. Pat Nixon, wife of Pres. Richard Nixon, graduated in 1929. (Courtesy of John Echeveste.)

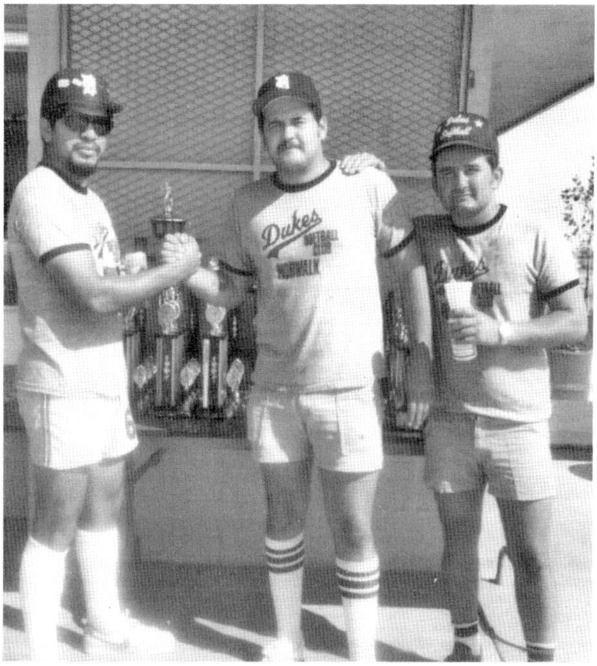

From left to right are John Lemos and brothers Tomás and Joe Espinoza at Zimmerman Park in Norwalk in 1984. After returning from the military, Tomás played regular softball games and decided to organize the Dukes. In 1981, he met Lemos, and by 1984, the Dukes were winning highly competitive games in tournaments. They established a state and national reputation with outstanding hitting, strong defense, speed on the base paths, and solid pitching. The team became a member of the US Slow Pitch Softball Association (USSSA), winning championships before disbanding in 1990. (Courtesy of Tomás Espinoza.)

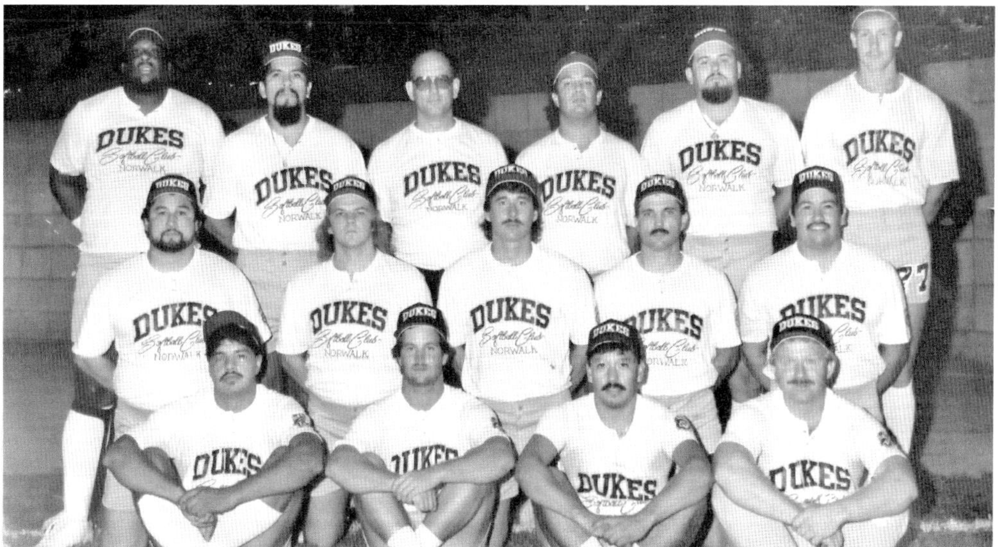

In 1988, the USSSA preseason rankings had the Norwalk Dukes number one for the C Division, which included the Southern California Softball Association state championship in Northern California. Team sponsor Jerry Ramsey paid for out-of-state trips. The team won the 1989 USSSA B Western Region Championship and went to the world tournament in Wilmington, North Carolina. The 1987 team is, from left to right, (first row) Issac "Chito" Alvídrez, Tommy Burgess, David Gallegos, and Steve Copeland; (second row) Dave Rangel, Dave Barrett, Tommy Garner, Jeff Sherman, and Steve Hernández; (third row) Ron "Big" Jones, John Lemos, Jerry Ramsey, Keith Phillips, Tomás Espinoza, and Greg Spatz. (Courtesy of John Lemos.)

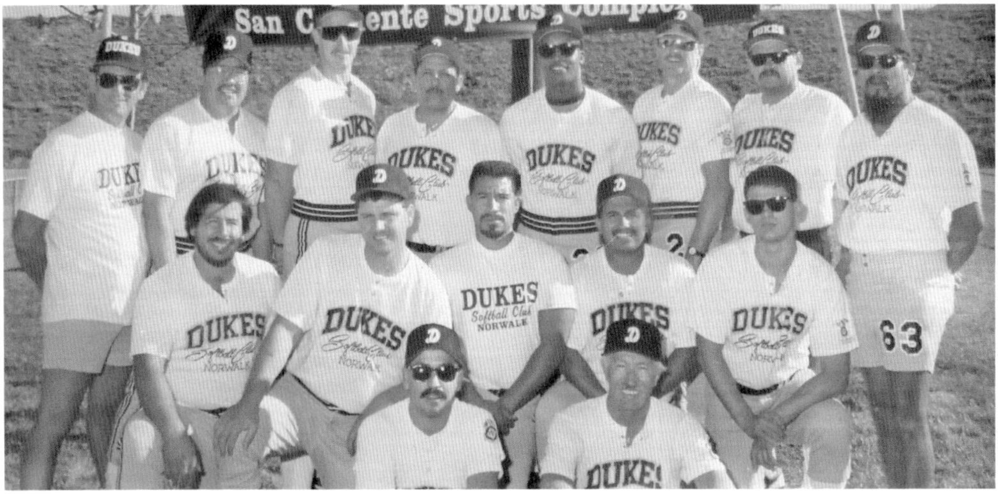

The Norwalk Dukes, pictured in 1989, were started in 1980 by Tomás Espinoza. In 1985, John Lemos and Espinoza entered the Dukes into their first tournament at Lake Arrowhead, where the team finished in a strong second place. By 1987, the team was entering the USSSA tournaments with much success. From left to right are (first row) David Gallegos and Larry Bowser; (second row) Tony Hernández, Billy Loard, Mando Correa, Louie Monreal, and Napolean Espinoza; (third row) Jerry Ramsey, Steve Hernández, Gregg Spatz, Jerry González, Dennis Moss, Zachary Darr, Tomás Espinoza, and John Lemos. (Courtesy of John Lemos.)

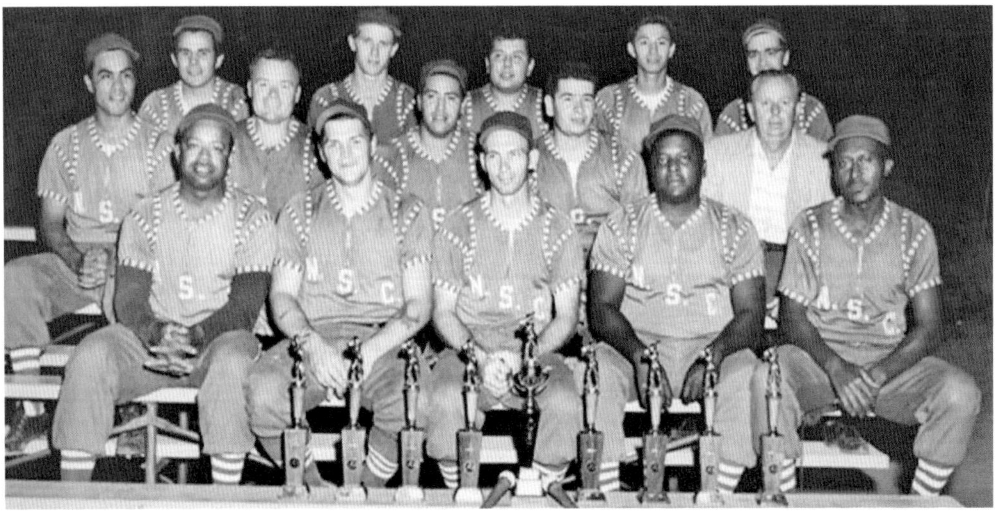

Ramiro Gallegos Jr. was born in 1940 in Michigan, where his family picked sugar beets and cherries. Families from San Antonio, Texas, worked the fields during the summer. Ramiro Sr. played baseball in the 1930s in San Antonio for the Pan American League, which included Arizona, New Mexico, Mexico, and Cuba. He also played ball at Lanier High School. He was killed during World War II as part of a tank corps unit. Ramiro Jr. (second row, second from right) played on this San Diego Navy Supply Center team in 1960 along with his wife's brother Julian Trujillo (second row, center) and brother-in-law Alfonso Don (second row, far left). (Courtesy of Ramiro Gallegos Jr..)

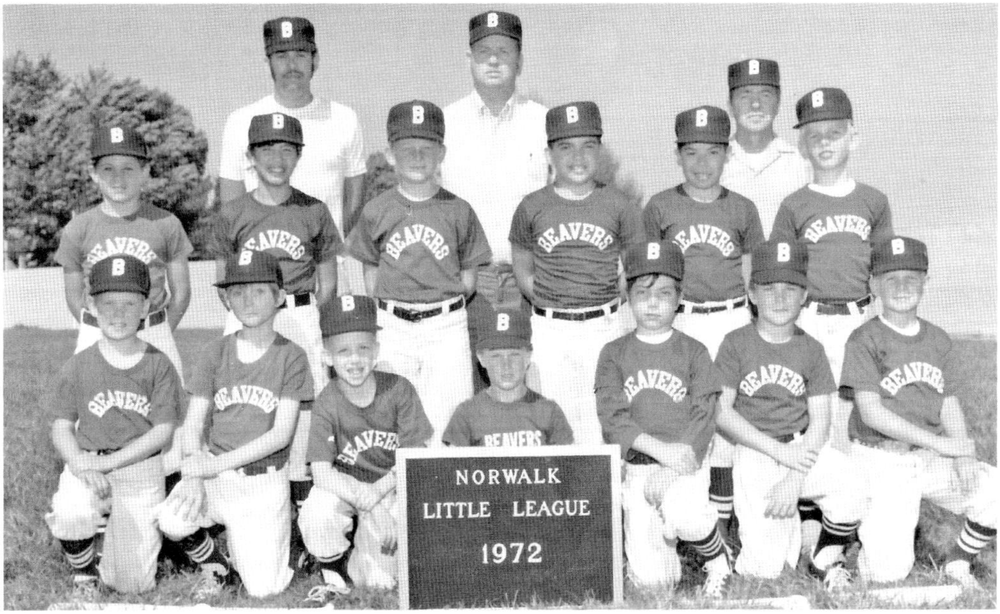

Ramiro "Chico" Gallegos III (second row, second from left) played for the 1972 Norwalk little league Beavers at O.K. Harrison Field. The Beavers were in the American League Division, which played the majority of its games at Corvallis Middle School. Ramiro played shortstop and first base and pitched. He struck out 16 players in one game. Ramiro III played four years of Pony-Colt ball at Holifield Park and also played at Norwalk High School. His first team was the Falcons. After his playing days, he helped his dad, Ramiro Jr., coach little league, Pony, and Colt Leagues. (Courtesy of Ramiro Gallegos III.)

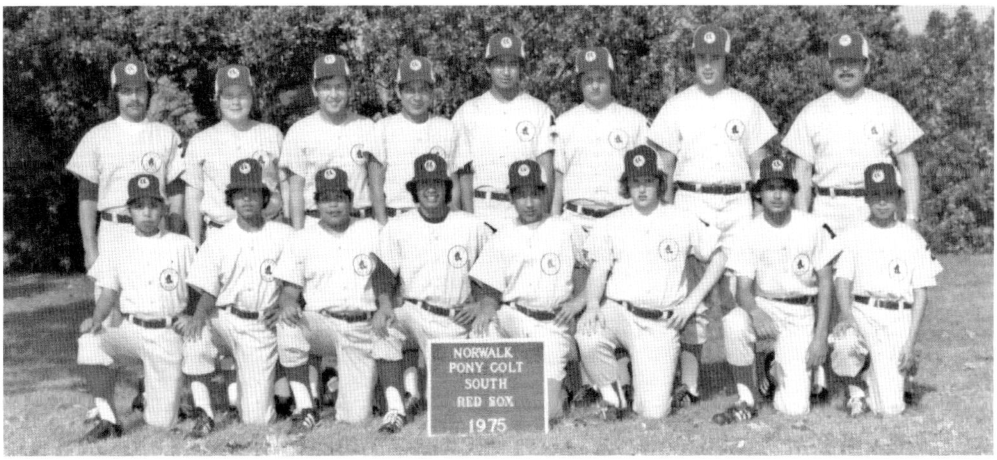

The 1975 Norwalk Pony League Red Sox played at Holifield Park. Players included Ramiro "Chico" Gallegos Jr., Ronnie Salcedo, Adrían De La Osa, Reyes Orozco, and Dirk Álvarez. These players represented several junior high schools and later would play ball at Excelsior, Norwalk, John Glenn, and St. Paul High Schools. Reyes Orozco was born with one hand, similar to Jim Abbot, and played first base. He was one of the team's best hitters. Saucedo played at the University of Arizona and was drafted by the Baltimore Orioles. (Courtesy of David Gallegos.)

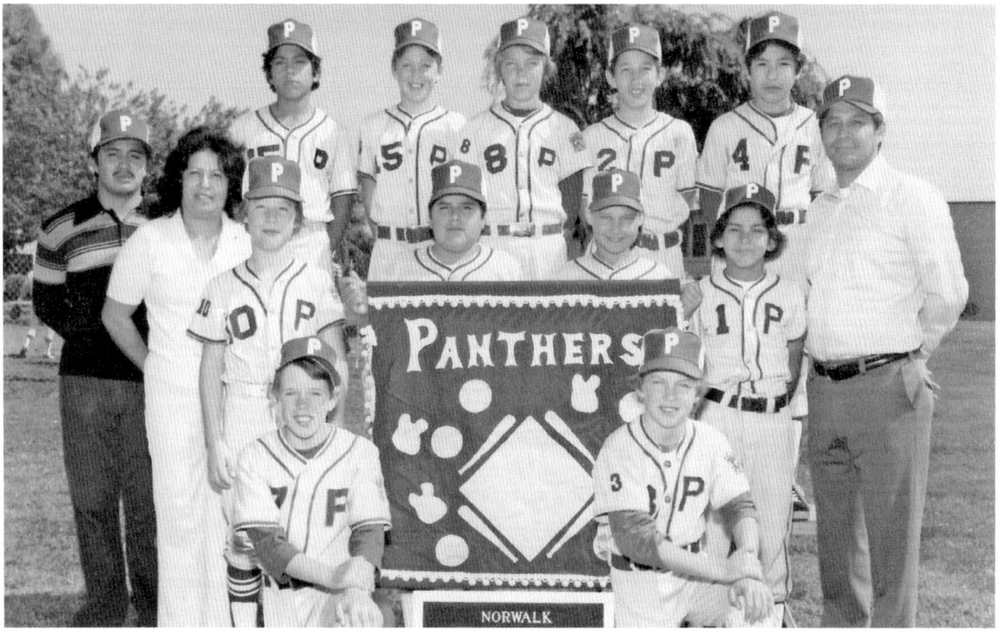

The Gallegos family has been active with youth sports in Norwalk since the 1960s. Ramiro Jr. (standing, far right) is pictured with wife and team mom Lucy (standing, left) and their two sons David (third row, far right) and coach "Chico" Ramiro III (standing, far left). Other players include Ben Ponce, Mark Kronc, Sean Wilcher, Richie Bush, Ignacio López, and Omar Ramírez. David played baseball with the Norwalk little league (1975–1979) and Pony-Colt League (1980–1983), and played football and baseball at Norwalk High School (1982–1984). In 1983, Norwalk reached the CIF finals at Anaheim Stadium. (Courtesy of David Gallegos.)

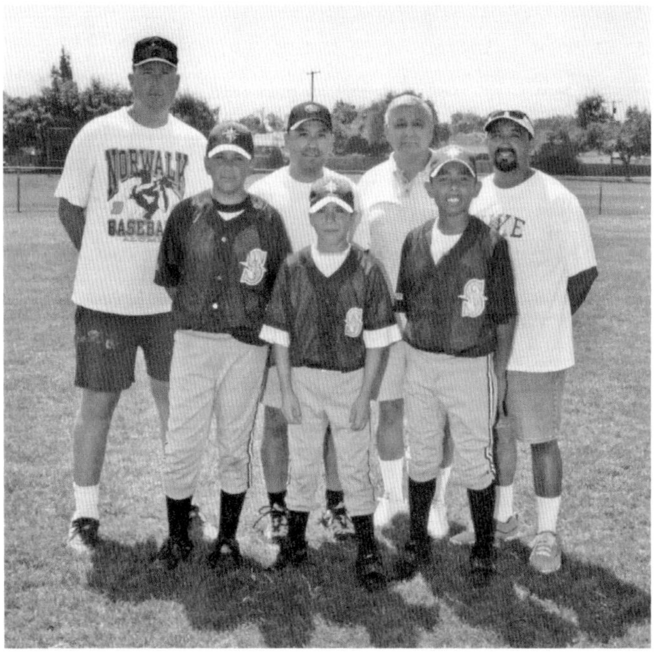

The outstanding 2000 Norwalk little league Major Division Mariners are, from left to right, (first row) Martín Wenrick, José Anthony Pérez, and Adrían Gallegos; (second row) John Wenrick, David Gallegos, Ramiro Gallegos Jr., and Ramiro "Chico" Gallegos III. Martín is the son of John, José is the nephew of David, and Adrían is the grandson of Ramiro Jr., the son of "Chico" Ramiro III, and the nephew of David. (Courtesy of David Gallegos.)

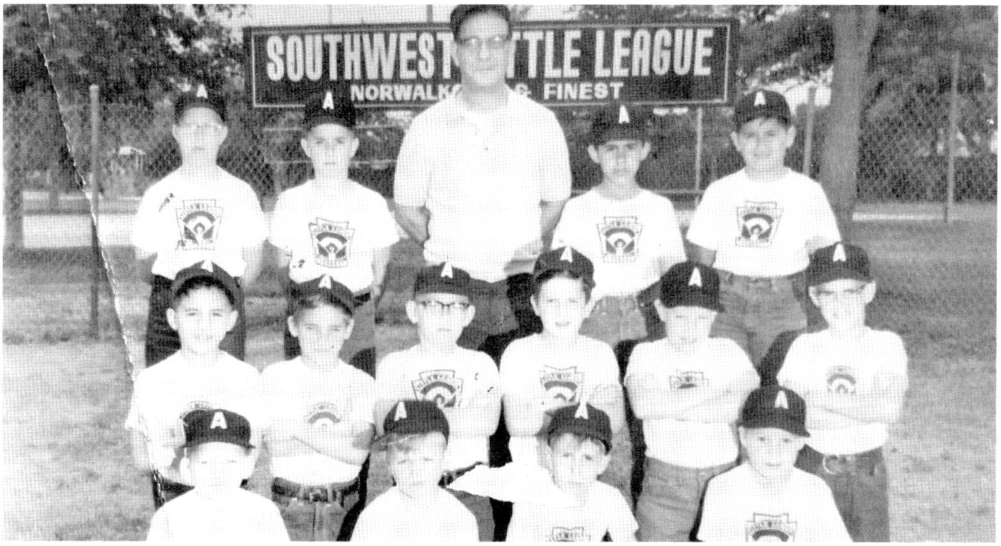

Tomás Espinoza (third row, far right) played catcher on this 1967 Southwest little league Norwalk team. He was born in Gardena, California, and his family moved to Norwalk in 1966. His father, Jose, was born in Batuc, Sonora, Mexico, and his mother, Artemisa, was born in Douglas, Arizona. Tomás had one brother, Joe, and three sisters, Artie, Linda, and Laura. Tomás attended Glazier Elementary School, Los Alisos Middle School, and Excelsior High School, graduating in 1976. He served in the Army from 1976 to 1980 as a tank commander. (Courtesy of Tomás Espinoza.)

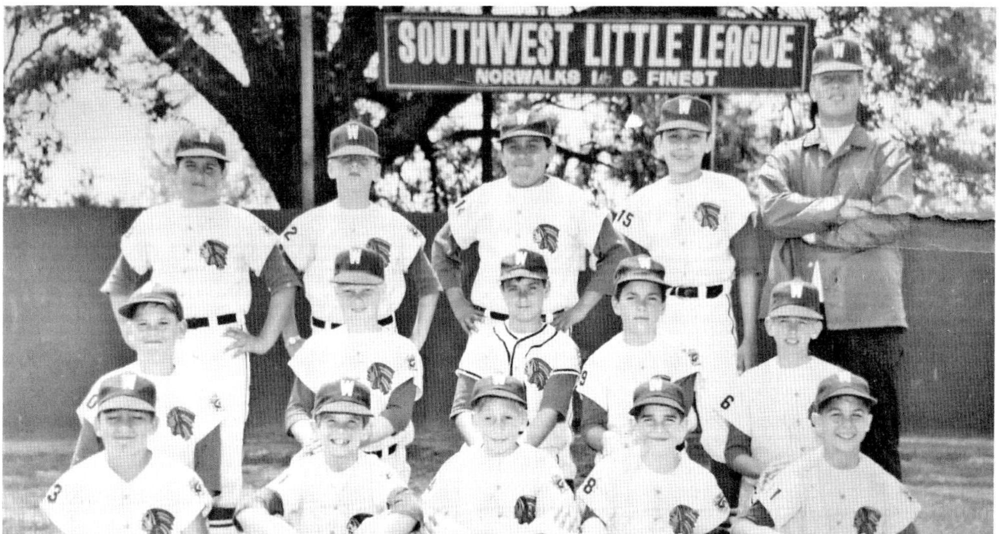

Tomás Espinoza (standing, left) and his brother Joe played little league, Pony League, and high school ball in Norwalk. They played at Excelsior High School in the 1970s, Tomás as a catcher and Joe at second base. Tomás played for the Warriors in the Southwest League in 1968, making the championship game. His boyhood friends included Ken Dicolla (first row, second from right) and David Almaro (second row, far right). After high school, Tomás was stationed at Fort Hood, Texas, with the 1st Cavary Division and served his last tour in California. (Courtesy of Tomás Espinoza.)

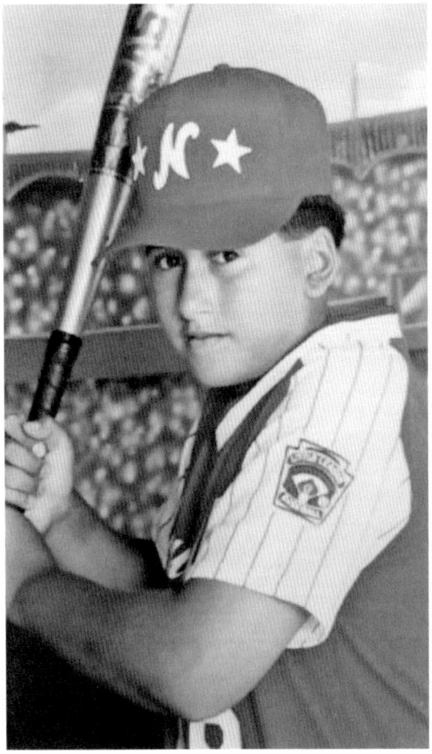

Tómas Espinoza II is the son of Tómas Espinoza, a longtime player and coach in the Norwalk area. The younger Tómas, like his brother Mike and sister Sofía, was born and raised in Norwalk, and started playing baseball at the age of five with the South West little league and Norwalk little league, where he played on both championship and all-star teams. Tómas II played football and baseball at Richard Gahr High School in Artesia. His father made sure that sports were a major part of his children's upbringing. Part of this baseball upbringing is to pass on the rich and long history of baseball and softball in Norwalk. The elder Tómas often shares with his children and others stories about the great Dukes teams from the 1980s, especially those players who are now playing on the big softball diamond in heaven—Steve Acedo, Eli Amaya, David Rangel, Ron "Big" Jones, Rudy Flores, and Larry "Doc" Bowser. Their memories will live on as long as there are softball fields in Norwalk. (Courtesy of Tómas Espinoza II.)

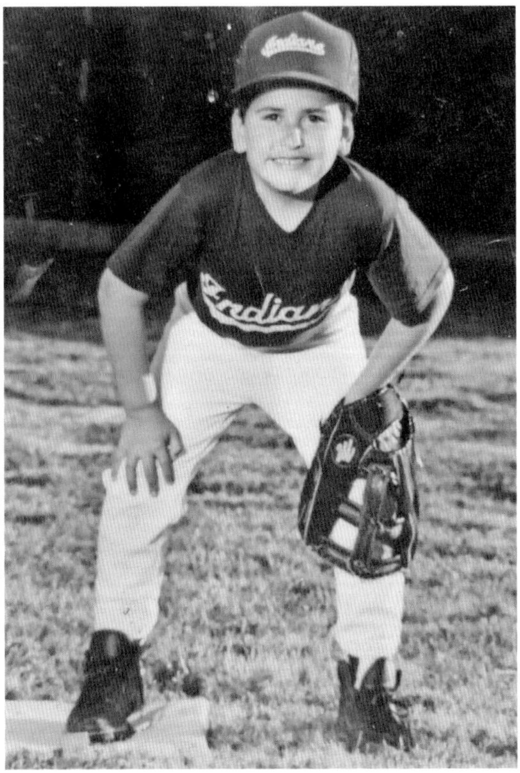

Mike Espinoza was born in Orange but raised in Norwalk. He says he grew up in the park and that his dad's softball buddies called him "Monster Mike" because he was a handful. At four, he started playing T-ball with both the Southwest and Norwalk little leagues; father Tomás was usually his coach. In high school, he ran track, wrestled, and played football. After high school, he worked in the music industry, including a 40-state tour with a rap group from Fresno. He has worked for major record labels and in 2018 works in radio, has his own podcast on a major network, and will soon be a father for the first time. (Courtesy of Mike Espinoza.)

5

Field of Dreams

The Latino Baseball History Project can trace its roots to California State University at Los Angeles in 2004. Chicano studies professor Francisco Balderrama, Pasadena public librarian Terry Cannon, and the dean of the library, César Caballero, organized a public exhibit at the John F. Kennedy Library on the remarkable history of Mexican American baseball and softball in East Los Angeles during its golden age between the 1920s and the 1950s. The exhibit was entitled From the Barrios to the Big Leagues. This well-thought-out presentation was two years in the making and was a huge success. Thousands of people from throughout California came to view vintage photographs, memorabilia, worn-out gloves, bats, and uniforms and to personally meet, honor, and pay tribute to the remarkable players, teams, coaches, sportswriters, umpires, and so many others who brought immense honor and never-ending pride to their families, friends, and fans.

A group of dedicated and passionate individuals who love both Mexican American history and baseball saw promise and a desperate need to collect, preserve, chronicle, and advance the full extensive story of Mexican American baseball and softball both in the United States and around the world. The project has integrated several strategies to make public this remarkable story, including the Mexican American baseball book series in partnership with Arcadia Publishing. Since 2011, this collaboration has resulted in 13 publications representing nearly 25 states and showcasing over 3,000 vintage photographs dating to the 1860s. Each book is a labor of love for the volunteer coauthors, editors, technicians, proofreaders, players, families, historical societies, students, community historians, and countless others.

Sorrowfully, scores of players who were the heart and soul of the project are now playing in the big diamond in the sky. Each of these books purposely finishes with a chapter entitled "Field of Dreams" to respect, treasure, and express gratitude to down-to-earth players now in the ninth inning of their lives or who are deceased. These once-bright stars in Mexican American communities are slowly growing dim. They will be deeply missed, but their well-documented heritage will live without end in the pages of this book series and in the hearts and minds of immeasurable generations.

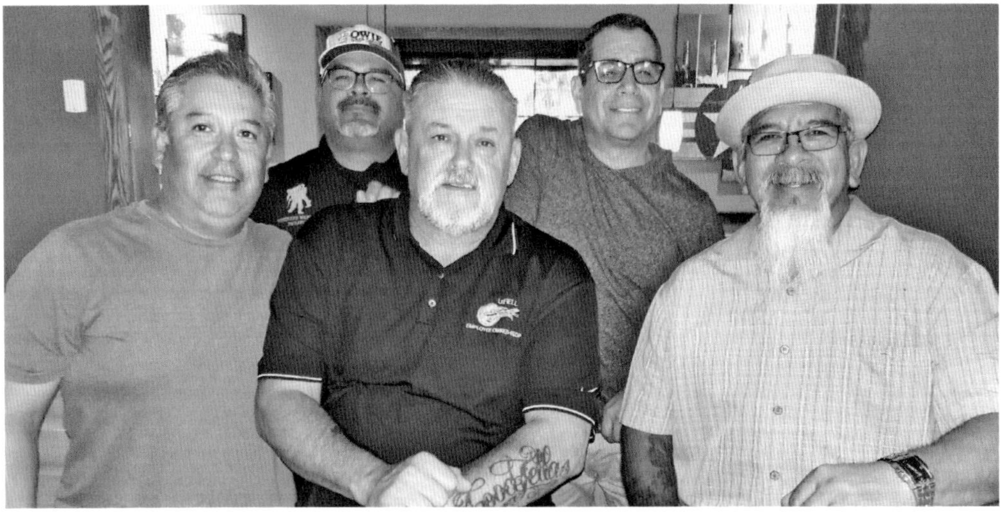

On January 15, 2018, a reunion of players and coaches took place in Norwalk. From left to right are David Gallegos, Tony Ríos, Tomás Espinoza Sr., Mike Álvarez, and John Lemos. Gallegos is the assistant baseball coach at Norwalk High School. Ríos is from El Paso and graduated from Bowie High School. Espinoza played and coached in Norwalk and surrounding communities. Álvarez grew up in Norwalk playing youth, high school, college, community, and semipro ball. Lemos coached in Norwalk, and his son John "Chopper" Lemos was an outstanding player at John Glenn High School. (Courtesy of Richard A. Santillán.)

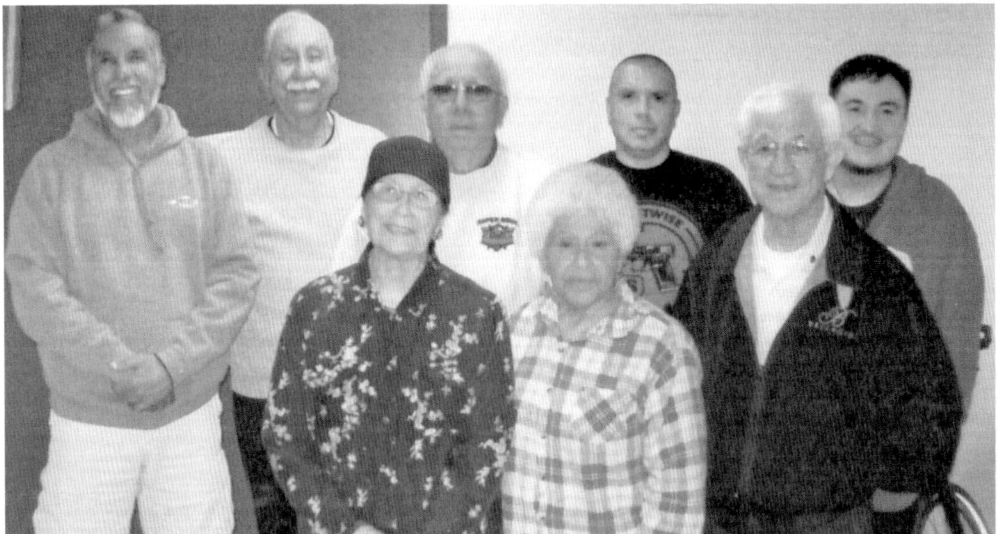

Generations of San Gabriel Valley baseball and softball players and coaches shared their recollections at the Montebello Historical Society in 2013. The stories were emotional and amazing for everyone in attendance. All of the speakers had several things in common, including pride, passion, and love for the game. From left to right are (first row) Consuelo Solís, Nora Morales, and Bob Lagunas; (second row) Phil Vásquez, Joseph Holguín, Armando Pérez, James Henninger Aguirre, and Davey Escobedo. (Courtesy of James Henninger Aguirre.)

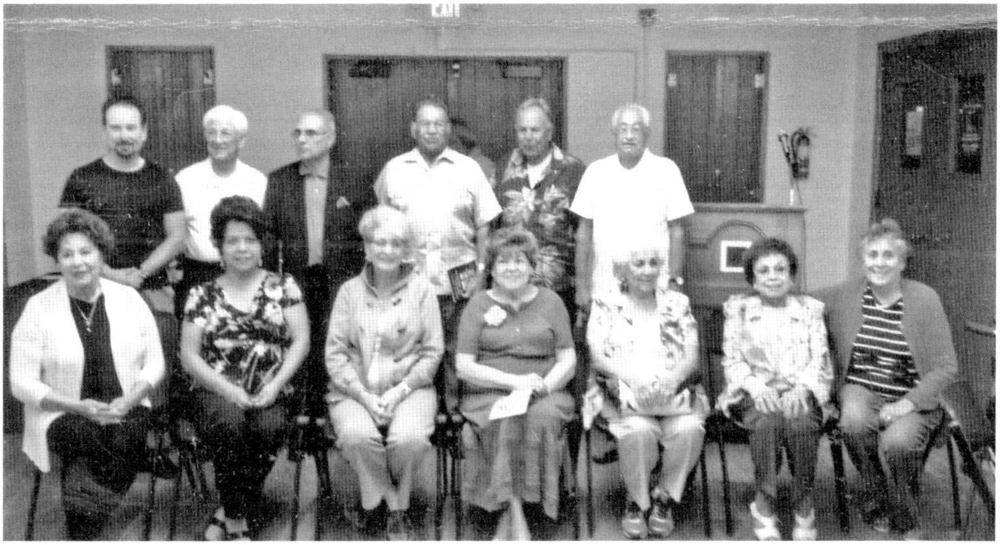

The San Gabriel Historical Association held a spring event in 2014 at the San Gabriel Grapevine Room to pay tribute to outstanding players and coaches from the San Gabriel Valley. From left to right are (first row) unidentified, Lucy Pedregón, Irene Aguirre Juárez, Margaret Barrera Sosa, Doli Juárez Acuña, Virginia Acuña Flores, and Camila Alva López; (second row) Enrique López, Bob Lagunas, Rod Martínez, Al Padilla, Carlos Salazar, and Tom Pérez Jr. Irene is the sister of Hank Aguirre, Margaret is the daughter of Joe Barrera, Virginia is the daughter of "Big" Joe Acuña, and Camila is the granddaughter of Mike Salazar. (Courtesy of Rod Martínez.)

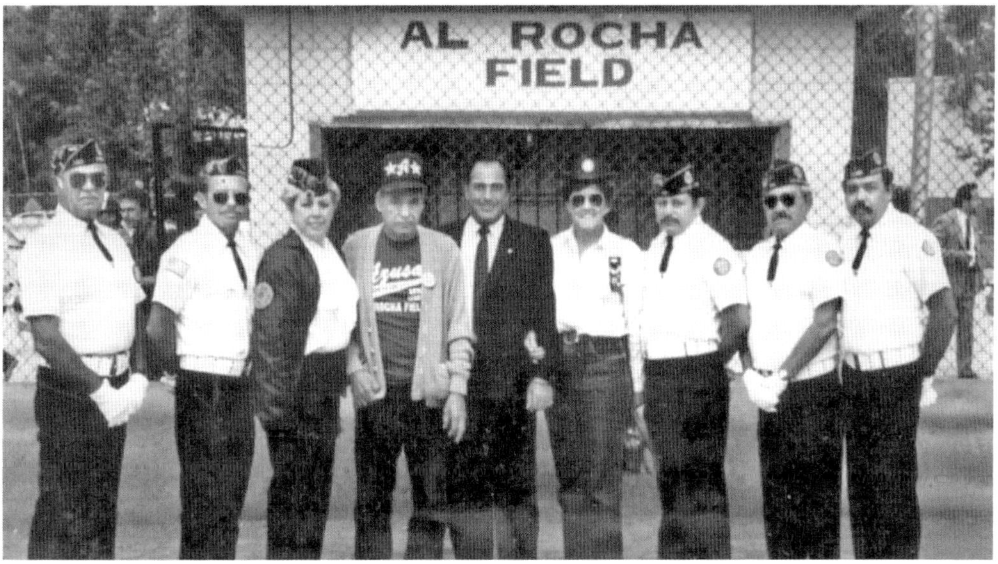

This 1986 photograph shows American Legion Post 180 at Zacatecas Park in Azusa. In 1979, the baseball field was named after outstanding citizen Al Rocha (1925–1987), who served as president, coach, business manager, and fundraiser for the Azusa American little league. Rocha served in the US Navy during World War II. He had five children: Susan, James, Jerry, Rosalie, and Al. Rocha (fourth from left) is standing next to Azusa mayor Eugene Moses (center). (Courtesy of Jerry Rocha.)

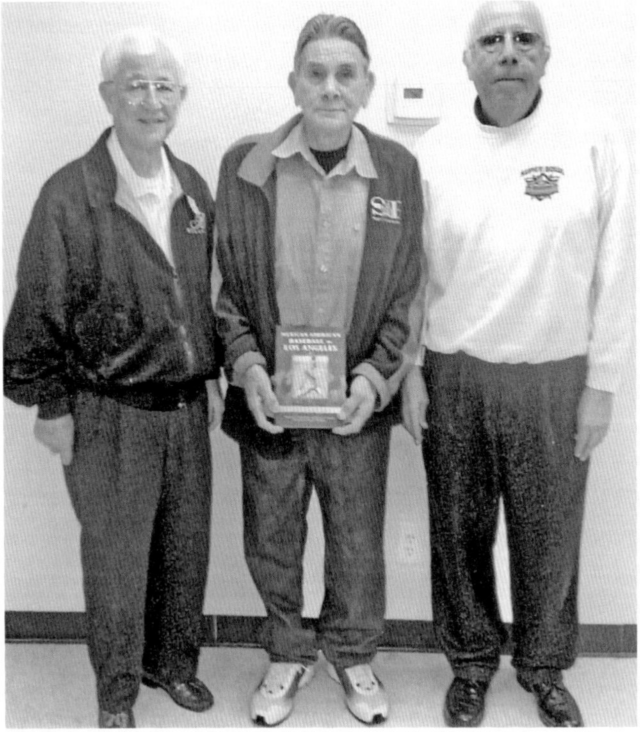

Generations of baseball and softball players shared recollections at the Montebello Historical Society on February 7, 2013. These players gave emotional testimony about their lives on and off the diamond. Their stories had an impact on all those who attended, regardless if they were young or old, because they spoke about how ball made a positive contribution to their personal and private lives. From left to right are Bob Lagunas, Julian Barry Aguirre, and Armando Pérez. Lagunas and Aguirre played ball and attended school together as children. (Courtesy of James Henninger Aguirre.)

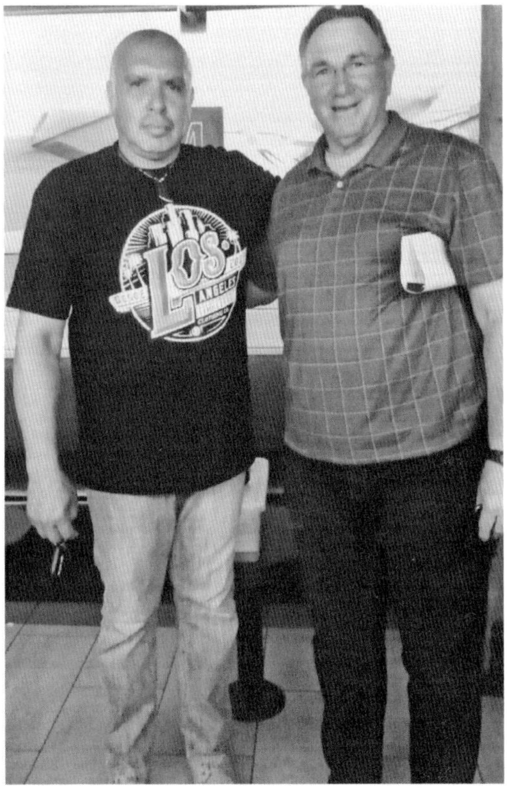

This 2016 reunion photograph shows former player James Henninger Aguirre (left) and his coach, Nicholas Jannis, after 35 years. Aguirre was a starting pitcher for the 1984 Bassett High School Olympians varsity team in Bassett, California. In 1985, he was the only walk-on starting pitcher to make the Rio Hondo College Roadrunners team in Whittier. Coach Jannis has been coaching baseball for more than 40 years and was instrumental in developing the mental and physical skills of his players. Coach Jannis's teams were often all Mexican Americans who could play different positions on the diamond. But his proudest accomplishment is that all of his former players became successful adults. (Courtesy of James Henninger Aguirre.)

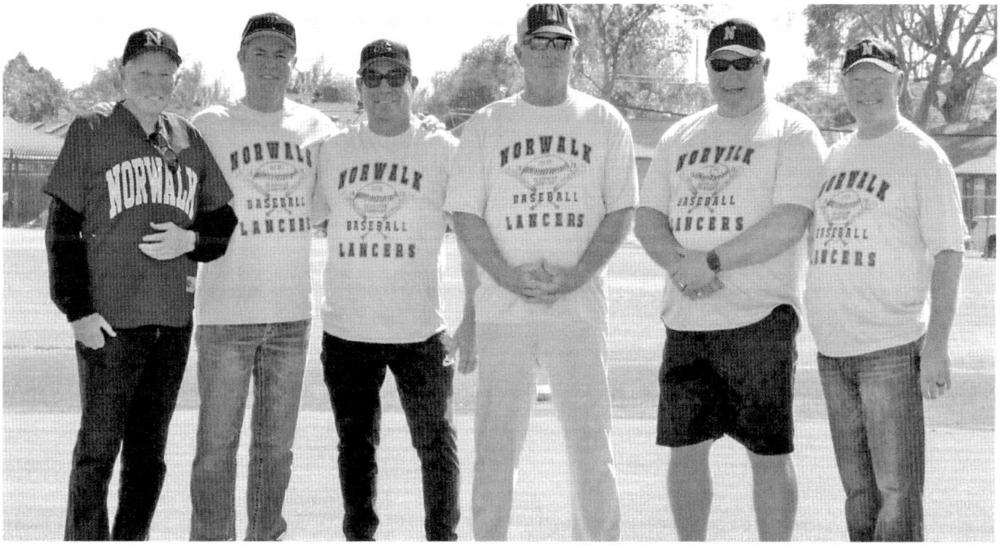

Members of the 1978 Norwalk High School CIF championship team are seen at their 40th anniversary on February 17, 2018. From left to right are coach Terry Bales, Greg Anderson, Mike Álvarez, Larry See, Mike Davis, and Phillip Davis. Bales also coached the 1982 team to a CIF championship. Anderson was a two-time CIF champion in football and baseball. Álvarez was a two-time all-league selection in baseball and a CIF champion. See was a two-time CIF champion in football and baseball and played for the Dodgers. Twins Mike and Phillip Davis were two-time CIF champions in baseball and football and played football at the University of Wyoming. (Courtesy of David Gallegos and Mike Álvarez.)

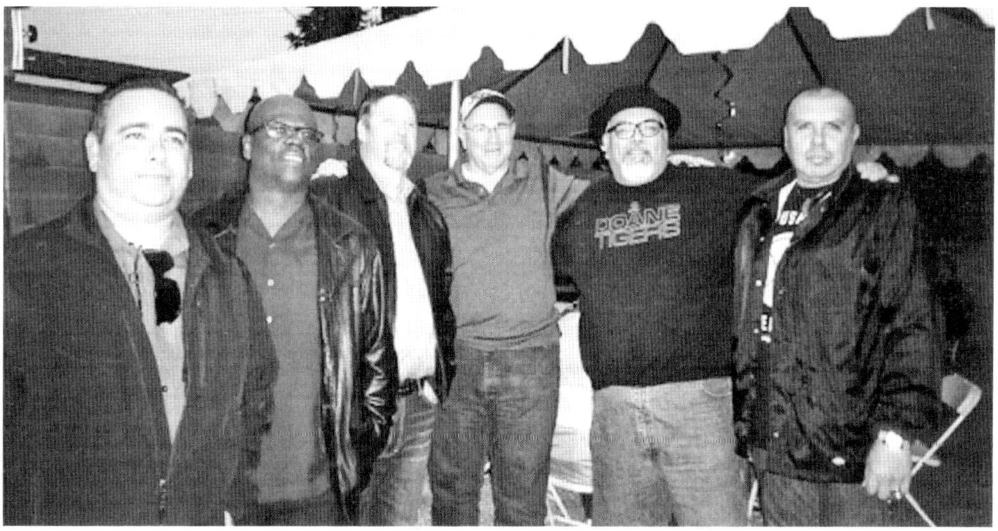

A few of the baseball players from the Bassett High School Olympians gathered in Bassett in 2016 after 30 years. They shared wonderful stories about their playing days and about their families and jobs, but they mostly spoke passionately about their coach, whom they still love and respect to this day. From left to right are Manuel Martínez, Gary Haley, Eddie Dean Ramos, coach Nicholas Jannis, Edward Hidalgo, and James Henninger Aguirre. (Courtesy of James Henninger Aguirre.)

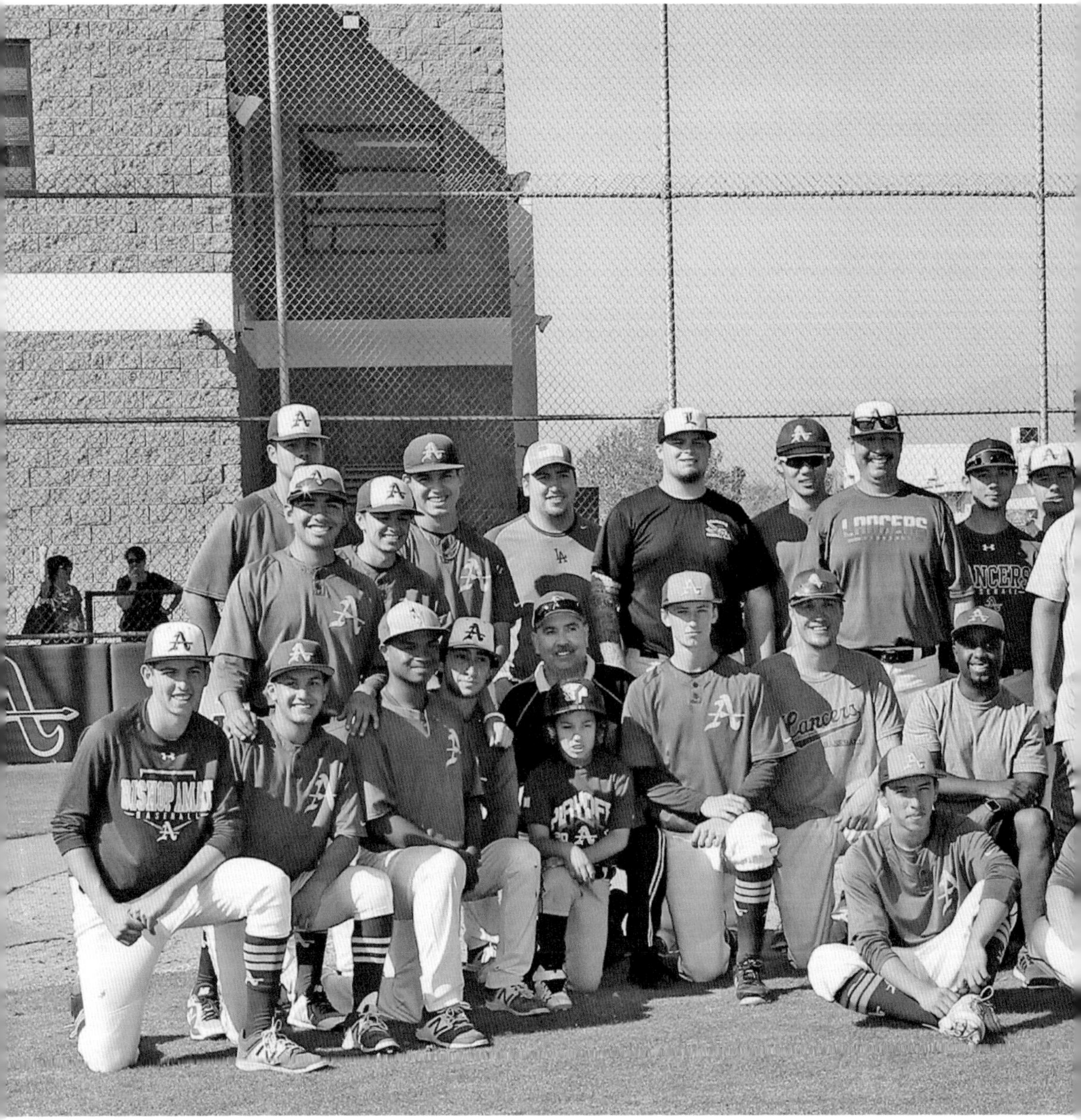

Bishop Amat Memorial High School is a coed Catholic school serving the San Gabriel Valley in the Archdiocese of Los Angeles. It was founded in 1957. The campus is located in La Puente, approximately 20 miles east of downtown Los Angeles. The student body comprises approximately 1,520 students in grades nine through 12, making Bishop Amat the largest private high school in

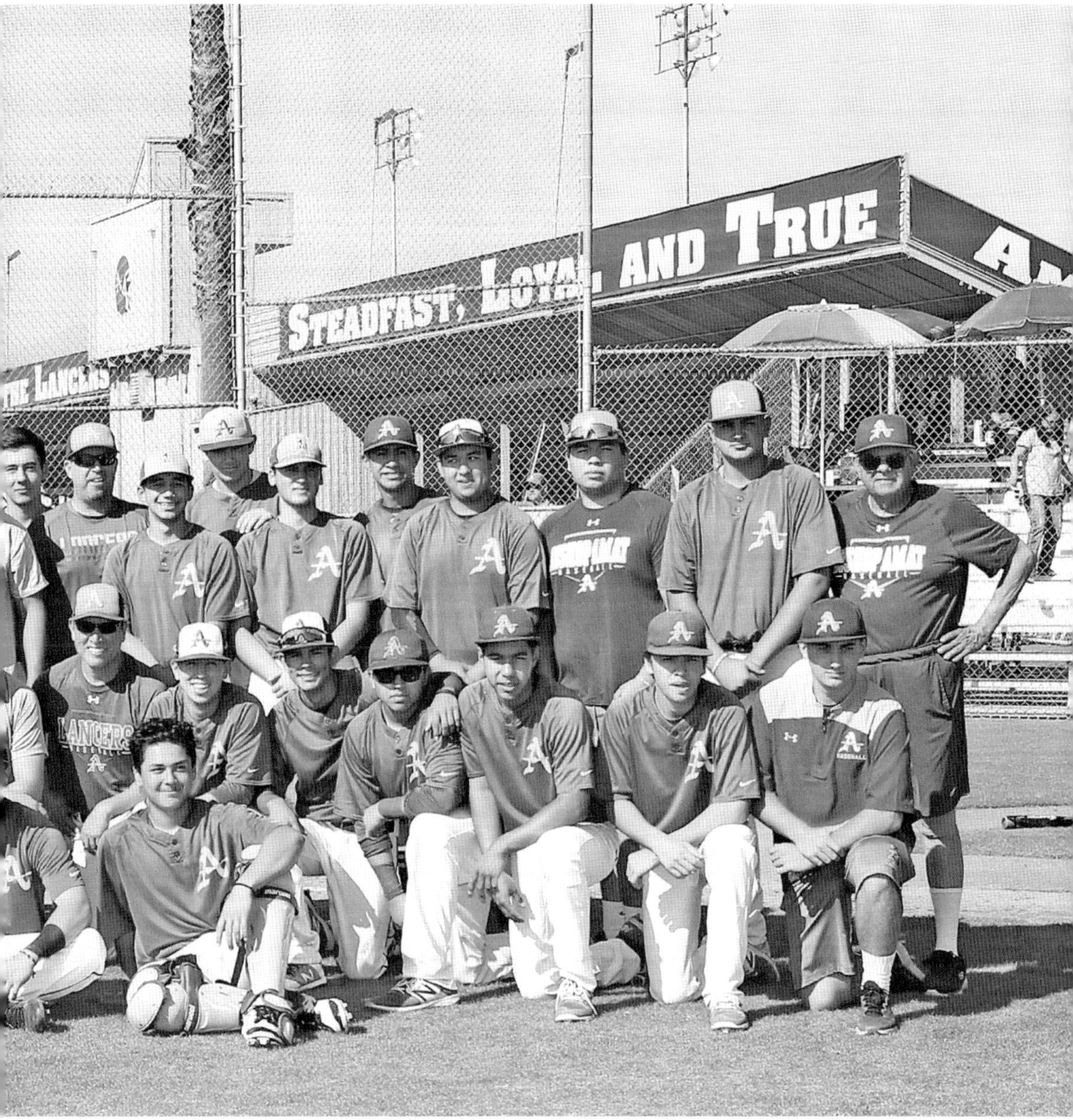

Los Angeles County. It is the only Catholic high school in the county that offers the international baccalaureate diploma program. The Bishop Amat baseball program has produced several major-league players. (Courtesy of Mark R. García.)

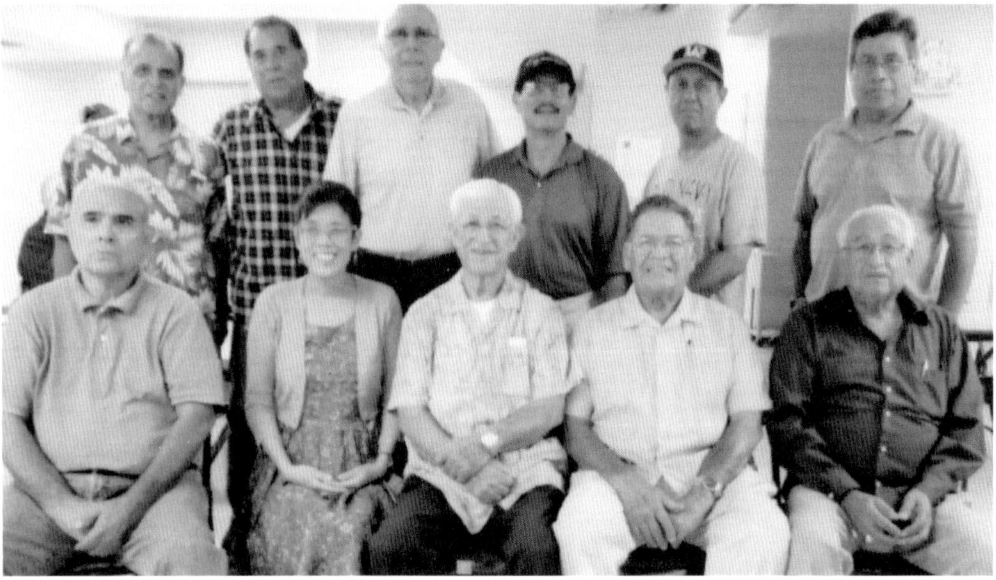

The Montebello Historical Society sponsored a Mexican American baseball event in September 2015. Wonderful stories were shared, photographs were displayed, and a book signing took place. From left to right are (first row) Rod Martínez, Mimi Poon, Bob Lagunas, Al Padilla, and Tom Pérez Jr.; (second row) Ray Ramírez, Ray Loya, Armando Pérez, Fidel Elizarrez, and Al and Frank De La Rosa. (Courtesy of Richard A. Santillán.)

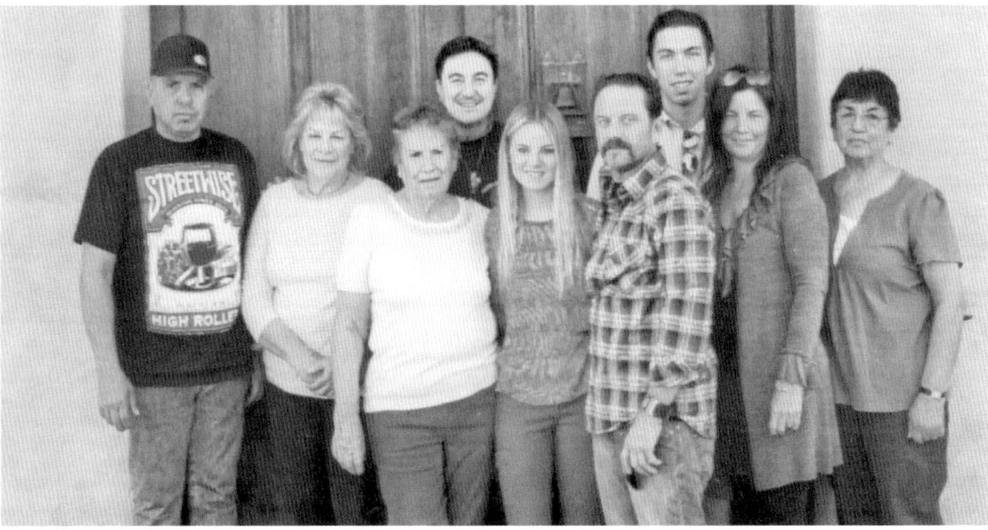

The Aguirre, Henninger, De La Ossa, Jeffredo, Escobedo, Macías, Bateman, and Belleville families have a rich tradition of playing baseball in the San Gabriel Valley for over 100 years. These and other original families continue to pass on this remarkable sports legacy to younger generations to preserve, protect, and promote their baseball heritage. From left to right are James Henninger Aguirre, Judy Bateman, Billie Henninger Jeffredo, Davey Escobedo, Lexi Macías, Phillip Macías, Cory Belleville, Stephanie Belleville, and Lucille Henninger Aguirre. (Courtesy of James Henninger Aguirre.)

Seen here are three fathers with their children. From left to right are Yogi Flores with son Issac, Rafael Gutíerrez with son Ryan and daughter Julianna, and Victor Durán with son Kevin. Rafael Gutíerrez coached both Yogi Flores and Victor Durán when they played high school baseball at Montebello High School in the 1990s. Both his protégés have coached Gutíerrez's son Ryan, Flores in 2017 and 2018 with the Blue Jays, and Durán for three seasons with the Twins. Yogi and his son are second basemen, Victor played shortstop and his son second base, Ryan plays first base, and Julianna plays shortstop and first base. (Courtesy of Rafael Gutíerrez.)

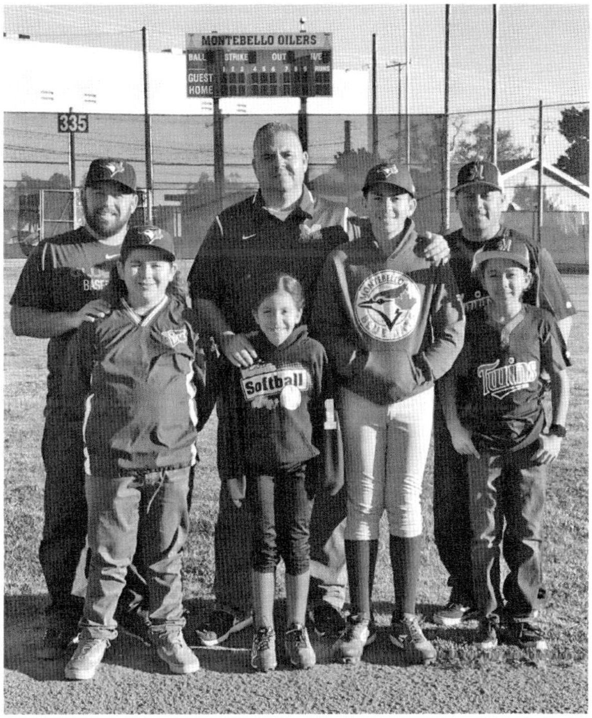

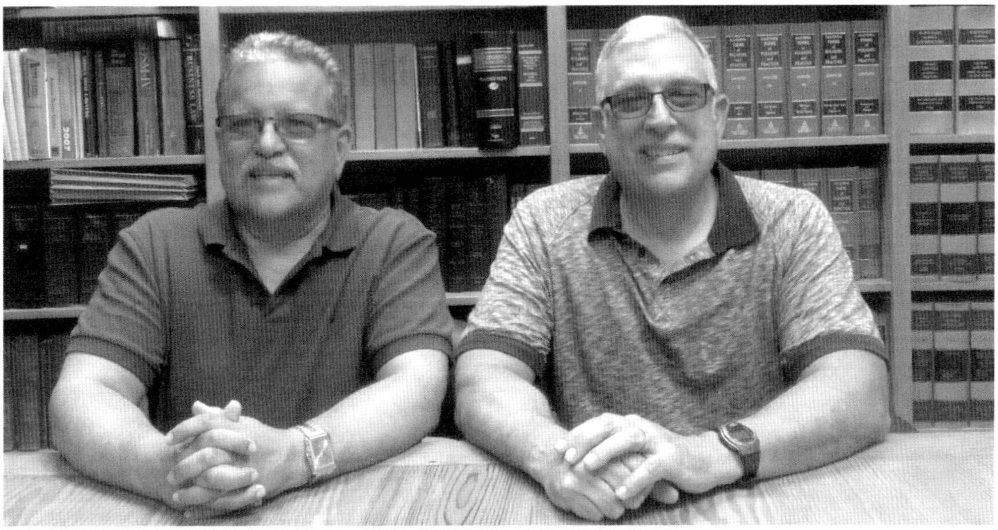

Francisco Suárez (left) was born in 1955, and his brother Mario Miguel Suárez was born in 1956. Both played youth little league on baseball diamonds around South San Gabriel at Rebels Field in Rosemead. Both attended Schurr High School in Montebello. Francisco attended California State University at Los Angeles, where he played in the intramural baseball league. He eventually graduated from the University of La Verne College of Law. He works as a personal injury and criminal defense lawyer and also with non-profit and for profit small businesses. Miguel graduated from Chaffey College and the University of Phoenix and has had a long career as an advertising executive. (Courtesy of Francisco and Mario Miguel Suárez.)

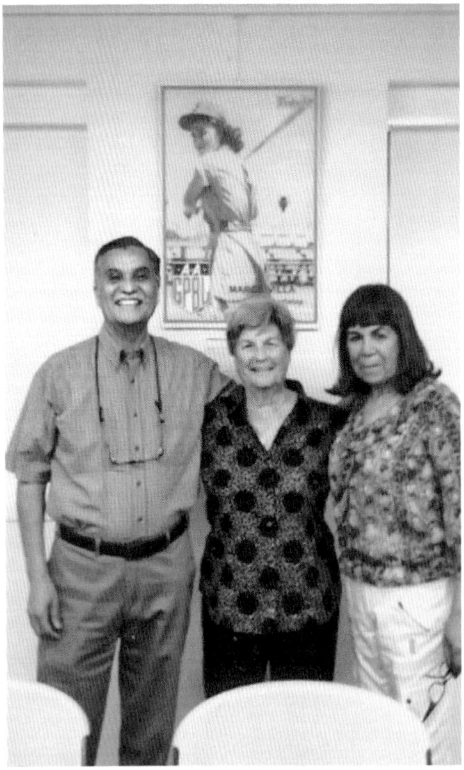

Margaret "Marge" Villa Cryan (center) was raised near the Simons Brickyard, now Montebello, and the City of Commerce. Her two brothers, Ernie and Tony, were outstanding baseball and softball players throughout the San Gabriel Valley. Marge enjoys attending reunions of the All-American Girls Professional Baseball League Players Association (depicted in *A League of Their Own*), held every few years at the Baseball Hall of Fame in Cooperstown, New York. She is part of the Women in Baseball permanent exhibit and has been invited to speak about her experiences with the Kenosha Comets in 1946. In her early 90s, she still enjoys golfing, tosses batting practice at her grandsons' little league games, and spends countless hours responding to requests for her autograph. She is pictured with Richard A. and Teresa M. Santillán at a 2016 event saluting her and other Mexican American women at California State University at Channel Islands. (Courtesy of Richard A. Santillán.)

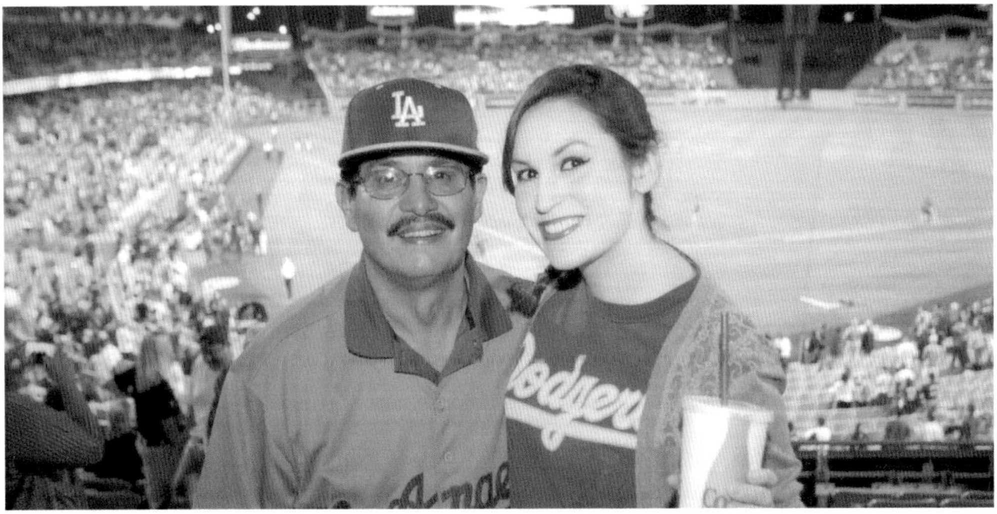

Fidel Elizarrez is seen here in 2017 with his daughter Andrea at Dodger Stadium on Father's Day. Andrea was born in 1984 at Kaiser Hospital in Anaheim Hills, California. In 1995, she played Little League softball in Walnut and graduated from Diamond Bar High School, later attending Loyola Marymount University from 2002 to 2003. She graduated from Boston College in 2006 with a bachelor's degree in English literature and went to graduate school studying theology and ministry from 2007 to 2009. She and her husband, Ryan Bethke, reside in Hemet, California. She pursued a career as an artist and designer. (Courtesy of Fidel Elizarrez.)

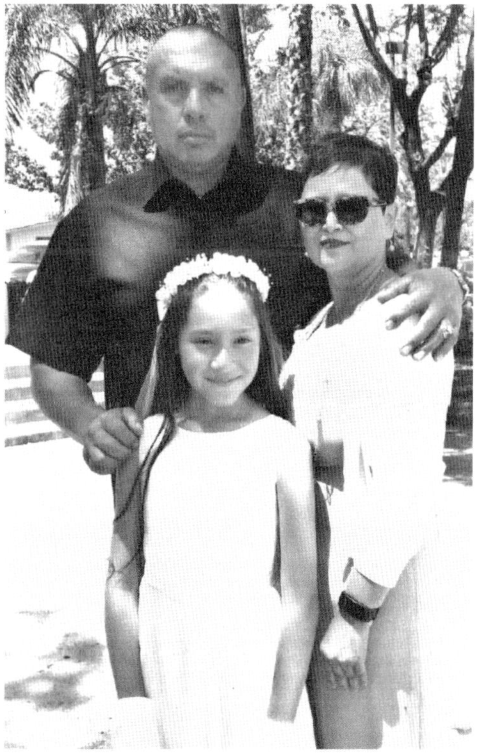

James Henninger Aguirre and Donna Galván are seen in 2017 with their goddaughter Alanna "Tatonka" Longoria at her First Communion at Resurrection Academy. All of their families have been involved with baseball, softball, football, and basketball in the San Gabriel Valley for over a century. James was a successful baseball player in little league, high school, and college. He is also a successful author whose focus is Native Americans. Donna graduated from El Rancho High School in Pico Rivera and attended Whittier College with a duel major in political science and economics. She attended the University of California Berkeley School of Law and passed the California bar exam. Alanna is a straight A student, receiving many certificates and awards, and aspires to receive scholarships in high school and college. (Courtesy of James Henninger Aguirre.)

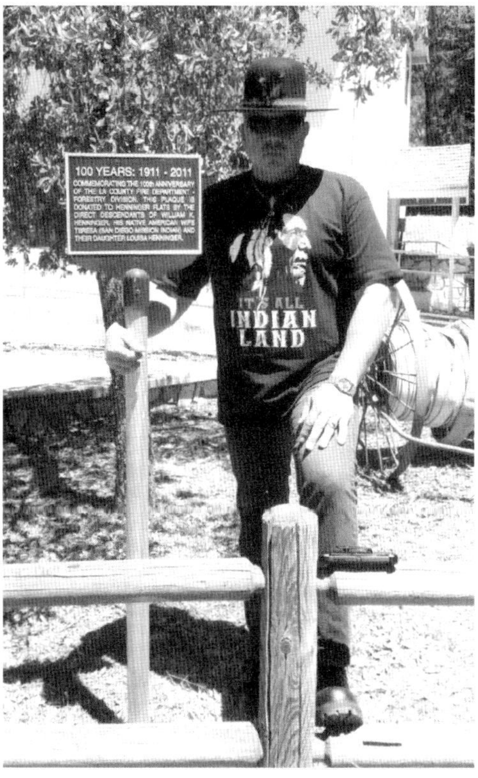

James Henninger Aguirre refers to himself as the "Warrior with a Pen" because of his writings on the long and rich history of Native Americans, especially in the San Gabriel Valley. He is seen here standing near a bronze marker donated by his family at the Henninger Flats Museum in the San Gabriel Mountains. Aguirre donated family photographs, newspaper articles, and a self-published book about William K. Henninger and his Native American wife Teresa. William K. Henninger was a pioneer and gold prospector who homesteaded a property named after him in 1894. He married Teresa Serrano, a full-blooded "Kumeyaay" San Diego Mission Indian at the San Gabriel Mission in 1858 They had four daughters named Natividad, Louisa, Susana, and Josefa. Louisa eventually became the family matriarch, purchasing property in San Gabriel in 1899 that is still owned by the family. (Courtesy of James Henninger Aguirre.)

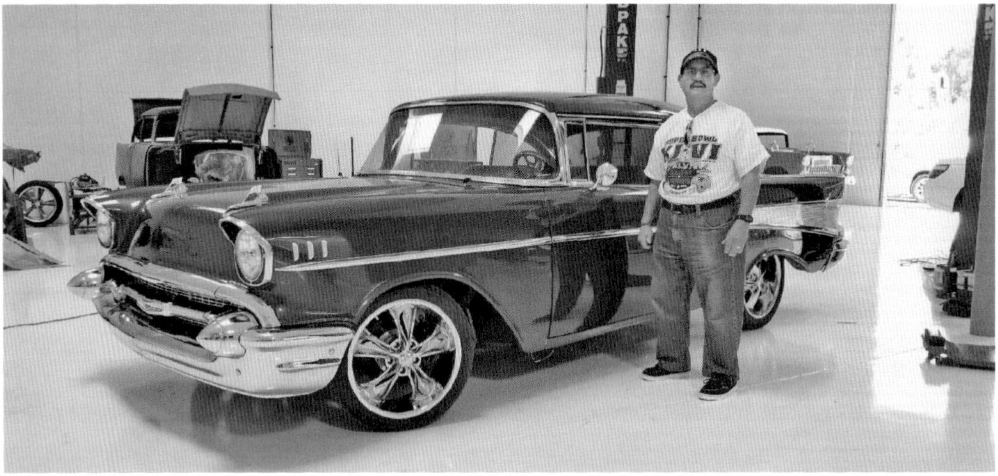

Fidel Elizarrez purchased his first 1957 Chevy Bel Air—his dream car—in 1968. He loved to cruise Whittier Boulevard in East Los Angeles. However, his father sold that car in 1970 while Fidel was serving in Vietnam. Fidel promised himself to restore another 1957 Bel Air to enjoy again. After 14 years, his car is ready for cruising. The car is painted Dodger blue and is ready for car shows. His wife, Jenny, loves to travel around the world with Fidel. She was the prom queen at Sacred Heart of Mary in Montebello and taught in the Montebello School District for 33 years. (Courtesy of Fidel Elizarrez.)

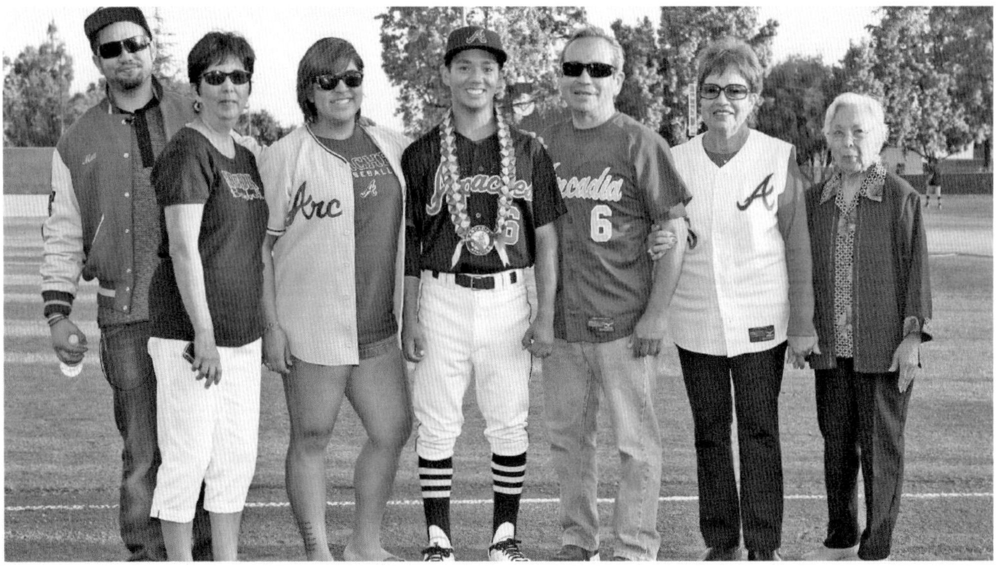

Matthew Morales is flanked by parents, Diane and Bob, at his final baseball game at Arcadia High School in 2013. Bob graduated from Loyola High School in 1973 and earned his bachelor's and master's degrees from USC, where he received the Hubbard Award for the most outstanding Mexican American graduate. He has worked on several political campaigns and is currently vice president of public affairs for Learn4Life Charter Schools. Diane graduated from San Gabriel Mission High School, won the Mexican American GI Forum Scholarship, and received her bachelor's degree from California State University at Los Angeles. (Courtesy of Diane and Bob Morales.)

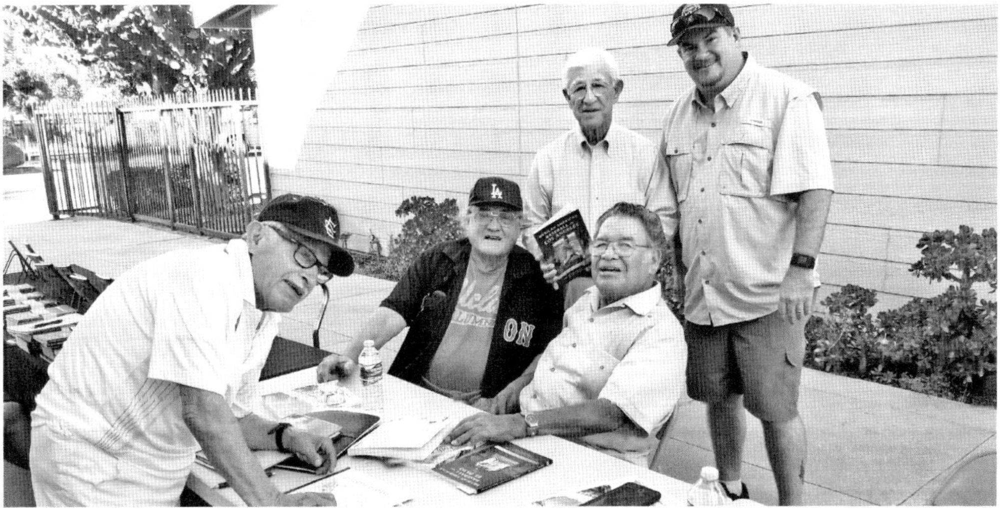

In August 2017, the San Gabriel Historical Association sponsored a book-signing event. From left to right are (first row) Bill Castellanos, Conrad Muñatones, and Al Padilla; (second row) Bob Lagunas and Joe Thompson. Castellanos played ball at Berkeley High School in Northern California and later was batboy for the old Pacific Coast League San Francisco Seals. Conrad Muñatones played ball at the University of California at Los Angeles and was one of the first Mexican Americans signed by the Los Angeles Dodgers. Padilla and Lagunas are legendary players and coaches in Southern California, and Thompson was a coauthor of *Mexican American Baseball in Houston*. (Courtesy of Richard A. Santillán.)

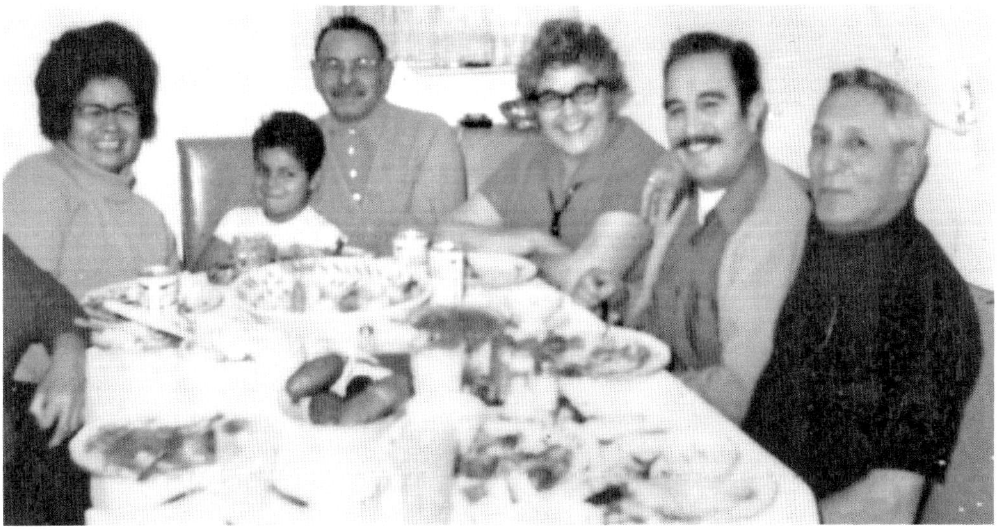

From left to right in 1971 are Adela Pérez Domínguez, Arthur Gutíerrez, Pomposo Domínguez, Bea Salazar, Henry Alva, and Louis Porras. Bea and Henry are the parents of Camila Alva López, coauthor of this book and museum curator and trustee of the San Gabriel Historical Association. Bea is also the daughter of Mike Salazar, an extraordinary player and coach in San Gabriel. Henry is the uncle of Hank Aguirre, who played for the Tigers, Indians, and Dodgers. Adela and Bea are descendants of the Gabrieleño-Tongva Band of Mission Indians. (Courtesy of Camila Alva López.)

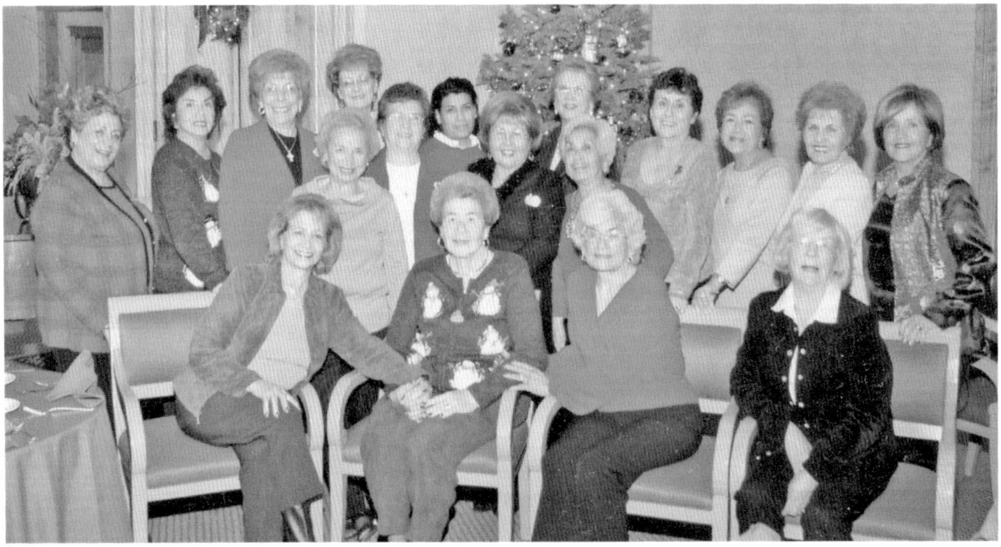

The San Gabriel Girls and Childhood Friends are seen here in 2005 at the San Gabriel Country Club. From left to right are (first row) Susan Ruela, Lorena Rodríguez Cerda, Cecilia Landa González, and Carmen Boli Pérez; (second row) Margaret Díaz Gallegos, Janet Domínguez Gutíerrez, and Rosie González Zuñiga; (third row) Margaret Murietta Alderete, Kathy Rodríguez Stepner, Alice Manríquez Vargas, Irene Aguirre Juárez (sister of Hank Aguirre), Melinda González, Ruth Moreno, Camila Alva López (granddaughter of Mike Salazar and cousin of Hank Aguirre), Louise Montaño Hernández, Celia Manríquez, and Arlene Márquez Kemp. (Courtesy of Camila Alva López.)

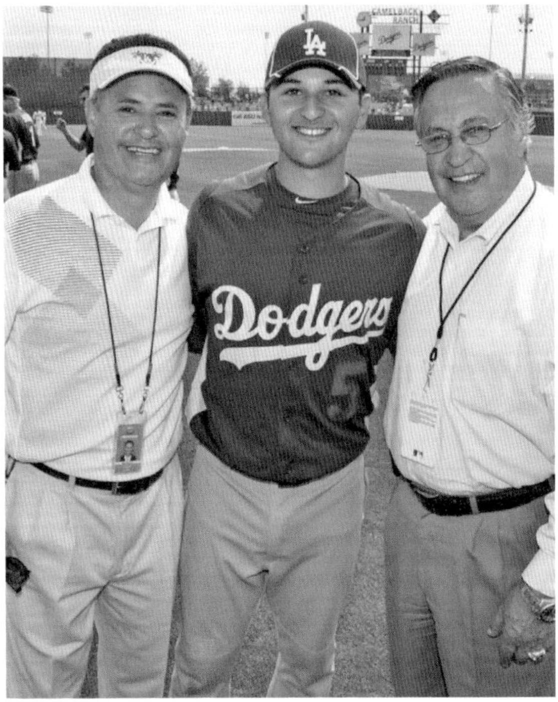

Three generations of the Jarrín family are seen here. Jaime (right) is the legendary Spanish-language broadcaster for the Los Angeles Dodgers since 1959, winner of the Ford C. Fricke Award in 1998, and Baseball Hall of Fame inductee. His son Jorge (left), now a Spanish broadcaster alongside Jaime, has worked for the Dodgers since 2003. Jorge's son Stefan (center) is a three-time Mission Valley All-League second baseman for the Gabrielino High School Eagles from 2006 to 2008 and twice Mission Valley League champion in 2007 and 2008. Stefan was drafted by the Dodgers in 2011 and played two years of minor-league ball. He works for the Dodgers as an inside sales associate. (Courtesy of Joe Laski.)

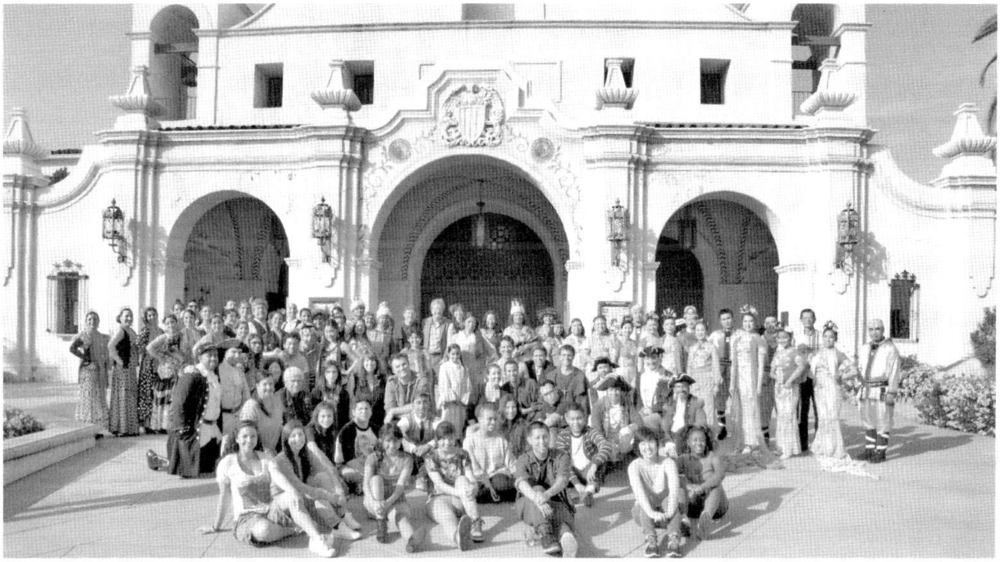

The Mission Playhouse was built in 1927 near the San Gabriel Mission. It presented the pageant *The Mission Play*, the epic story of the rise and fall of the California missions. The play was written by John Steven McGroarty, poet laureate of California, and introduced to the public in 1912 in a small open-air theater on grounds known today as Plaza Park. McGroarty built the larger Mission Playhouse in 1927. The play was performed until 1932 and was revived in 1947 and 2013, the centennial year of San Gabriel. The Mission Playhouse is actively used for entertainment and festivities. (Courtesy of the San Gabriel Historical Association Museum archives.)

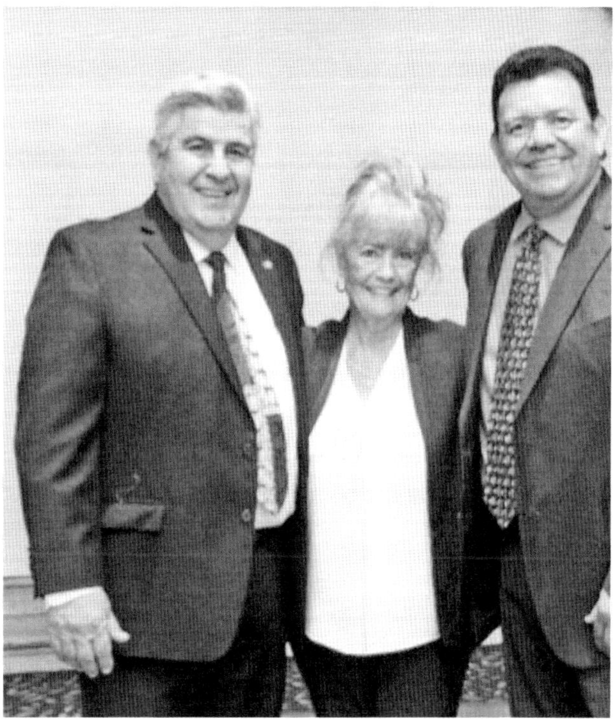

A fundraiser was held at the Biltmore Hotel in downtown Los Angeles in 2017 for the Weigart YMCA in East Los Angeles. The honored guest was Fernando Valenzuela (right), a former Dodgers pitcher and current color commentator for Dodger Spanish-language broadcasts. Valenzuela is a true legend and one of the great Dodgers of all time. He was being recognized for his unselfish community service dating to his playing days, when he helped launch a stay-in-school program and promoted reading at home. He is seen here with Tony and Diane Ortega. (Courtesy of Tony Ortega.)

BIBLIOGRAPHY

Acosta, Dan. *Iron River.* El Paso, TX: Cinco Puntos Press, 2018.

Aguirre, James Henninger. *William K. Henninger, His Native American Wife Teresa and Their Legacy.* Self-published, 2010.

———. *The Barry Family Legacy, A Personal Journey.* Self-published, 2011.

———. *Through Native Eyes: Talking Leaves.* Self-published, 2012.

———. *Warrior with a Pen.* Self-published, 2018.

Andrade-Aguirre, Frank M. *A Bibliography: Reyner Didn't Come Home.* San Gabriel, CA, Self-published, 2002.

Arnold, Richard. Images of America: *San Gabriel.* Charleston, SC: Arcadia Publishing, 2013.

Bustillos, Ernesto. *Creating Community: The San Gabriel Barrio.* Unpublished paper, 2018.

Chavez, Francis. *Old Mission Tales.* North Charleston, SC: CreateSpace Independent Publishing Platform, 2013.

Copley, Robert E. *The Tall Mexican: The Life of Hank Aguirre.* Houston, TX: Pinata Books, University of Houston, 2000.

Johnston, Bernice Eastman. *California Gabrielino Indians.* Los Angeles, CA: Southwest Museum, 1962.

Jurmain, Claudia and William McCawley. *O My Ancestor: Recognition and Renewal for the Gabrielino Tongva People of the Los Angeles Area.* Berkeley, CA: Heyday Books, 2009.

Ling, Susie. "History of the City of San Gabriel." susieling.wordpress.com/san-gabriel. June 13, 2013.

Macias, John. *Spanish Myths and Mexican Realities.* Claremont Graduate University, CA: doctoral dissertation, 2012.

Miller, Bruce W. *The Gabrielino.* Los Osos, CA: Sand River Press, 1991.

Moreno, Lorraine. *Shhh…!* Bloomington, IN: Xlibris, 2012.

Read, Nat. *Don Benito Wilson: From Mountain Man to Mayor, Los Angeles 1841 to 1878.* Santa Monica, CA: Angel City Press, 2008.

Santillan, Richard A. et al. *Mexican American Baseball in the Central Coast.* Charleston, SC: Arcadia Publishing, 2013.

Spitzzeri, Paul. *The Workman and Temple Families of Southern California, 1830–1930.* Dallas, TX: Seligson Press, 2008.

Teutimes, Ernest Salas et al. *Joan of Arc of California.* San Gabriel, CA: Kizh Tribal Press, 2010.

Young, Paul R. *The Farm, McKinley School and a Big Bit More.* San Gabriel, CA: Self-published, 2017.

LATINO BASEBALL HISTORY PROJECT ADVISORY BOARD